CRITICAL POLITICAL THEORY
AND RADICAL PRACTICE

Mainstream political theory has been experiencing an identity crisis for as long as I can remember. From even a cursory glance at the major journals, it still seems preoccupied either with textual exegesis of a conservatively construed canon, fashionable postmodern forms of deconstruction, or the reduction of ideas to the context in which they were formulated and the prejudices of the author. Usually written in esoteric style and intended only for disciplinary experts, political theory has lost both its critical character and its concern for political practice. Behaviorist and positivist political "scientists" tend to view it as a branch of philosophical metaphysics or as akin to literary criticism. They are not completely wrong. There is currently no venue that highlights the practical implications of theory or its connections with the larger world. I was subsequently delighted when Palgrave Macmillan offered me the opportunity of editing Critical Political Theory and Radical Practice.

When I was a graduate student at the University of California, Berkeley, during the 1970s, critical theory was virtually unknown in the United States. The academic mainstream was late in catching up and, when it finally did during the late 1980s, it predictably embraced the more metaphysical and subjectivist trends of critical theory. Traditionalists had little use for an approach in which critique of a position or analysis of an event was predicated on positive ideals and practical political aims. In this vein, like liberalism, socialism was a dirty word and knowledge of its various tendencies and traditions was virtually nonexistent. Today, however, the situation is somewhat different. Strident right-wing politicians have openly condemned "critical thinking," particularly as it pertains to cultural pluralism and American history. Such parochial validations of tradition have implications for practical politics. And, if only for this reason, it is necessary to confront them. A new generation of academics is becoming engaged with immanent critique, interdisciplinary work, actual political problems, and more broadly the link between theory and practice. Critical Political Theory and Radical Practice offers them a new home for their intellectual labors.

The series introduces new authors, unorthodox themes, critical interpretations of the classics, and salient works by older and more established thinkers. Each after his or her fashion will explore the ways in which political theory can enrich our understanding of the arts and social sciences. Criminal justice, psychology, sociology, theater, and a host of other disciplines come into play for a critical political theory. The series also opens new avenues by engaging alternative traditions, animal rights, Islamic politics, mass movements, sovereignty, and the institutional problems of power. Critical Political Theory and Radical Practice thus fills an important niche. Innovatively blending tradition and experimentation, this intellectual enterprise with a political intent will, I hope, help reinvigorate what is fast becoming a petrified field of study and perhaps provide a bit of inspiration for future scholars and activists.

STEPHEN ERIC BRONNER

Published by Palgrave Macmillan:

Subterranean Politics and Freud's Legacy: Critical Theory and Society
Amy Buzby

Politics and Theatre in Twentieth-Century Europe: Imagination and Resistance
Margot Morgan

The Radical Humanism of Erich Fromm

Kieran Durkin

palgrave
macmillan

First published in 2014 by
PALGRAVE MACMILLAN®
in the United States—a division of St. Martin's Press LLC,
175 Fifth Avenue, New York, NY 10010.

Where this book is distributed in the UK, Europe and the rest of the world,
this is by Palgrave Macmillan, a division of Macmillan Publishers Limited,
registered in England, company number 785998, of Houndmills,
Basingstoke, Hampshire RG21 6XS.

Palgrave Macmillan is the global academic imprint of the above companies
and has companies and representatives throughout the world.

Palgrave® and Macmillan® are registered trademarks in the United States,
the United Kingdom, Europe and other countries.

ISBN: 978–1–137–43639–9

Library of Congress Cataloging-in-Publication Data

Durkin, Kieran.
    The radical humanism of Erich Fromm / Kieran Durkin.
        pages cm.—(Critical political theory and radical practice)
    Includes bibliographical references and index.
    ISBN 978–1–137–43639–9 (hardback)
        1. Fromm, Erich, 1900–1980. 2. Humanism—Philosophy.
    3. Humanistic psychology. 4. Psychoanalysis. I. Title.

BF109.F76D87 2014
150.19'86—dc23   2014008946

A catalogue record of the book is available from the British Library.

Design by Newgen Knowledge Works (P) Ltd., Chennai, India.

First edition: September 2014

10 9 8 7 6 5 4 3 2 1

Contents

Acknowledgments

This book was a long time in the making. Because of this, many have influenced it—many more than it is possible or even conceivable to mention. As an undergraduate student in what seems like a different age, Scott Meikle and Harvie Ferguson jolted me out of my complacency in their own, very different ways, placing profoundly conflicting worldviews with their attendant problematics and problems forefrontal in what was then my youthful deliberating mind. Though this tribute may not wholly please them—so different are many of the positions I take in these pages from their own (this particularly applies to Harvie)—they nevertheless influenced the tangents of my thinking at a crucial stage in my intellectual development to such a degree that I would find it hard to overstate their importance.

In terms of the construction of the book itself, two people in particular stand out for special mention. Bridget Fowler and Andy Smith took the time to read the entire manuscript in its various guises, providing invaluable commentary and suggestions that have surely saved it from the worst of fates that might have befallen it—that it might not experience the best of fates is, of course, not their responsibility. Again, while not everything in these pages will be to their tastes, Bridget and Andy were highly influential and supportive throughout, showing exemplary human qualities alongside impressive intellectual acumen. I would also like to acknowledge the encouragement and advice given by Daniel Burston, Lawrence Wilde, Annette Thomson, Matthew Waites, Matt Dawson, and the disruptions to the rigidity of my thinking caused by Stephen Jackson and Lisa Bradley. During the long-drawn-out process of composing this book, where I had to constantly fight the irresistible tendency to become lost in my own tortured monologue, engagement with other thinkers possessing productively similar (or not so similar) views to my own was a much needed form of nourishment and challenge.

A central acknowledgment must be offered to Rainer Funk, whose friendly and encouraging hospitality while I was at the Fromm Archives in Tübingen was gratefully received. Dr. Funk gave up significant time to field my many and varied questions, both while I was in Germany and by email after I had returned. His work as sole executor of Fromm's literary estate, alongside his own publishing career, has been and is the greatest service to Frommian thought outside of that of Fromm himself.

Finally, and above all, I would like to thank my partner, Jodie, for her forbearance, love, and support during the writing process, and for sticking with me through the ups and downs of a small lifetime together. This book is dedicated—if it matters at all that I say this—to her, to our daughter, Heidi, and to my parents, Dermot and Linda, whose example to me as I was growing up led in no small way to my finding myself here and to the enduring pull of Erich Fromm.

Introduction

Writing in 1986, John Rickert, an American philosopher, remarked of Erich Fromm that he had "long been out of fashion" (Rickert, 1986: 1). Almost three decades since Rickert's observation—and with the publication of a number of book-length studies dedicated to Fromm's thought[1]—it seems that this lack of fashionableness has not proved terminal. But while a terminality has failed to set in, Fromm remains a fairly anonymous figure in contemporary academia, his name generally absent from most mainstream social theory and his ideas markedly under-utilized in social scientific and humanitarian thought. Caught between the "analytic" and "continental" philosophical traditions and their advocates in the human sciences, Fromm's thought is generally neither wanted nor respected—its overt humanism a seemingly permanent embarrassment, its psychoanalytic genealogy a peculiar anathema, and its accessible style a more or less effective barrier to high regard. This is unfortunate, given the condition of contemporary social theory, and, in fact, symptomatic of this very condition. For despite signs that significant change may be possible, social theoretical thought seems largely to still be adversely affected by the anti-humanism and other excessively relativistic tropes characteristic of the linguistic turn and of structuralist and poststructuralist thought more generally. This anti-humanism centrally reduces to an overstated attack on the axiomatic precepts of humanism—namely, the idea of "man" (or the human being), "the subject," "the self," and of history as the realm in which human perfectibility (or flourishing) can manifest itself. As Roy Bhaskar has shown, the philosophical underpinning of most academic thought today is influenced either by the "empirical realism" of positivism (and the related idea that we can only know about what we can experience or test) or by the "super-idealism" of "postmodern" thought (and the related idea that we create or change the world with our theories), or of unintentional combinations of the two (Bhaskar, 2011: 13). These positions, which are misrepresentations of the ontological and epistemological realities, have led to a peculiarly high-minded reductionism that is hard to displace, effective in all spheres up to and including the ethical and political.

What Fromm's thought can offer, in spite of its unfavorable reputation, is a vital and generally overlooked contribution to the rectification of this situation. His mixture of essentialist and constructionist aspects, which was the direct result of his policy of refined continuation in relation to classical humanist thought (particularly as he saw it as manifested in Judaism, Marxism, and Freudianism), is potentially greatly instructive in relation to the task of recovering the central categories of humanist thought that have been put out of use over the past 50 years or so. Writing in the middle part of the last century, and spurred on by the intellectual challenge of grappling with and accommodating the differing imperatives of a wide variety of thought systems, Fromm advances a qualified form of essentialism compatible with the central ideas of constructionist thought that have increasingly dominated large swathes of the academy. Based on an unfashionable old idea—namely, that there *is* such a thing as a "human nature," which is, however, variously manifested in different social and cultural contexts—Fromm's thought seeks to account for, and raise to a central analytical status, the idea of a basic psychological dynamism that underlies human experience and that figures as a fundamental variable in the social process. Crucially, such a dynamic account is premised on the idea that the psychological is not only the refraction of aspects of social experience but also the interaction of these refracted aspects with basic human drives or "existential needs," as Fromm terms them. As such, the dynamism that informs Fromm's thinking is based on a form of human universalism that leads to a productive concern with ethical normativism, objective values statements, and, ultimately, a realistic and achievable form of democratic socialism based on resolutely humanist criteria.

What ought to be stressed here is that Fromm's writings are *primarily* an expression of humanism. Although often framed in psychoanalytic language and generally set up as sociopsychoanalytical project, they are first and foremost the expression of his underlying religio-philosophical premise, while at the same time helping to define it. To say this is not to deny that psychoanalysis was an absolutely central feature of Fromm's thought: analyzing almost daily for 50 years, Fromm always approached issues with the dynamism of the psyche in mind. What I am saying is that Fromm's thinking, including the psychoanalytic framework he generally employed as central to it, is constituted by a prior and deeper humanism that characterizes his corpus *as a whole*. In making this contention I am explicitly and self-consciously opposing the suggestion, proffered by Martin Birnbach, and then by Don Hausdorff, that Fromm's humanism arrives unheralded in 1947 with the publication of *Man for Himself*. Based on what seems to me to be a failure to appreciate the subtlety of Fromm's qualified essentialism in *Escape from Freedom*, Birnbach and Hausdorff suggest that there is a shift in Fromm's thought—brought about by the barbarity and destructiveness of the Second World War—from what they take to be the stringent cultural relativism of *Escape from Freedom* to the undeniable ethical and normative humanism of *Man for Himself* (Birnbach, 1962: 81; Hausdorff, 1972: 38).[2] While it is almost certainly the case that the horrors of the Second World War affected Fromm's thinking, perhaps prompting him to place more direct and explicit stress on ethical and normative humanist aspects, it is surely not a consistent reading of Fromm to suggest that this was a rupture in his thinking. Fromm had talked of the "nature of man" as far back as 1932, in one of his programmatic articles for the Frankfurt *Institut für Sozialforschung* (Institute for Social Research), returning to this idea in *Escape from Freedom* in a self-conscious and explicit attempt to tread the line between complete malleability and complete fixity. As such—and as I will argue in the subsequent chapters—Fromm's thought can legitimately, and in fact most adequately, be described as consistently humanist, and, in particular, as consistently *radical* humanist. Having said this, Fromm's usage of the phrase "radical humanism" dates, in fact, to the middle-to-end of his career, appearing as a description of his intellectual project for the first time in *You Shall Be as Gods*, in 1966 (prior to this point Fromm had spoken of "normative humanism," "socialist humanism," "Renaissance humanism," "Enlightenment humanism," "dialectic humanism," as well as plain "humanism"). Although Fromm was to adopt the description explicitly only at this point, it can nevertheless be legitimately seen as a retroactive descriptor that fits to his work, considered as a whole. To claim this is not to ignore the differences that obtain in Fromm's thought at different periods (although there are comparatively few consequential differences in what is a generally strikingly homogeneous body of work). It is, rather, to claim that "radical humanism" can be understood as the appropriate categorization of Fromm's entire intellectual edifice, irrespective of the differences that obtain between periods; indeed, part of the argument advanced in these pages is that radical humanism can be seen as the *hermeneutic center* or *nucleus* of Fromm's thought, the circumference of this thought encompassing the various evolutionary forms that his movements from the center take on.

The thinking that informs Fromm's writings, and which I take to consistently do so, is radically humanist in the first instance by virtue of the fact that it seeks to go to the root. As a radical humanism, then, it is a humanism that seeks for consistency and that is self-consciously grounded on a metaphysical realism/essentialism that recognizes the existence of the human being as an entity possessed of certain properties, the said properties constituting the ground upon which value for human beings exists and upon which the very idea of ethics makes sense. As such, it is a humanism that is centrally motivated by a commitment to the belief in the dignity and unity of humankind and in the possibility of the unfolding toward perfection of human nature. Having such a commitment, it is also a humanism that is centrally focused on the individual and on the development of the characteristically human powers of the individual that are compatible with flourishing and well-being. In particular, it is a humanism that places a marked stress on the goal of achieving authentic selfhood, the stripping away of illusions, achieving inner and outer harmony. In being such a humanism, then, Fromm's radical humanism is a humanism that tries to restore, in a manner similar to Ernst Bloch, Adam Schaff, Leszek Kolakowski, and the Yugoslav Praxis philosophers, the early Marx's focus on the individual and ethics to the forefront of socialist thought, focusing primarily on the experience of the subject as the pivotal factor in social change. It is characteristic of Fromm's radical humanism, over and above these proximate accounts, that it confronts the false individualism that reigns today, as well as the pathology of normalcy that sustains it—alienation and idolatry in all their secular forms—and that it does so by proceeding on the basis of a depth psychology concerned with the importance of value and ethical problems for the understanding of human psychic and social life. It is characteristic also in that Fromm's is not merely a philosophical humanism, but one related to the applied understanding of "actually existing real men," both in the sense of being simultaneously personally and societally relevant (the creation of a New Man and New Society) and in the sense that it enables the reinstating of humanist analytical categories in social analysis. The overall concern, which encompasses these issues, is a concern with challenging the "forgetting of humanism" that dominates both the intellectual and wider culture today and which prevents the main goal of the renaissance of humanism.

Reclaiming Humanism

It is unfashionable in most respected intellectual circles today to talk of humanism. If not for what is taken as the irredeemably protean nature of the term itself—the contention, as Michel Foucault puts it, that "the humanistic thematic is in itself too supple, to diverse, too inconsistent to serve as an axis for reflection" (Foucault, 1984a: 44)—then the fact of its association with the acts of terror and barbarity committed in its name is enough for most to steer well clear of it. Beyond this, the influence of Martin Heidegger looms large here, his famous "Letter on 'Humanism,'" with its argument for an antimetaphysical form of philosophy and the Nietzschean belief that there is no hope of establishing universal moral ethical standards of value. These aspects, added to the highly influential idea that "langauge is the house of being" (Heidegger, 1998: 239), are the bedrock for most anti-humanisms that followed in Heidegger's wake. In light of such opposition, the desire to resurrect and advance a humanist scheme of thought will no doubt seem strange and ill-advised to many. It is my contention that this assumption is misplaced, and that there *is* a point in reclamation in relation to humanism. For rather than continually reinventing, moving farther and farther into tortured neologistical territory, we can (and should) seek to clarify, purify, and ultimately reclaim humanism, thereby preventing serious damage to our understanding by becoming lost in terminological muddles. In this process we need to denounce what is wrong in the idea as it has come to be expressed but remain resolute in praise of what was right in the idea all along, always seeking to ensure a consistent interpretation that can deal with the attacks brought against it on the basis of naïve or nefarious applications. The act of reclamation here seems especially apt, considering the intuitive conceptual link that exists between the label "humanism" and the kind of "humanistic" experience it is generally assumed to refer to. As such, maintaining the continued separation between the label and the experience, and thus the natural expressive power the notion possesses, will ensure that progressive social theory will remain all the poorer and all the more restricted for it.

The term "humanism" (*humanismus*) was most likely devised by Friedrich Immanuel Niethammer, a nineteenth-century German educationalist, to describe the German high school and university curriculum based on what had been known since the Middle Ages as the "humanities"—the study of ancient Greek, Latin, and the literature, history, and culture of those who spoke these languages (Davies, 2008: 10). While this is so, the term has taken on much wider usage, most consistently seen as referring to certain central as aspects of the humanistic thought systems of the predominant figures of the Renaissance and Enlightenment, particularly the passionate belief in the unity and "perfectibility of man" as realizable through commitment and effort. For Fromm, in fact, it was possible to read humanism back into human history, at least as far back as the turn to monotheism in what Jaspers (1951) has described as the "axial age"—something Fromm does through the imputation of a common ideational core that can be identified in this history and that is perennially worth reclaiming. As Daniel Burston has eloquently put it:

> Whatever form it takes and whenever it appears, humanism always emphasizes the fundamental unity of the human species, the singularity and worth of persons, and our duty to defend and promote human dignity and welfare in our time, rather than in kingdom come. Furthermore, humanism (in all its forms) emphasizes that human beings are not just the passive playthings of Fate—or of language, ideology, and so on. It allows for the existence of a degree of selfdetermination which is not trivial, and must never be overlooked. By the humanist account, people can (and must) take an active role in shaping their own destinies and their own identities, if they wish to be truly free. Freedom, by this account, is not the mere absence of external constraint, or something that someone else can bestow on you. It is something that is earned or achieved through reflection and diligent self-development. (2014: 916)

Though it may be "almost impossible to think of a crime that has not been committed in the name of humanity" (Davies, 2008: 141), it should be similarly difficult to fail to recognize that the vast majority of these crimes were committed in direct contravention of the central principles of humanist thought interpreted in consistent and robust fashion. The fact that it can be said of all humanisms that "until now [they] have been imperial" (Davies, 2008: 141) is the very point in returning to Fromm's *radical* humanism, and the point in reclamation more broadly.

It is the contention of this book that the best way to affect this reclamation is by a deeper and fuller restatement of Fromm's radical humanism alongside a sustained critique of the ideas that would seek to oppose it. To suggest "restating" here, however, is slightly disingenuous in that Fromm never really offers an account of radical humanism in a systematic form. As such, my intention is to offer a forensic investigation of the claims that underlie Fromm's radical humanism in its fullest expression and to thereby provide conceptual clarity on radical humanism as a system of thought taken in itself—the importance of the latter point has been noted by Rainer Funk, who said of Fromm that "his own presentation frequently suffers from an imprecise and inconsistent use of concepts and too limited a systematic interest" (Funk, 1982: xiv). That there are clear pitfalls in such an undertaking is readily acknowledged. The syncretic nature of Fromm's radical humanism is such that it unites various trends from different intellectual traditions, pulling together influences from the philosophic and hermeneutical traditions of Judaism and Christianity, Marxism and Freudianism, and aspects of Enlightenment and Romantic thought, as well as from the disciplines of anthropology, neurobiology, and evolutionary biology. As Funk puts it:

> To evaluate Fromm fairly, to arrive at a final judgement, one would need to be competent in all the various disciplines and sciences, for to Fromm's credit, he risked a global view of man and his history at a time when the sciences were becoming ever more specialized. His scientific work, its understanding and critique, propose a task one can never discharge in a wholly satisfactory manner. (1982: 6)

As much as this is true, the syncretic nature of Fromm's thought is where its real importance lies—and, therefore, where I have tried to go.

Others have gone before me, of course. The clearest precursor to the present study is Lawrence Wilde's excellent *Erich Fromm and the Quest for Solidarity*.[3] Both the present book and Wilde's study put forward a positive assessment of Fromm's thought and make reference to the salience of his essentialism and ethical normativism. Both also contextualize it in relation to current issues/thinkers. The singular and concerted focus on "radical humanism" as an *explicit* social theory undertaken here, however, is unique, as is its distinctive contextualization via the thinkers of what I term the "anti-humanist paradigm" (in particular, Althusser, Adorno, Lévi-Strauss, Foucault, Lacan, Derrida, Lyotard, and Rorty). In addition to this, the present book gives greater space to a discussion of theological, psychological, and anthropological issues pertaining to radical humanism as a system of thought taken in itself, engaging in a generally more sustained level of argumentation in favor of humanism (and its related essentialism), whereas Wilde's focus is geared more toward the explication of Fromm's ideas in relation to political thought and practice. A further important difference between the two works is the greater stress in the present work on excavating Fromm's significant debates with Marcuse, Horkheimer, and Adorno, showing his positions here to be highly relevant to contemporary understandings of these thinkers as well as Marx, Freud, and the theorization of social change more generally. All things considered, I hope that the present study might be capable of acting as a companion to Wilde's recent Fromm scholarship, complementing this work by helping to fill out radical humanism as a developed system of thought.

Perhaps the best studies of Fromm, apart from Wilde's more recent offering, are Rainer Funk's *Erich Fromm: The Courage to be Human* and Daniel Burston's *The Legacy of Erich Fromm*. Funk's book is, in many senses, the basic Fromm textbook.[4] Like the present book, it is a full-length attempt to explain Fromm's thought in its totality, placing particular stress on the

Judaic underpinnings of Fromm's thought. In so doing, Funk has shown deep and lasting similarities between the underlying form of his thought and that found in Hasidic thinking. I have sought to build on Funk's holistic account of Fromm, attempting also to map out the depth of the Judaic influence (especially in relation to Hermann Cohen and other aspects of biblical analysis, where I think I have unearthed some particularly strong explicit connections not stressed by Funk) and to make sustained linkages through Marx and Freud to radical humanism as a position in itself. Although both Funk's study and the present one offer a sympathetic account of Fromm's thought, I locate more tensions—and do so in different places—than Funk does, while seeking to contextualize his thought in relation to social theory more generally, which Funk does not.

Burtson's impressive intellectual biography tackles Fromm's thought primarily from a psychoanalytic angle, although he does also make some important connections to the social and philosophical thought that Fromm was exposed to in his intellectual development. Stressing Fromm's position as one of what he terms Freud's "loyal opposition," having significant connection to, but remaining crucially distinct from, Adler, Jung, Rank, and Ferenczi, Burston shows Fromm to be a pivotal yet unrecognized figure in the development of interpersonal psychoanalysis. Partly because Burston has done this so well, and partly because my focus is less on Fromm's connection to the psychoanalytic tradition and more on Fromm as a humanist thinker, I have generally avoided detailed discussion of Fromm's similarities to his close psychoanalytic predecessors and colleagues. I have, however, sought to resurrect and flesh out Fromm's much underutilized critique of Freud's underlying mechanistic philosophy and bourgeois biases, contextualizing it in relation to his ultimately fractured relationship with Horkheimer, Adorno, and Marcuse. Aspects of this fractured relationship—and various points of comparison—recur throughout the book, hopefully to revealing effect.

Outside of these studies, there are several other accounts that deserve mention. Annette Thompson's *Erich Fromm: Explorer of the Human Condition* is a good, short, critical introduction to Fromm, written primarily from a psychological and social-psychological angle. My account offers a more detailed and laudatory assessment of Fromm's humanism and has a greater concern to place his thought in the social theoretical canon. Svante Lundgren's *Fight against Idols: Erich Fromm on Religion, Judaism and the Bible* is a good account of Fromm's views on religion, but does not deal with social theory or humanism per se. Gerhard P. Knapp's *The Art of Living: Erich Fromm's Life and Works* is a weaker effort on Fromm, showing reliance on outmoded assumptions absorbed through what seems to be an overly strong affiliation to Marcuse and Adorno. Lawrence Friedman's *The Lives of Erich Fromm: Love's Prophet*, the long-overdue first full-length biography of Fromm, manages to bring out certain aspects of Fromm's personality that illuminate the potential psychological basis of some of his theoretical proclivities. As important as Friedman's study is, it is of a quite different overall nature to the present study, with nothing in terms of content that pits Friedman's work against what I am arguing here.

Besides these studies, there are a few accounts of Fromm to be found in textbooks on the "Frankfurt School" and critical theory—Douglas Kellner in *Critical Theory, Marxism and Modernity* and, particularly, Stephen Eric Bronner in *Of Critical Theory and its Theorists*, offering perceptive and balanced appraisals of Fromm's contribution. Martin Jay's *The Dialectical Imagination: A History of the Frankfurt School and the Institute of Social Research 1923–1950* and Rolf Wiggershaus's *The Frankfurt School: Its History, Theories and Political Significance* touch on Fromm's thought, offering a mixture of astute analysis (particularly Jay) and pejorative misreadings (particularly Wiggershaus) of Fromm. Either way, the focus in these works is generally on the Frankfurt School, considered from the point of view of its eventual critical theory than from the point of view of Fromm's thought taken in itself, with the attendant limitations this entails. Neil McLaughlin, writing primarily from a sociological angle, has done much to argue for Fromm's contemporary relevance in relation to social scientific thinking. In a series of important articles (1996; 1998; 1999; 2000; 2001; 2007), McLaughlin has helped to draw out many of the reasons as to why Fromm is an unfairly "forgotten intellectual" today (McLaughlin, 1998) while simultaneously helping to draw attention to the prescient and groundbreaking nature of much of Fromm's social-psychological thought. I echo much of McLaughlin's appraisal of Fromm, but seek to draw out even further the social theoretical importance of his social psychology, particularly in relation to stressing the potential for a social theoretical reappropriation of his idea of social character.

Over and above these accounts I have sought to present Fromm as a consistent and before-all-else *radical humanist* operating with a qualified form of essentialism. I have tried to show that his humanism is sensible, viable, and desirable, and that the essentialism that underlies it is crucial to its success—enabling him to avoid the excesses of extreme relativism or absolute essentialism. In addition to this, I have tried to show that he is a unique contribution within the streams of Marxian and psychoanalytic theory, that his attempt at fusing Marx and Freud into a radical humanist form of social psychology deserves to be returned to, offering as it does the opportunity of ensuring the retention of the analytical categories of humanist thought in relation to social analysis. I have also tried to resurrect his call for a renaissance of humanism, for a New Man and a New Society in which we practice the "art of living" based on the theoretical "science of man," confronting in the process the firmly held opposition to such apparently simplistic "objectivism." Further to this, I have tried to portray his gradualist socialism and secular messianism as unique though crucial contributions to genuine and feasible revolutionary progress, and that a concern with the ethical well-being and commitment of the individual is the basis of this progress. Finally, I have tried to show that his normative humanism and mysticism are productive and, in the latter case, surprising aids to this progress; that a concern with ethics need not be moralism, and that the deeply ingrained opposition to theological thought in contemporary secular societies has pernicious effects wider than its intention (and wider than is good for critical thinking). If I have achieved any of the above to a significant degree, Fromm ought to be seen as eminently worth returning to, and radical humanism ought to be seen as an appealing social theoretical position from which to commence social analysis.

Outline and Structure

In what follows I have striven to ensure that as little complexity as possible is lost in the inevitably truncated discussions that are characteristic of any expositive account. There are undoubtedly some ultimate insufficiencies, some curtailed and unsettled arguments, etc.; but, while this is the case, I hope there is also definite progression in the task of trying to make more understandable and palatable the underappreciated salience of Fromm's thought. As much as the point was to be faithful to Fromm, it was also to be faithful to the *spirit* of Fromm and to try to move his thought forward wherever possible so that it could more readily face the malaises of twenty-first-century social theory. Part of the intention, then, was to search for the strongest and most consistent account of Fromm's thought (particularly his radical humanism as manifested in this thought), and thereby to recover something of its progressive and constructive power. Naturally, as a text-based study, my methodological deliberations were not massively complex—it was plain that the study would consist of the analysis of Fromm's texts and the ideas contained within them. The only serious deliberation was *what* to study. From a fairly early stage it was decided that a focus on the length and breadth of Fromm's writings would be the most appropriate and revealing approach. Despite the challenges this posed (voluminous as these writings are), this seemed the only way to really get close to the heart of what radical humanism is, in Fromm's writings. The fact that Fromm's writings present a fairly unitary front meant that the difficulty was lessened somewhat, although it did mean that vigilance was required in noting conceptual changes (not always stressed by Fromm) and in always seeking to weigh up what Fromm meant at a particular point as well as what his position could be said to be overall. In the process of researching for the present book, I visited the Fromm Archives in Tübingen, where I was given the opportunity to peruse Fromm's often lengthy correspondences, as well as unpublished papers and visual and audio recordings. This exploration of Fromm's unpublished writings and old audio and visual recordings was a crucial supplement to the textual analysis. This—added to the pursuit of every possible publication of Fromm's—was borne of the belief that the breadth and depth of a writer's thought is not necessarily contained in full in his or her published works, that their often private and less formalized utterances provide glimpses of a revealing truth in relation to that writer, aiding the appreciation and adequate representation of the totality of their thought. I believe that this policy helped greatly in piecing together a clearer idea of Fromm and his thought.

In terms of structure, I decided to open the book with an intellectual biography of Fromm. Chapter 1, then, consists of a summative account of Fromm's thinking, focusing on his major publications and the central events in his life. This is apt not only because of the general lack of awareness with regard to Fromm and his contribution to twentieth-century thought, but also by virtue of what is a generally continuous development of a central nucleus of ideas throughout his various writings. An intellectual biographical sketch, therefore, reveals something of the subtle shifts that took place in the development of Fromm's thought and which contribute to the radical humanist position that emerges from his body of work, providing in the process the unifying basis for later more substantive chapters. As part of this discussion, I offer an account of the formative role of the Judaic tradition as Fromm experienced it in his family milieu and as part of the Jewish community of early twentieth-century Frankfurt, as well as his conversion to psychoanalysis and eventual move away from orthodox psychoanalysis toward the development of his own distinctive psychoanalytic position. In addition to this, I offer an account of Fromm's largely unrecognized role in the early period of the *Institut für Sozialforschung* in Frankfurt (including an account of his fractured relationship with Horkheimer, Adorno, and Marcuse), his rise to "public intellectual" status in America (including his influence on the American political scene—from activist to presidential level), and his return to Europe and influence on Green-alternative movement there.

Chapter 2 is concerned with outlining the trajectory of Fromm's radical humanism in inaugural form, seeking, in the process, to provide conceptual clarity on what can be said to be the roots of radical humanism as a system of thought taken in itself. The discussion here centers on the development of Fromm's radical humanism from its beginnings in the philosophical and hermeneutic traditions of Judaic thought, through the philosophical and sociological thought of Karl Marx and the psychoanalytic theory and practice of Sigmund Freud. What I have sought to convey here is Fromm's radical humanist *inversion* of Judaic principles and their unfolding into materialist and psychological domains. As part of this discussion I focus on Fromm's reading of the Old Testament and its later tradition as a humanistic development in thought, as well as a discussion of the influence of the mysticism of Habad Hasidism, showing how the spiritual autonomy and self-sufficiency Fromm finds embedded in these traditions can be said to form the central injunction of his radical humanism: namely, the idea that man must "develop his own powers" and reach the goal of complete independence, "penetrating through fictions and illusions to full awareness of reality." This discussion is then supplemented with an account of how Marx's thought can be said to represent the inversion of these Judaic influences, his penetrating engagement with Hegel and Feuerbach leading to an anthropological, materialist humanism that in many senses, mirrors Fromm's own. The chapter ends with a discussion of Freud as representing, in certain crucial respects, a development of Marx's materialism, offering what Fromm saw as the basis of a "science of the irrational" and, thus, a radical humanist conceptual instrument for more fully understanding "really existing active men."

Chapter 3 consists of a discussion of Fromm's radical humanist understanding of psychoanalysis relative to that of Freud and to his colleagues at the *Institut für Sozialforschung*. It opens with an account of what Fromm takes to be Freud's insufficient picture of relatedness, before moving on to offer a discussion of his "existential" view of the human condition and an account of the delineation of what he contends are the central "existential needs" common to humanity (central to this discussion is the conveyance of the fact that Fromm views the characteristic human passions not as the result of frustrated or sublimated physiological needs but as the "attempt to make sense out of life and to experience the optimum of intensity and strength under the given circumstances"). This is followed by an account of Fromm's own "science of character," demonstrating how it is built on but crucially diverges from Freud's prior theory, i.e., as deriving from the specific kinds of relatedness to the world gained in the process of living as opposed to the relatively closed and instinctually determined forms of relatedness posited by Freud. In addition to this, I engage in a thorough discussion and analysis of Fromm's own complex character typology (or characterology), including his account of the "marketing character," as well as the "biophilia/

necrophilia" and "having/being" alternatives. The chapter finishes with a defense of Fromm's overall psychoanalytic position against the criticisms of his ex-colleagues at the *Institut für Sozialforschung*.

Chapter 4 is concerned with outlining Fromm's psychoanalytic social psychology, including his concepts of "social character" and "the social unconscious" and his various social psychoanalytic case studies. Here I explain the genesis of Fromm's whole sociopsychoanalytical enterprise as found in his attempt to produce a functioning synthesis of Marx and Freud and how this effective melding of historical materialism and psychology seeks to deal with the problem of the extent to which the personality structure of the individual is determined by social factors and, conversely, with the extent to which psychological factors themselves influence and alter the social process. As part of this discussion I explain how the goal of psychoanalytic social psychology is centered on discerning the psychic traits common to the members of a group and to explaining their unconscious roots in terms of shared life experiences (to "investigate how certain psychic attitudes common to members of a group are related to their common life experiences"). I also discuss Fromm's introduction of the idea of the "socially conditioned filters" of *language, logic*, and *taboos*. The chapter finishes with a qualified defense of Fromm's psychoanalytic social psychology, praising it as a radical humanist, Marxian attempt to improve upon the sexual reductionism of the early psychoanalytic researchers and to extend Weber's analyses into regions where he had not ventured (and thus as pointing out the right path for a Marxian social psychology, despite the fact that his analyses may have sometimes fallen short of fulfilling the demands that he set for them).

Chapter 5 essentially consists of a defense of (Fromm's radical) humanism against what can be called the "anti-humanist paradigm" that is prevalent in many sectors of the social sciences and humanities today. As part of this paradigm, I discuss the anti-humanism of Louis Althusser, Theodor Adorno, Michel Foucault, Claude Lévi-Strauss, Jacques Lacan, Jacques Derrida, Jean François Lyotard, and Richard Rorty, showing how their thought is constructed in opposition to the axiomatic precepts of humanism (namely, the idea of "man," of "the subject," and of "the self," etc.). What I then try to show is how the positions of these thinkers—which are concerned at base with the problematization of the naïve ethnocentricity of the classical humanist constructs—have a tendency to get caught up in this very problematization, in excessive attributions of linguistic and cultural determination or one-sided stresses on fragmentation and discontinuity, and which consequently tends to lack any significant reference to the human being and, thereby, a convincing account of subjectivity. I finish the chapter with a defense of the idea of the subject and the self (citing Margaret Archer,

Antonio Damasio, Clifford Geertz, Melford Spiro, Nancy Chodorow, and Gananath Obeyesekere) against the idea that the self is wholly a product of socialization and against the idea of multiple selves, which implies that there can be no dominant and "authentic self," and, therefore, no sovereign subject.

Chapter 6 seeks to resurrect Fromm's call for a "renaissance of humanism" as manifested in the creation of a New Man and a New Society. It begins with an account and defense of Fromm's reading of humanism back into Western history (based on the identification of what Fromm took to be its central idea and experience namely, man as an end) as well as a defense of this account from potential accusations of "historical solecism" or "teleological thinking." From this discussion, it moves on to an account of what can be said to be Fromm's narrative of the "forgetting of humanism" that has taken place over the past three centuries or more, including his account of the loss of the religio-philosophical worldview, with its characteristic questioning of existence, of our ability to connect with our existence and to recognize the norms and values which follow from it (his normative humanist or naturalistic ethical position is stressed). After this, it deals with Fromm's account of what he takes to be the profound *indifference* to the human individual which predominates in our age, cloaked by an illusory individualism that conceals a "pathology of normalcy." Central to this discussion is what Fromm identifies as our idolatrous worship of things, and the greed, narcissism, and destructiveness that goes with it, as well as his descriptive account of alienation in various spheres of life, including detachment from real, meaningful participation in work and politics and the triumph of reified ethics. The chapter finishes with a defense of the pertinence and salience of Fromm's call for inner and outer transformation and for the normative humanist philosophy that underpins it, warding off criticisms of outmodedness, conformity, utopianism, and authoritarianism, and lauding his idea of the "paradox of hope."

In the conclusion, I stress the underlying sophistication of Fromm's radical humanist thought and its potential to act as the basis upon which the reclamation of the central analytical and normative categories and schemas of traditional humanism is possible. In particular, I stress Fromm's policy of refined continuation in relation to the classical humanist tradition and how this policy allows a fruitful mixture of essentialism and constructionism that can accommodate concerns over naïveté and ethnocentrism. In addition to this, I stress the distinctness of Fromm's radical humanism as well as showing how it relates to previous forms of humanism, and how it can facilitate a renaissance of humanism that is stronger than was found in these previous forms. As part of this discussion, I describe Fromm as primarily a beginning, as opposed to a terminus, but a fertile beginning who calls us on to further development. I end the piece with a discussion of the idea of a contemporary "science of man" filled with the humanistic spirit, and capable of helping social theory progressing toward its historical role of realizing a more effective and enlightened praxis.

Note on Terminology

From the early stages of writing I was confronted with the terminological problem of rendering consistent, but also appropriate, my discussion of the central proposition of humanist thought: namely, "the human," or, in the older language of Fromm and his influences, "man." This was an issue that proved difficult to resolve satisfactorily, considering my reliance at certain points on quoted material (and paraphrased discussion next to this quoted material), and which ultimately led to my use of the gender-biased noun "man" at times when I would otherwise not have done so. Wherever possible—that is, when not connected to a discussion of an older author for whom "man" was a regular feature of their discussion, or when a change in terminology did not disrupt the conceptual flow of the discussion—I have tried to speak of "humans," "human beings," "Homo sapiens," "humankind," "us," "our," etc. I was partly encouraged to adopt this approach of accommodation in light of Fromm's explanation as to why he persisted in using the gender-biased "man" despite awareness of, and sympathy with, the argument against this usage. Citing the lack of a common gender third-person singular noun in English (his adopted language) and his prior usage of the generic, sexless *Mensch* in his native German, Fromm explains that, though aware of the issue of sexism in language, he wanted to retain the term "man" as "a term of reference for the species *Homo sapiens*." "The use of "man" in this context," he states, "without differentiation of sex, has a long tradition in humanist thinking, and I do not believe we can do without a word that denotes clearly the human species character. No such difficulty exists in the German language; one uses the word *Mensch* to refer to the non–sex-differentiated being. But even in English the word 'man' is used in the same sex-undifferentiated way as the German *Mensch*, meaning human being or the human race. I think it is advisable to restore its nonsexual meaning to the word 'man' rather than substituting awkward sounding words" (2008 [1976]: xx). While not in full agreement with Fromm here, I was somewhat reassured by his explicit discussion of the issue, and have therefore sought to follow his practice where it seemed most appropriate to do so.

CHAPTER 1

The Life and Writings of a Radical Humanist

Considering the comparative disregard of Fromm's thought with that of other thinkers from the same period—particularly his Frankfurt School associates and contemporaries, Adorno, Marcuse, Benjamin,[1] and also slightly later thinkers such as R. D. Laing, Michel Foucault, Jacques Derrida, etc.—there is particular benefit in engaging in an intellectual biographical account of Fromm at the outset. This is apt not only because of the general lack of awareness with regard to Fromm and his contribution to twentieth-century thought, but also by virtue of the impressive degree of continuity that characterizes his writings. An intellectual biographical sketch can therefore reveal something of the subtle shifts that took place in the development of Fromm's thought and that contribute to the radical humanist position that emerges from his body of work. Inclusion of a biographical sketch is of particular importance in the case of Fromm in that, as someone for whom human worth was measured by actions and deeds as much as by words, it will reveal something of the extent to which he attempted to enact his philosophy in his personal life, or at least reveal something of his preoccupation with humanism in both theoretical *and* practical terms. There is also a more utilitarian reason for opening with such a sketch: outlining Fromm's intellectual biographical details, including a broadly chronological listing of his major publications, will help to situate the discussion of the later chapters in relation to his life, thereby freeing up these chapters for more substantive and unencumbered discussion.

Most of what is written in this chapter has been drawn from Rainer Funk's *Erich Fromm: His Life and Ideas—An Illustrated Biography*. Lawrence Friedman's recent full-length biography—*The Lives of Erich Fromm: Love's*

Prophet—and some unpublished correspondence sourced from the Fromm archives provided some important and illuminating additions. Other than Funk's and Friedman's biographies, there has been relatively little written about Fromm's life. Although it is true that there are bits and pieces of biography to be found in certain publications, they are generally found in studies of Fromm that are rarely read, or in studies of the Frankfurt School that generally tend to consider Fromm from the point of view of the School itself, and particularly as part of the narrative of his departure from it. I have sought to ensure that Fromm's role in the early period of the *Institut für Sozialforschung* features as an important part of the present discussion, but that it does so from the point of view, and as part, of the story of Fromm's life taken in and of itself.

Beginnings

Fromm was born to Orthodox Jewish parents in Frankfurt am Main on March 23, 1900. His father, Naphtali, a wine merchant, was the son of a rabbi and descended, as did his mother Rosa, from a distinguished line of rabbinical scholars, notable among who was Rabbi Seligmann Bär Bamberger, author of numerous halakhic works and a central figure in the nineteenth-century Orthodox Jewish movement. Crucially, while Fromm was still a child, his great-uncle, Ludwig Krause, a renowned Talmudist from Posen, came to stay in the family home, during which time he gave Fromm his first scriptural lessons. As Fromm makes clear in a rare autobiographical sketch, what interested him in these lessons were the prophetic writings of the Old Testament and, in particular, their vision of "the End of Days" or "Messianic Time":

> I was brought up in a religious Jewish family, and the writings of the Old Testament touched me and exhilarated me more than anything else I was exposed to. Not all of them to the same degree; I was bored by or even disliked the history of the conquest of Canaan by the Hebrews; I had no use for the stories of Mordecai or Esther; nor did I—at that time—appreciate the Song of Songs. But the story of Adam and Eve's disobedience, of Adam's pleading with God for the salvation of the inhabitants of Sodom and Gomorrah, of Jonah's mission to Nineveh, and many other parts of the bible impressed me deeply. But more than anything else, I was moved by the prophetic writings, by Isaiah, Amos, Hosea; not so much by their warnings and their announcements of disaster, but by their promise of the "end of days," when nations "shall beat their swords into ploughshares and their spears into pruning hooks: nation shall not lift sword

against nation, neither shall they learn war anymore"; when all nations will be friends, and when "the earth shall be full of the knowledge of the Lord, as the waters cover the sea." (2006 [1962]: 2)

These writings, with their vision of an age of universal peace and harmony "between man and man and between man and nature" (1992 [1963]: 212), which made their initial impression on Fromm as early as 12 years of age, offered what was to become a lifelong "inexhaustible source of vitality" (1986 [1983]: 89), testimony to which is strewn throughout his numerous mature writings.

At the age of 16, while attending services at Frankfurt's Börneplatz synagogue, Fromm made the acquaintance of Rabbi Nehemiah Nobel, the then leader of the Orthodox community and the next decisive influence upon the trajectory of his thought. A former student of Hermann Cohen—who Fromm was to describe later as the 'last great Jewish philosopher' (2005: 143)—and a follower of Hasidism, Nobel imparted to Fromm a deeper and an extended understanding of the ideals of the prophets, mixing their thought with ideas from the German Enlightenment, and particularly with Goethe's idea of humanitarianism (Fishbane, 1997: 12). This example of the fusion of the modern and the old was to greatly influence Fromm, showing him that it was possible to connect the "medieval" (1986 [1983]: 98) environment of his home and family life with the contemporary world without violating the principles of the former in the process. As Fromm was to later remark, in a statement that in many ways captures the tenor of his whole intellectual enterprise, "I became an eager student of everything that created this link between the old and the new" (1986 [1983]: 100).

After the death of Nobel in 1922, Fromm began a period of study with Salman B. Rabinkov, his third and final rabbinical teacher. Formally trained as a rabbi, Rabinkov waived his right to take up office, preferring instead to teach the Talmud to a group of students on a private basis, inclusive of who were Ernst Simon, Nahum Goldman, Salman Schasar, and Hermann Struck (Funk, 1990: 3). During their six years of study together, Fromm and Rabinkov saw each other almost daily, when they would be characteristically engrossed in interpretation and discussion of the Talmud, the Old Testament, and the wider Jewish tradition—particularly Habad mysticism (a form of Hasidism) and the thought of Maimonides and Hermann Cohen. Rabinkov, who was noted as being a man of extreme humbleness, also had strong socialist sympathies, sympathies that, no doubt, influenced both Fromm's turn to Marxism and the formation of his view of Marx as a secular messianic prophet. Speaking of Rabinkov some years later in a letter to Lewis Mumford (dated April 29, 1975), Fromm remarked of him: "He influenced my life more than any other man, perhaps, and although in different forms and concepts, his ideas have remained alive in me."[2]

So important were the ideas of the Judaic tradition to Fromm's intellectual development that on leaving school his first wish was to go to Lithuania to become a Talmud scholar (Funk, 2000: 17). Only his father's explicit prohibition, prompted by an apparent desire to ensure that he remain close to the family in Frankfurt, prevented Fromm from realizing his wish. Frustrated in this respect, Fromm embarked on an academic path, setting out initially to study jurisprudence at the University of Frankfurt in 1918 but subsequently transferred to Heidelberg's Ruprecht-Karls University in 1920, where he finally enrolled in the department of National Economics (which would soon become known as "sociology"). Here Fromm studied under Karl Jaspers, Heinrich Rickert, Hans Driesch and, most importantly, Alfred Weber. Speaking of Weber in a letter to Lewis Mumford (April 29, 1975), Fromm described him, in contrast to his brother Max, as "a humanist not a nationalist, and a man of outstanding courage and integrity… the only one of my university teachers whom I considered a real teacher and master." At university, Fromm attended classes on the history of philosophy and psychology, social and political movements, and the theory of Marxism (Funk, 2000: 50–52). As a result of this period—and in addition to his studies with Nobel and Rabinkov—Fromm became systematically acquainted with the classics of the German intellectual tradition, which included, in addition to the thought of Karl Marx and the philosophical classics, the more contemporary, social scientific thought of Werner Sombart, Ferdinand Tönnies, Max Weber. These modern, Germanic, influences can be said to feature, or at least be implied, in his mature thought, interacting productively with the Judaic ideas he had encountered during his studies with Krausse, Nobel, and Rabinkov.

For his doctoral dissertation, Fromm undertook a study of the social and psychological functions of Jewish Law in the Diaspora community—the Karaite, Reform, and Hasidic sects in particular—attempting to explain how it was that they survived as Jews despite the absence of national religious institutions (Funk, 2000: 56–58). Lacking a developed psychological framework or mechanism to anchor its analysis, the study nevertheless attempted an inquiry into the psychological function of the religious ethos and other forms of solidarity within the Jewish community. Fromm saw—in a manner that clearly presages his later work on social character—how it is that ethical forms are internalized by members of groups and turned into ways of life that become definitive for those groups. Notably, the study concluded with a positive appraisal of Hasidism's ability to maintain its integrity in face of the ever-increasing encroachment of liberal-bourgeois and capitalistic values

(Funk, 1988). During his time at university, alongside Georg Salzberger, a liberal rabbi, Fromm helped set up a Jewish teaching institute (the *Freies Jüdisches Lehrhaus*), the aim of which was to counteract the widespread ignorance of Jewish religion and history among the Diaspora community. It operated through the provision of free classes taught by—in addition to Fromm and Salzberger—Rabbi Nobel, Franz Rozenweig, Martin Buber, Gershom Scholem, Leo Baeck, and Siegfried Kracauer (Funk, 2000: 41; Funk, 1988).

Despite encouragement from Alfred Weber, Fromm decided against an academic career, a decision motivated primarily by the feeling that it would constrain his development (letter to Lewis Mumford, April 29, 1975). Instead, Fromm's interests began to move toward psychoanalytic matters—a move that was facilitated in large part through his relationship with Freida Reichmann, a well-known psychoanalyst whom he married in 1926 (hereafter Freida Fromm-Reichmann). A friend since his time in Frankfurt, Fromm-Reichmann's influence on Fromm was considerable. It was with her that he first underwent psychoanalysis, introducing him to what would become an indispensable framework for his thinking for the remainder of his life. It was with her too that he discovered Buddhist thought, an encounter he would later describe as "one of the greatest experiences in my life" (1986 [1983]: 105). Lastly, it was with her that he would formally renounce Judaism—a renunciation symbolically conveyed through the eating of leavened bread on Passover (Fromm-Reichmann in Funk, 2000: 61).

Prior to this renunciation, Fromm had, together with Fromm-Reichmann, opened a sanatorium in Heidelberg for the specific psychoanalytic treatment of Jewish patients. As part of this venture, Fromm spent a year in Munich with Wilhelm Wittenberg, undertaking psychoanalytic training and attending lectures given by Emile Kraepelin, among others. After this, Fromm spent a period of analysis with Karl Landauer in Frankfurt before moving to Berlin, where he was taught by Hans Sachs and Theodore Reik at the Berlin Psychoanalytic Institute and where he was to open his first psychoanalytic practice in 1928. While in Berlin, Fromm was an attendee at Otto Fenichel's famous *Kinderseminar*, a gathering point for young dissident psychoanalysts interested in exploring the relevance of psychoanalysis for matters pertaining to socialism. Other attendees at the regular meetings included Wilhelm and Annette Reich, Edith Jacobson, and George Gero (Jacoby, 1983: 66–69). In addition to this, Fromm was an acquaintance of Paul Federn, Ernst Simmel, and Siegfried Bernfeld, all high-profile psychoanalysts and socialists with whom he shared ideas on the connections between Marxism and psychoanalysis. During this time, Fromm made his first attempts at the public communication of his ideas, publishing a psychoanalytic account of "Der Sabbat"

(The Sabbath) in *Imago* in 1927 and giving lectures on *Die Psychoanalyse des Kleinbürgetums* (The Psychoanalysis of the Petty Bourgeois), among other subjects (Funk, 2000: 61, 67).

Development and Separation

In 1929, Fromm returned to Frankfurt, where he founded the Frankfurt Psychoanalytic Institute of the South-West German Psychoanalytic Association along with Karl Landauer and Heinrich Meng. In his role at the Psychoanalytic Institute, Fromm taught courses on the relationship between psychoanalysis and sociology, giving a lecture on the same subject at the inauguration of the institute in which he laid out in brief form some of the fundamental ideas of his developing social psychology. In this lecture Fromm particularly stressed the need "to investigate what role the instinctual and unconscious play in the organization and development of society and in individual social facts, and to what extent the changes in mankind's psychological structure, in the sense of a growing ego-organization and thus a rational ability to cope with the instinctual and natural, is a sociologically relevant factor" (1989 [1929]: 38). Later that year, Fromm was invited, through his connections with Karl Landauer and Leo Löwenthal (a school friend married to Fromm's former fiancé Golde Ginsburg), to participate in the research program of the Frankfurt *Institut für Sozialforschung* (hereafter generally "Institut"), which happened to be housed in the same building as the Psychoanalytic Institute. The Institut's director, Max Horkheimer, had also seen the importance of psychoanalysis for understanding sociological issues, his influence stimulated, in fact, by Löwenthal—who had himself been analyzed by Freida Fromm-Reichmann—and by informal conversations with Fromm and the other members of the Psychoanalytic Institute (Funk, 2000: 72; Jay, 1996: 87). Fromm was immediately given the task of leading an innovative empirical study of the attitudes of German manual and white-collar workers in relation to fascism. The study—the methodology and theoretical focus of which informed the Institut's *The Authoritarian Personality* study some twenty years later—purported to have found evidence of unconscious authoritarian and conservative character traits among the supporters of the Social Democratic and Communist parties, pointing toward the relative acquiescence of the general populace that was to characterize Hitler's reign. For reasons that will be discussed in due course, the study was not published until the 1980s (appearing under the title *Arbiter ind Angestellte am Vorabend des Dritten Reiches: Eine sozialpsychologische Untersuchung*—subsequently published in English as *The Working Class in Weimar Germany: A Psychological and Sociological Study*), and Fromm's pivotal role in the development of authoritarian studies was largely forgotten.

Fromm's first monograph, *Die Entwicklung des Christusdogmas, Eine Psychoanalytische Studie zur Sozialpsychologischen* (*The Dogma of Christ*), was published in 1930, being translated into English in 1963. Exhibiting certain obvious similarities to the previously mentioned criminological studies, Fromm was concerned in this work with the sociopsychoanalytical analysis of the early Christian sects that sought "to determine the extent to which the change in certain religious ideas is an expression of the psychic change of the people involved and the extent to which these changes are conditioned by their conditions of life" (1992 [1963]: 10). Attempting to fuse Marxian and Freudian insights once more, Fromm attempted to map the morphology of Christian Dogma by relating the ideas it conveys, relative to each stage of its development, as expressions of the socioeconomic situation and psychic attitude of its followers (to which end he introduces the explanatory-descriptive idea of "character matrix" common to most members of a particular group, class, or society). In addition to this, Fromm engaged in a theoretical explanation of the rationale behind his proposed psychoanalytic social psychology, especially how it should be used in application and also in terms of how to understand the relationship between individual psychology and social psychology.

Fromm's next publications were two critiques of the criminal justice system—"Der Staat als Erzieher: Zur Psychologie der Strafjustiz" ("The State as Educator: On the Psychology of Criminal Justice"), which appeared in *Zeitschrift für Psychoanalysche Pädagogik* in 1930, and "Zur Psychologie des Verbrechers und der strafenden Gesellschaft" ("On the Psychology of the Criminal and the Punitive Society"), which appeared in *Imago* in 1931. In these articles, which were only made available to an English-speaking audience by Kevin Anderson in *Erich Fromm and Critical Criminology: Beyond the Punitive Society*,[3] Fromm combines Marxian and Freudian analyses to revealing effect. Breaking new ground in the criminological thought of the time by applying Marxian-inspired psychoanalytic thought to the study of crime, Fromm argued in these articles that the criminal justice system fails to realize its stated goals of reform and correction because of that fact that its focus on influencing criminals is pitched at the conscious as opposed to the unconscious level, therefore bypassing the dynamic drives that help structure behavior. Considering the ineffectual nature of penal sanction in this regard, Fromm stressed the legitimating functions of the criminal justice system for the capitalist state, showing how this system sought to "influence the masses psychologically in the sense desired by the rulers" (2000 [1930]: 126–127), and also how the use of power by the police and military could only fulfill its repressive function on the basis of "the psychic readiness of the great majority to adjust to the existing society and to subordinate themselves to the ruling powers" (2000 [1930]: 125).

In 1932, while recuperating from tuberculosis in Switzerland, Fromm was made a tenured director of the Institut, in charge of the fields of psychoanalysis and social psychology (Funk, 2000: 73). His article of that year, "Über Methode und Aufgabe einer Analytischen Sozialpsychologie. Bemerkungen über Psychoananlyse und historischen Materialismus" ("The Method and Function of Analytic Social Psychology"), a further development of the theory laid down in *The Dogma of Christ* and in his 1929 lecture, was published in the first edition of the *Zeitschrift für Sozialforschung*, (hereafter *Zeitschirft*) the periodical for the Institut, appearing alongside another article on "Die psychoanalytische Charakterologie und ihre Bedeutung für die Sozialpsychologie" ("Psychoanalytic Characterology and its Relevance for Social Psychology").Taken together, these articles, with their stress on the importance of psychoanalysis for historical materialism, effectively outlined the Institut's research program for the following ten years, including the 1936 *Studien über Autorität und Familie* (*Studies on Authority and the Family*) in which Fromm expanded his work on the authoritarian character.

Despite having received his primary psychoanalytic training from strictly orthodox psychoanalytic figures, Fromm had long harbored doubts over certain aspects of Freud's theory. As far back as 1926, he had made the acquaintance of Georg Groddeck, Sándor Ferenczi, and Karen Horney—three analysts who had voiced concerns over certain aspects of orthodox psychoanalysis. During regular trips with Fromm-Reichmann to Groddeck's home in Baden-Baden, where they were often joined by Ferenczi and Horney, Fromm came to see that some of Freud's clinical and metapsychological ideas might be challenged. He explored these insights further during his period of convalescence in Switzerland through a concerted study of the anthropological accounts of matriarchy found in the works of Johann Jakob Bachofen, Lewis Morgan, and Robert Briffault. His article on Bachofen's *Mother Right*, "Die sozialpsychologie Bedeutung der Mutterrechtstheorie" ("The Theory of Mother Right and Its Relevance for Social Psychology"), which appeared in the 1934 edition of the *Zeitschrift*, argued in a similar manner to Wilhelm Reich that matriarchal theory acted to underline the specificity of the bourgeois social structure and of all psychic complexes resulting from it. Stress again fell on the need for more attention to be given to the particular social-psychic milieu of the society under study. By this time Fromm had separated from Fromm-Reichmann and was engaged in a relationship with Karen Horney. Still suffering the effects of tuberculosis, he travelled to the United States in 1933, having been invited by Horney to give a series of lectures at the Chicago Institute of Psychoanalysis. Although returning briefly to Europe at the end of 1933, by May of the following year Fromm had decided to leave Europe and immigrate to New York where, largely on the back of his preparatory work, the Institut had reassembled. Here, Fromm made the acquaintance of Ruth Benedict, Margaret Mead, Edward Sapir, William Silverberg, Clara Thompson, and Harry Stack Sullivan, among others.

In the 1935 edition of the *Zeitschrift*, Fromm published "Die Gesellschaftlichte Bedingtheit der Psychoanalytischen Therapie" ("The Social Determinants of Psychoanalytic Therapy"), an article in praise of Groddeck's and, particularly, Ferenczi's analytic approach over Freud's analytically neutral "medical-thera-peutic procedure" (Funk, 2000: 111–112). In the article Fromm describes the difference between Ferenczi and Freud as "the difference between a humane, kind attitude which wholeheartedly promotes the well-being of the patient, in contrast to a patricentric-authoritarian, basically misanthropic 'tolerance'" (Fromm, quoted in Funk, 2000: 112). He notes of Ferenczi that "as positive features of an analyst he demanded tact and kindness. He mentions as an example the ability to recognize 'when the silence (of the analyst) causes unnecessary torment to the patient.' He did not force the patient during the analysis to lie down and have the analyst invisible behind him. He analyzed also in cases where the patient was unable to pay. He often prolonged a session to avoid the shock of a sudden interruption" (Fromm, in Funk, 2000: 112). The conclusions at which Fromm arrives here, while clearly indebted to his association with Fromm-Reichmann, Groddeck, Ferenczi, Horney, and Reich, were also, to some definite degree, encouraged through his friendship with Harry Stack Sullivan. Sullivan, who had learnt depth psychology through Clara Thompson, who had in turn learnt from Ferenczi, was famed for his work on schizophrenia and for his stress on the intricacy and uniqueness of individual experience. He had also made attempts to construct a new methodology that would force the researcher's attention onto the person suffering from the pathology as opposed to the researcher's own preconceived formulations and explanations, and whose major function he felt was to impart an illusory sense of power, knowledge, and "objectivity" (Greenberg and Mitchell, 1983: 84). Perhaps most crucially, Sullivan conceived of psychiatry as the study of "interpersonal relations" in which the human being would be approached as a "psychobiological organism, social in orientation" within "a world of cultural emergents" (1936 letter to Fromm, quoted in Funk, 2000: 105). This conception had great resonance with Fromm's own approach, which was beginning to take definite shape at the same time— something that can be seen in the following proclamation, made by Fromm in a letter to Karl August Wittfogel, dated December 18, 1936: "The problem within psychology and sociology is the dialectic intertwining of natural and historical factors. Freud has wrongly based psychology totally on natural factors" (quoted in Funk, 2000: 94). In a separate letter to Robert Lynd in the same year, Fromm outlined the task of psychoanalytic theory as the attempt "to understand the structures of character and instincts as a result of adaptation to the given social conditions and not as a product of the erogenous zones" (quoted in Funk, 2000: 93). Sullivan was also responsible for securing for Fromm a teaching position at the New York Branch of the William Allanson White Institute of Psychiatry, allowing him a platform upon which he could further develop and expound his own theory of psychopathology.

By 1937 Fromm's questioning of Freud had crystallized into opposition in a pivotal article submitted but rejected for publication in the *Zeitschrift*. Appearing in print for the first time in a 2010 edited collection of Fromm's psychological writings under the title "Man's Impulse Structure and Its Relation to Culture," the piece was a fundamental reexamination of Freud, which lays out, in many respects, the basis of Fromm's mature psychological position.[4] As well as accusing Freud of a psychologism that confuses the middle-class character with that of all humans, and thereby giving up "the historical, that is to say, the social principle of explanation" (2010: 23), Fromm puts forward the idea of a revision of the theory of drives in which the psychic structure of a person is to be understood by reference to the life-situation of that person (his way of life, activity, and relations to himself and others) and not as the direct or sublimated product of the impulses themselves (2010: 46). Despite seeming to follow the sociological logic of Marxian analysis, Fromm's prospective article met with broad resistance from his Institut colleagues. Theodor Adorno, who had been invited to join the Institut in February of 1937, and who shared a mutual dislike with Fromm,[5] was particularly vociferous. In a letter to Horkheimer dated March 23, 1937 (quoted in Funk, 2000: 97), Adorno criticized Fromm for "putting psychology and society on the same level in Adlerian sense"—by which he meant raising society to the level of biology, a repeated charge laid at the door of those who deviated from strict adherence to libido theory. Horkheimer, whose own position had increasingly come to mirror that of Adorno, responded in agreement, warning that Fromm was in danger of "sliding into revisionism" (Horkheimer to Adorno, April 6, 1937, quoted in Funk, 2000: 98). In addition to this, Horkheimer refused to accede to Fromm's desire that the German worker study—the analysis of the questionnaires for which Fromm had been working through from 1935 to 1938—be published (Funk, 2000: 88). The official line given for this refusal, repeated by Martin Jay in his study of the Frankfurt School, was that the research design was flawed and that many questionnaires had become lost in the move to the United States (Jay, 1996: 117). Fromm disputes this, suggesting in a letter to Jay that to his knowledge no interview was ever lost (Fromm to Jay, dated May 14, 1971, in Kessler and Funk, 1992: 249–256); he suggested, in fact, that Horkheimer was disinclined to publish the study for fear of its "leftist" pretensions (letter to Bottomore, March 26, 1974).[6]

A further factor, discussed by Rolf Wiggershaus, represents what was perhaps Horkheimer's strongest motivation: namely, the development of his thought away from the ground he once shared with Fromm and toward a new position more closely aligned with that of Adorno. As far back as June 1934, Horkheimer had, in a letter to Friedrich Pollock, said of Fromm that he "does not particularly appeal to me. He has productive ideas, but he wants to be on good terms with too many people at once, and doesn't want to miss anything. It is quite pleasant to talk to him, but my impression is that it is quite pleasant for many people" (quoted in Wiggershaus, 1994: 162). The conclusion to be drawn is that Horkheimer was looking to get rid of Fromm—a drain on money and an impediment to the theoretical direction that he now saw as most adequate for the Institut's work.[7] Fromm himself saw this, accusing Horkheimer of changing his position and becoming a "defender of orthodox Freudianism," a change he accorded at least partly to the influence of Adorno (Fromm to Jay 1971 in Kessler and Funk, 1992: 254, quoted in McLaughlin 1998: 8). The fact that, a year later, in October 1939, on the pretext of insufficient funds, Fromm was relieved of his tenured directorship lends support to this account. Although it is certainly accurate to say that Institut was struggling financially at the time, the fact that Adorno was accepted as a tenured member only a year or so before does suggest that the financial situation was not so bad and that the growing relationship between Horkheimer and Adorno seems to have been the overriding reason for the separation.

What is certain is that, following his split from the Institut, Fromm's erstwhile colleagues did their best to play down his central role in its early history. In addition to this, they presented a series of public criticisms of Fromm's thought which, in time, became received wisdom where he was concerned. Initially, perhaps motivated by Horkheimer's fear that Fromm would set up a rival institute with other former members and in the knowledge that Fromm had so far refrained from overt criticism of his former colleagues (Funk, 2000: 98), these criticisms remained private, restricted to communications such as Horkheimer's 1942 letter to Leo Löwenthal accusing Fromm of "commonsense psychology" and of "psychologiz[ing] culture and society" (October 31, 1942, quoted in Funk, 2000: 99). This pact was broken, however, by Adorno's implicit criticism of Fromm in a lecture given in 1946, in which he spoke out on the dangers of the "neo-Freudian" revision of libido psychology (Jay, 1996: 104). Horkheimer then expanded his earlier private criticism in a letter to the publishers of the *Philosophical Review* in 1949, accusing Fromm of "revisionism" and of "sociologizing"

Freud (Horkheimer, in Funk 2000: 100). This was followed by further criticism on the part of Adorno in *Minima Moralia*, published in 1951, and, most notably, by Marcuse in an article in *Dissent*, "The Social Implications of Freudian 'Revisionism,'" and in *Eros and Civilization*, both in 1955, in which Fromm was accused of mutilating Freud's theory. Finally, Adorno extended his implicit criticism of Fromm in certain sections of *Negative Dialectics*, published in 1966, before delivering a critique of Fromm (and Horney, Hartmann, and Parsons) in *New Left Review*, 1967–8, in which Fromm was accused of denying the negative dialectic between drive and society, and, consequently, the harmonization of actual conflict.

Despite the fact that these are somewhat strange positions for supposedly Marxian thinkers to adopt—seeking as they did, in one way or another, to maintain the strict biological materialism of Freud over Fromm's sociological revision—these criticisms did great damage to Fromm's legacy in social-theoretical circles. In the case of Adorno and Marcuse, they were accompanied by accusations of conformism, Fromm cast as a "business-like revisionist" and "sermonistic social worker" (Adorno, 2005: 60; Marcuse, 1966 [1955]: 6). Through the popularity of critical theory, and particularly of Adorno and Marcuse, from the mid-to-late 1960s onward, the view of Fromm proffered by his Institut ex-colleagues came to be adopted by the majority of social theorists and radicals in academia and beyond (of particular note here is Russell Jacoby's *Social Amnesia: A Critique of Conformist Psychology from Adler to Laing*, which reads like a direct extension of Adorno and Marcuse's thinking in relation to Fromm). Since then, Fromm has rarely been seen without the distorting lens of this criticism, and the attempt to play down his role in Frankfurt School history has—a few notable exceptions aside—continued, Fromm being replaced by Marcuse, Adorno, and even Benjamin in the "Origin Myth" of the Institut (McLaughlin, 1999).

New Beginnings

After leaving the Institut, Fromm began to write and publish in English, developing further his revision of Freud. His first major work of this period, *Escape from Freedom*, was published in 1941 to critical acclaim. Focusing on the themes of authoritarianism and conformism, the work was an account of "the meaning of freedom for modern man" (1969 [1941]: xiv), which sought to explain the increasing sense of aloneness that characterized the post-Reformation world. Conceived while Fromm was still a member of the Institut, the study also built on the substance of his reconceptualization of Freud proposed in the rejected article of 1937 and on two subsequent articles, "Zum Gefühl der Ohnmacht" ("The Feeling of Powerlessness") (1937) and "Selfishness and Self-Love" (1939), the latter of which appeared in English in Sullivan's *Psychiatry* journal. In these articles, Fromm argues that the need for related-ness and avoidance of aloneness—needs that can be met through sadomasoch-istic subservience-dominance patterns, forms of destructiveness, conformity to a larger whole, or by the development of the capacity for spontaneity and love—be instantiated in place of libido as the primary human motivations (as connected to this discussion, and pulling him further from Freudian ortho-doxy, Fromm clearly stressed what he saw as the need for psychoanalysts to see the relevance of moral problems for the understanding of a personality). In opposition to what he takes as the conflation of self-love and selfishness found in Luther, Calvin, Kant, and Freud, Fromm argues that self-love and selfishness are in fact incompatible and that genuine self-love, and the true individualism which flows from it, is lacking, not overflowing, in our society. The book also contains an appendix in which Fromm introduces his concept of the "social character," an extension of Freud's dynamic concept of character which holds that every society or group has a common character structure (or at least the nucleus of one) that is a social adaptation of the individual character to the objective conditions that shape that particular society.

Considered in methodological terms, *Escape from Freedom* was an impor-tant continuation of the social-psychological stipulations Fromm had laid down in *The Dogma of Christ* and *Zeitschrift* articles. The study found res-onance with the burgeoning "culture and personality" tradition, its focus on the psychology of Nazism fitting alongside the work of Ruth Benedict, Margaret Mead, Abram Kardiner, and Ralph Linton. It was also, in this regard, an influence on Talcott Parsons, Robert Merton, Erik Erikson, David Riesman, and Michael Maccoby (the latter two, in particular, bas-ing much of their approach to social psychology on Frommian principles) and played a largely unrecognized role in helping to inaugurate the detailed sociopsychoanalytical study of emotions (McLaughlin, 2007: 762). In addi-tion to this, the book also acted as a founding work in the field of political psychology, elevating Fromm to "public intellectual" status and opening avenues for the wider dissemination of his ideas. Most of Fromm's publica-tions over the next 40 years had a similar mass appeal, increasingly drawing out his sociocultural analytical skills and deeper prophetic instincts.

Fromm's relationship with Karen Horney, which had been highly influ-ential in the development of his thought, particularly in relation to his revi-sion of psychoanalysis, started to come to an end during the last years of the 1930s. During this time Fromm became involved in an affair with Katherine Dunham, the famous concert dance artist and civil rights activist from whom he gained a firsthand appreciation of the Black Atlantic exchange of talent and ideas (Friedman, 2013: 94),[8] and, in 1944, he was married to Henny Gurland, a fellow émigré who had accompanied Walter Benjamin on his fated attempt to cross the France-Spain border in 1940, witnessing and seemingly covering-up his subsequent suicide (Funk, 2000: 122). Apparently stung by the success of *Escape from Freedom* relative to her own work, and effectively signaling the end of friendly relations, Horney blocked Fromm's application to a hold a seminar based on technical issues at the Association for the Advancement of Psychoanalysis on the grounds that Fromm was not medically qualified to do so (Funk, 2000: 116–117). Despite attempts at mediation, Fromm left the association and joined the Washington-Baltimore Psychoanalytic Society, co-formed with Clara Thompson, who had resigned her role as president of the association in protest at the treatment given to Fromm (Funk, 2000: 117). Fromm worked at the Psychoanalytic Society (renamed William Alanson White Institute of Psychiatry, Psychoanalysis, and Psychology, in 1946) as a training analyst and supervisor for many years.

In addition to his training and supervisory role at the William Alanson White Institute, Fromm was employed as a lecturer at the New School for Social Research in New York, and at Bennington College, Vermont, where he taught courses on Aristotle and Spinoza, among other subjects (Funk, 2000: 124). Through these teaching roles, Fromm was able to further develop his own theoretical approach, the fruits of which are evident in his next work, *Man for Himself: An Inquiry into the Psychology of Ethics*, published in 1947. In the foreword to *Escape from Freedom*, Fromm had stated that during the writing of that work he had been forced "to refer frequently to certain concepts and conclusions without elaborating on them as fully as [he] would have done with more scope" (1969 [1941]: ix–x).[9] *Man for Himself* attempted to rectify this situation, offering a more systematic account of ontogenetic psychological development and his own character typology (which contains his notion of "the marketing character," with its depiction of the commodification of personality). As is suggested by the subtitle, the work goes beyond the bounds of a standard psychological discussion and enquires into the connections that obtain between psychology and ethics. Fromm's earlier discussion of the conflation of selfishness and self-love is greatly expanded here, framed by an explicit humanism that makes it clear—if it was not clear before—that his thought is situated firmly within the humanist tradition.

What characterizes Fromm's writings from this period onward is a more direct ethical humanism that draws together his sociological and psychological insights with his understanding of Judaeo-Christian (and Buddhist) humanism into an explanatory and evaluative social philosophy that he would eventually term "radical humanism." Considered in biographical terms, this represents something of a reconciliation for Fromm, and particularly so in relation to his understanding of religion. Whereas in his earlier works religion is viewed in the spirit of the early Freud as a superfluous childish illusion, Fromm now comes to see it as a necessary condition for personhood, a part of the human condition (although what he means by religion is not what it is ordinarily understood in Western thought). Stripped of its inconsistent theistic designation, religion comes to be understood by Fromm in broader terms that encompass theistic, nontheistic and even anti-theistic conceptualizations.[10] It comes to designate any frame of orientation or object of devotion (particularly, although not exclusively, shared ones), which offers the individual a sense of meaning and purpose in relationship to the world. Understood thus, the question is not *whether* religion, but *which kind* of religion.

This reconciliation, which was largely connected to Fromm's anterior break with orthodox Freudianism and his studies on authoritarianism, was instantiated in *Man for Himself* but developed more fully in *Psychoanalysis and Religion*. Published in 1950, on the basis of material delivered during a visiting professorship at Yale University, *Psychoanalysis and Religion* denotes "religion" as "any system of thought and action shared by a group which gives the individual a frame of orientation and an object of devotion" (1950: 21). A few pages later, Fromm reverses the Freudian idea that every religion is a collective childhood neurosis by positing that every neurosis is "*a private form of religion*" (1950: 27), qualifying the group-based stipulation contained in the previous definition. What is important for Fromm is to understand the human reality underlying the thought system: given that we are all involuntarily "religious," what matters is whether the thought system has a *humanistic* or an *authoritarian* effect on the individual, whether the individual's capacities for reason, love and autonomy are furthered, or stunted. In a resurrection of his earlier studies of Herman Cohen, and with clear parallels to the thought of Feuerbach, Fromm argues that in theistic humanistic religions God stands as a symbol for man's powers and not as an authority placed above him. He sees this as a feature of early Christianity, and of Judaism more generally, existing as it did beyond the bounds of real secular power, which gives way in large part to the authoritarianism of the Roman church. He sees it too in Buddhism— minus what he calls its "historically accidental elements" (belief in rebirth, etc.)—and in the mystical traditions of Judaism, Christianity, and Islam. Fromm's thought itself, in fact, comes in many ways to resemble a kind of *ethical mysticism*, placing a stress on what might be called an "experiential humanism" based on the idea of the art of living.[11] In this he is closer to Albert Schweitzer than to Ernst Bloch or Walter Benjamin—although he is much closer to Bloch than he is to Benjamin. As with Schweitzer, mysticism for Fromm does not equate to irrationalism and submission to authority but involves, rather, the assertion of one's own powers and a spirituality relating to life itself. Authors such as Spinoza and Meister

Eckhart feature more centrally in his writings, alongside his social criticism and social psychology, as do certain ideas from Buddhist (particularly Zen Buddhist) thought. Quotes from—and references to—Biblical, Talmudic, and mystical sources increase, such that well before he speaks of the need for a humanistic "religiosity" in *To Have or To Be?*, it is clear that the centrality of his interest in religion had never quite left him, only become temporarily muted, to now be realized in inverted nontheistic humanist form.[12]

Exile and Productivity

Later the same year in which *Psychoanalysis and Religion* was published, Fromm moved from the United States to Mexico, largely on account of the ill health of his wife. Tragically, Fromm's wife died two years later, apparently taking her own life (Friedman, 2013: xxviii). In spite of this, Fromm remained permanently based in Mexico until 1973, marrying his third wife, Annis Freeman, in 1953. During his time in Mexico, Fromm held the position of professor at the National Autonomous University in Mexico City, establishing the psychoanalytic section at the medical school (*Sociedad Psicoanalítica Mexicana*) there in 1956. He also established an independent psychoanalytic institute (*The Instituto Mexicano de Psicoanálisis*) in Mexico City in 1963. Through his teaching roles at these institutions, Fromm came to influence a whole generation of Mexican psychoanalysts. Although Fromm's decision to remain in Mexico removed him somewhat from the academic community in the United States, he did retain some teaching commitments there, coming to New York each spring to teach, until 1959. This arrangement was followed by a number of similar arrangements, enabling the rise rather than decline of Fromm's profile in the American public scene.

The Sane Society, a study of the affluent alienation of twentieth-century industrial-capitalist society, appeared in 1955. Centered on the notion of the "pathology of normalcy," it argued that contemporary Western societies were fundamentally sick, that in them man was "dead", buried under social and economic apparatuses allied to the industrial machine. These sentiments chimed with many who felt the sterility of mass culture and who identified with Fromm's extended description of the marketing character. For a society to be sane, Fromm argues, it must correspond to the objective needs of man, to which end he speaks of the importance of a "normative humanism" which can stipulate universal criteria for mental health. As part of this discussion he outlines a typology of basic needs which stem from the conditions of human existence, characterizing mental health as consisting in "the ability to love and to create, by the emergence from incestuous ties to clan and soil, by a sense of identity based on one's experience of self as the subject and agent of one's powers, by the grasp of reality inside and outside of ourselves, that is, by the development of objectivity and reason" (2002 [1955]: 67). Importantly, the work also undertook an analysis of prescriptions for change, underlining the idea that change cannot occur in one sphere alone but must take place in all spheres simultaneously.

The Sane Society was followed in 1956 by The Art of Loving: An Inquiry into the Nature of Love. In this work, which became an international best seller, Fromm argues that the social structure of contemporary Western civilization and the spirit resulting from it are not conducive to the development of love. Rather, he argues, contemporary Western society is characterized by a number of forms of pseudo-love that hide the underlying reality of the disintegration of love. Fromm defines love as "the achievement of interpersonal union" based on the preservation of one's integrity/individuality in the overcoming of human separateness (1956: 17). Central to this conception is the idea that love is an active, not a passive process in which one strives for care, respect, and knowledge of as well as responsibility toward the other person and to the world as a whole. Fromm stresses that love is an *art* that needs to be practiced, and which consists essentially in an attitude and orientation toward the world, as opposed to an exclusive attachment to another person, as it is normally understood. Crucially, while Fromm sees that genuine love is rare in capitalist society, it is not, he argues, impossible: "I am of the conviction that the answer of the absolute incompatibility of love and 'normal' life is correct only in an abstract sense. The *principle* underlying capitalistic society and the *principle* of love are incompatible. But modern society seen concretely is a complex phenomenon. Even if one recognizes the principle of capitalism as being incompatible with the principle of love, one must admit that 'capitalism' is in itself a complex and constantly changing structure which still permits of a good deal of non-conformity and of personal latitude" (1956: 118–119). Nevertheless, for love to be possible for the majority of society, humanistic concerns must come to govern our socioeconomic arrangements and be worked into character.

Taken together, The Sane Society and The Art of Loving reaffirm Fromm's place in the humanist tradition. In 1957, a year after publishing The Art of Loving, Fromm wrote a draft constitution for a prospective Institute for the Study of Man. In the document, posthumously published as "The Humanistic Science of Man" in Wissenschaft vom Menschen-Science of Man: Jahrbuch der Internationalen Erich-Fromm-Gesellschaft, 1990, Fromm states that "there is a great need for rational and demonstrable proof that there is indeed such a thing as man and human nature beyond the purely anatomical and physiological realm" (1990 [1957]: 3). In particular, Fromm envisaged concerted collaborative study seeking to establish the concept of human nature by integrating our knowledge of historical human cultures with what we know of human cultures in the present day, calling explicitly for going beyond a descriptive anthropology to try to get at the basic forces behind the various different cultural manifestations. Fromm's main concern in the proposing of such an institute was his dissatisfaction with contemporary academic thought, particularly what he saw as its facile operational separation between fact and value, as well as his conviction that we need to see human being as not only a biologically but also a *psychologically* definable entity. As such, in the constitutional draft he explicitly stipulates that the study of man "must be based on certain humane concerns, primarily those which have been the concern of the whole humanistic religious and philosophical tradition: the idea of the dignity of man and of his potentialities for love and reason which can be actualized under favorable circumstances" (1990 [1957]: 2).

Prior to this venture, and only a year after moving to Mexico, *The Forgotten Language: An Introduction to the Understanding of Dreams, Fairy Tales and Myths* was published. An exposition of the ancient art of symbol- ism in relation to psychoanalysis, it shows Fromm emphasizing his distance from orthodox Freudianism and putting forward his own account of the nature of dreams, the unconscious, and of psychoanalytic interpretation in general. In this work Fromm deals in some detail with the respective merits of Freudian and Jungian psychoanalytic ideas, giving a generally positive appraisal of Jung over Freud at certain crucial points—in particular, Fromm stresses that he and Jung are in agreement to the extent to which they see that we are often wiser and more decent in our sleep than in our waking life (although for Fromm this is nothing to do with revelation stemming from a source transcending us). Drawing on Jung and Bachofen, in addition to Freud, Fromm puts forward an argument for symbolism as the "universal language" of the human race (linked as it is to role of the body in the expres- sion of inner experience), crucially stressing that this is a universal language that is instantiated through the varied and many "dialects" that arise in response to discrete historical and social situations.

The distinctness of Fromm's psychoanalytic approach received further emphasis with the publication of *Psychoanalysis and Zen Buddhism* in 1960. Stimulated by his friendship with D. T. Suzuki, one of the main popular- izers of Zen Buddhism in the West, it attempted to argue for the overall similarity in the aims of psychoanalysis and Zen. In an account that is per- haps as expressive of the development of his own position as it is of genuine commonalities between psychoanalysis and Zen, Fromm stresses what he sees as the shared concept of well-being implied in both systems: namely, the overcoming of greed and the aggrandizement of the ego, and the relations between the processes of derepression and enlightenment. Going over and above Freud, he posits didactic analysis as the beginning of a process of ever-increasing awareness, and Zen as offering the possibility of widening and deepening the horizon of psychoanalysis, helping it to arrive at a more radical grasp of reality as the ultimate aim of full, conscious awareness. The work also contains important additions to Fromm's social-psychological conceptual schema: namely, the idea of socially conditioned filters pertaining to language, logic, and taboo.

Between the years of 1957 and 1961, Fromm held the position of professor of psychology at Michigan State University. During this time *Sigmund Freud's Mission: An Analysis of His Personality and Influence* was published. In this tract, Fromm goes beyond the discussion of the methodological and epistemological aspects of psychoanalysis to engage in a direct appraisal of the psychoanalytic movement as set up and maintained by Freud and his disciples. Although placing Freud alongside Kant, Nietzsche, Marx, and Darwin in the great liberatory thrust of the past three centuries, Fromm was highly critical of what he saw as the authoritarian and fanatical nature of the movement, its dogmatic intolerance of dissention and idolization of Freud, which, in Fromm's view, led to the loss of its originally radical character. Concerned with its own preservation, it had largely reduced itself to a quasi-religious sect offering a confessional function for its middle-class patients who were more than happy to pay for the ritual.[13] Unsurprisingly, such a critical account from such a high-profile figure was not well received by the psychoanalytic establishment, who had already worked to ensure that Fromm was denied membership of the International Psychoanalytic Association. In spite of this, Fromm was appointed adjunct professor of psychology at the Graduate School of Arts and Sciences at New York University in 1962, and was instrumental in setting up the International Federation of Psychoanalytic Societies—a collection of dissident psychoanalytic groups, which included Fromm's Mexican group, The William Alanson White Institute, and the German Psychoanalytic Association, among others. Later that same year, *Beyond the Chains of Illusion: My Encounter with Marx and Freud* was published. This work was effectively a statement of Fromm's own thought as it stood at the age of 62, including formal conceptualizations of earlier aspects of his thought, such as the idea of the social unconscious, and a broadened account of the socially conditioned filters. Notably, the work stressed the particular importance of Marx in his thought relative to Freud. It also contained a plea for a renaissance of humanistic experience and of experiencing life as the paradoxical task of realizing individuality at the same time as union with others.

War, Peace, and Activism

Clearly much of Fromm's work can be read as deliberate pleas to conscience and attempts at advancing humanism in the world: in our institutions, politics, religion, and in our very relationship to life and being. In addition to this literary activity, Fromm had also been politically active for many years despite feeling that his personality was not suited for politics. As far back as the late 1940s he had persuaded Albert Einstein, Martin Buber, and Leo Baeck to publish a declaration in the *New York Times* demanding respect for the rights of the Arabs during the foundation of the state of Israel. The declaration, which he himself had written, explicitly called for the formation of a multinational Jewish-Arab state in Palestine and was wholly opposed to what he saw as the "nationalistic, militaristic, xenophobic, and reactionary elements" that characterized the approach of the modern Israeli state (*New York Times*, April 18, 1948). At the beginning of 1950s, Fromm had met several times with presidential candidates Adlai Stevenson and Senator J. William Fulbright, making donations to and offering suggestions for their respective campaigns. In addition to this, Fromm was a founding member of the anti-nuclear group SANE, and played a leading role in efforts at encouraging unilateral disarmament, an issue that had a great effect on him. There is evidence, in fact, that Fromm may have influenced President Kennedy's June 1963 American University Commencement Address, a talk that was crucial in paving the way for disarmament talks between the Soviets and Americans (Friedman, 2013: 210). In addition to all of this, Fromm was also a serious donor to a variety of social and political groups that aligned with his political convictions, including the American Civil Liberties Union.[14]

Increasingly, Fromm's political activity was reflected in the choice of theme for his works. *May Man Prevail? An Inquiry into the Facts and Fictions of Foreign Policy* was published in 1961 in a direct attempt to influence the nuclear debate between the United States and Soviet Union. *The Heart of Man: Its Genius for Good and Evil*, which was released in 1964, consisted of an extended analysis of our tendencies directed against life and those directed toward it. Here Fromm expounds on the concepts of "biophilia" and "necrophilia"—syndromes of growth and decay that form the ultimate human alternative: the love of life and the love of death—which he had formally introduced in the essay *War Within Man: A Psychological Inquiry into the Roots of Destructiveness* a year earlier. A humanist counterpoint to Freud's idea of the Eros and Death instincts that grew out his involvement in politics and the impending nuclear crisis, Fromm argues that the relative lack of fear of total destruction evident in the nuclear debate stems from a lack of real love for life, that is to say, from the fact that we have largely become *homo mechanicus*, gadget-men deeply attracted to "all that is mechanical, and inclined against that which is alive" (1980 [1964]: 56–58). He also introduces here his idea of social narcissism (sometimes referred to in later works as "group narcissism"). In addition to his involvement with the peace movement, Fromm was notably active in socialist politics. He had joined the American Socialist Party-Social Democratic Federation (SP-SDF) in the late 1950s, seeking to provide it with a new, revitalized program. His prospective manifesto, which advanced practical, humanistic-socialist directives, was ultimately rejected, despite drawing some support. It was, however, published later that year by the SP-SDF as a discussion piece for the socialist movement under the title *Let Man Prevail: A Socialist Manifesto and Program*. Fromm resigned from the party not long after due to what he saw as its lack of radicalism.

A year later, in 1961, *Marx's Concept of Man* was published. The work contained one of the first English translations of Marx's *Economic and Philosophic Manuscripts*, which at the time did much to challenge the widespread division of Marx into an earlier "humanist" and later "scientist." Around this time Fromm tried to organize a movement of humanist socialists, making contact with, among others, Ernst Bloch, Lucien Goldmann, Maximilien Rubel, Tom Bottomore, Bertrand Russell, Lewis Mumford, Karl Polyani, Raya Dunayevskaya, Adam Schaff, and the Yugoslav Praxis group, as well as leading religious figures such as Karl Rahner and Albert Schweitzer (Funk, 2000: 147–148). His idea of a magazine, prospectively titled *Humanist Studies*, that would unite humanist scholars of all hues, never materialized (Funk, 2000: 148). He did, however, publish *Socialist Humanism: An International Symposium* (1965), a collection of essays that attempted to clarify the problem of humanist socialism in its various theoretical aspects and to demonstrate its salience as a worldwide movement. Contributions to the volume came from many of those listed above, as well as from Herbert Marcuse and from Indian and African authors. This was followed a year later by *You Shall Be as Gods: A Radical Interpretation of the Old Testament and Its Traditions* (1966). An important source illustrating the continuity of Fromm's interest in religious thought, it contains his most detailed account of the sociohistorical evolution of the concepts of "God" and "Man" and a description of the experiential substratum behind all "religious" experience. Fromm expounds at length on what he takes to be the central humanist thrust of Judaic thought, seeking in part to highlight the stark disparity between the nature of this thought and the Zionist policies of the state of Israel. It was in this book that Fromm first coined the phrase "radical humanism."

The 1960s were a period of impressive demand and popularity for Fromm. On a three-week lecture tour in California in 1966, he spoke to over sixty thousand people. Not immune to the stress of such an undertaking, Fromm suffered a heart-attack that year, prior to speaking to an anti-Vietnam War rally at Madison Square Garden. Despite this, Fromm was soon active again, taking on the role of speech writer for Eugene McCarthy's campaign to win the Democratic nomination for President. Concerned to exert some added influence in the campaign and to further his goal of a humanized society, Fromm published the hastily written *The Revolution of Hope: Toward a Humanized Technology* in 1968, which contained a direct appeal to the radical social movements of the time. It is interesting to note in this connection that the FBI had files on Fromm that ran to over 600 pages (Funk, 2000: 145). In the wake of McCarthy's failed campaign, and perhaps with health concerns in mind, Fromm retreated somewhat from the forefront of public life to concentrate on his writing efforts, which continued with no immediate signs of declining productivity. *The Nature of Man*, a collection of philosophical writings ranging from the Upanishads to Alfred North Whitehead on what it means of be human, coedited with Ramon Xirau, was released in 1968. *The Crisis of Psychoanalysis: Essays of Freud, Marx and Social Psychology*, a collection of his essays spanning four decades, prefaced with a new lead essay on the current decline in interest in psychoanalysis, followed in 1970. This was followed later that year by *Social Character in a Mexican Village: A Sociopsychoanalytic Study*, a case study of a Mexican peasant village, which sought to demonstrate a new method for the application of psychoanalysis to social science, to test the efficacy of the theory of social character, and to discover data that might be useful for prediction and planning social change in peasant society. Carried out with the assistance of Michael Maccoby and a team of researchers, the study proffered the notion of *social selection* through character adaptation to the objective conditions obtaining in a society as explaining the different fortunes of respective social groups. Although generally overlooked as an innovative primer in social-psychological research, it did influence a handful of similar studies, such as Sonia Gojman (1992) and Sonia Gojman and Salvador Millán (2001, 2004).

Fromm's fame began to fade, particularly in the English-speaking countries, from the late 1960s onward. The influential culture and personality tradition to which Fromm was affiliated had suffered a decline from its heyday in the 1930s and 1940s, and Fromm's often didactic writing style and straightforward ethical humanism began to seem stuffy in comparison to Adorno and, particularly, Marcuse's writings, as well as the works of the Situationist, postcolonial and poststructuralist traditions. By this time, the attacks by his Institut ex-colleagues, their followers, and those of leading representatives of orthodox Marxism and Freudianism, began to coagulate, and his future reputation as a "revisionist," "moralist," and "simple popularizer" was more or less set. Despite this, Fromm remained primarily concerned with social and humanistic issues. Intentions for a four-volume work on humanistic psychoanalysis were diverted by events into the writing of *The Anatomy of Human Destructiveness*, which was released in 1973. A largely brilliant attempt to clarify the nature of human destructiveness and aggression, this work stands as one of Fromm's most detailed and rigorous works. Wide-ranging though focused, Fromm attempts the integration of psychoanalytic insights with findings from the fields of neuropsychology, animal psychology, paleontology, and anthropology, arguing, in contrast to Freud, Konrad Lorenz, and a whole range of sociobiologists, that "destructiveness and cruelty are not instinctual drives, but passions rooted in the total existence of man...one of the ways to make sense of life" (1997 [1973]: 113). A good summation and mature statement of his central ideas, it reads well—almost as impressive as his earlier German writings—and is placed in scientific relief to a far greater degree than in his more popular works. It also contains a revised version of his account of the primary human existential needs, and develops further his idea of the necrophilous character with the aid of case studies of Stalin, Himmler, and Hitler.

In the year following the publication of *The Anatomy of Human Destructiveness*, Fromm left Mexico for Ticino, Switzerland. It was here that he was to write his final major work, *To Have or To Be?*, which was published in 1976. In this work Fromm introduces the idea of *having* and *being* as "fundamental modes of existence," his naming of them drawing out what was implicit in his earlier theory. Not so much character orientations as "ultimate judgments" (Funk, 1982: 250), which antedate but characterize and determine the various character orientations, Fromm's discussion, characteristically mixing theory and praxis, illustrates the phenomenological reality of these modes at the level of daily existence and in the realm of social and political thought. Arguing that contemporary industrial-capitalist society is characterized by the ascendency of radical hedonism and unlimited egotism and facing the threat of ecological catastrophe, Fromm calls for the creation of a "New Man," a new ethic toward nature, and a new way of life based on characterological and socioeconomic change, offering practical suggestions for sane consumption, participatory democracy, and the humanistic constitution of work. The study was to become a fundamental catalyst for green-alternative movement, guaranteeing Fromm a brief resurgence in fame, particularly in Germany, Italy, and Spain, where Frommian groups remain to this day.

During his time in Switzerland, Fromm remained active in relation to social and political issues. He was involved in activism against the persecution of the Praxis group by Tito, contacting Ernst and Karola Bloch and the Yugoslav ambassadors in Washington and many other countries to try to secure a successful intervention. Ever affected by the nuclear power struggle between the United States and the USSR, he attempted to gather support for a denunciation of Alexander Solzhenitsyn's apparent promotion of the Cold War (Funk, 2000: 162). In an incident that suggests that Fromm's name was not completely blackened in "radical" circles, he was invited to appear as a defense witness at the Bader-Meinhof trial, unsurprisingly choosing to refuse the offer (Funk, 2000: 162). In 1977, however, Fromm suffered a second heart attack. This was followed the year after by a third and notably more severe one. Despite these health concerns, he managed to produce one final work, *The Greatness and Limitations of Freud's Thought*, a summative account of his interpretation of Freud; it appeared in 1979. A year later, on March 18, 1980, Fromm suffered a fatal fourth heart attack.

Since Fromm's death, a number of collections of previously unpublished writings have appeared, courtesy of the editorship of Rainer Funk. *The Revision of Psychoanalysis*, a compilation of related writings concerned with his dialectical and sociological revision of classical Freudian theory and practice (including an extended critique of Marcuse's attempt at "philosophical psychoanalysis"), appeared in 1992. This was followed later that year by *On Being Human*, a collection of writings based largely on lectures given during the last 20 years of Fromm's life that show his faith in humanity, in spite of what he saw as unprecedented levels of self-alienation. *The Art of Being*, consisting of sections dealing with "steps towards being," held back from publication in *To Have or to Be?* for fear that the book would be confused with a "self-help" manual, was published in 1993. *The Art of Listening*, a collection of transcribed lectures, interviews, and seminars dealing predominantly with technical psychoanalytic issues, and *Love, Sexuality, and Matriarchy: About Gender*, a collection of essays on the subjects mentioned in the title, were released in 1994 and 1997, respectively. *The Clinical Erich Fromm*, a collection of accounts of Fromm as a psychoanalyst from colleagues, students, and friends, including two pieces by Fromm on therapeutic practice and on the relationship to the patient, was published in 2009. *The Pathology of Normalcy* and *Beyond Freud: From Individual to Social Psychology* were published in 2010 by the American Mental Health Foundation. Consisting predominantly of transcribed lectures from across Fromm's career, the former contained the first publication of Fromm's seminal 1937 essay on the revision of Freud, and, the latter, a proposal for a prospective Institute for the Science of Man.

CHAPTER 2

The Roots of Radical Humanism

The fullest and most explicit definition that Fromm gives of radical humanism is found in the early pages of *You Shall Be as Gods*. Here he explains that "by radical humanism I refer to a global philosophy which emphasizes the oneness of the human race, the capacity of man to develop his own powers and to arrive at inner harmony and at the establishment of a peaceful world. Radical humanism considers the goal of man to be that of complete independence, and this implies penetrating through fictions and illusions to full awareness of reality" (1966a: 13). In an addition on the following page, he stresses that radical humanism recognizes the fact that ideas, "especially if they are the ideas of not only a single individual but have become integrated into the historical process, have their roots in the real life of society" (1966a: 14). In this rather uneven definition, which can be separated into a quartet of clauses (three of religio-philosophical origin and a fourth taken from sociological or social-psychological thought), Fromm bares his intellectual soul. It is, as will hopefully be shown, a definition that owes its primary debt to Fromm's interpretation of the philosophical and hermeneutic traditions of Judaic thought, but which is extended nontheistically in the philosophical and sociological thought of Karl Marx and the psychoanalytic theory and practice of Sigmund Freud. As well as uneven, this definition is also provisional, and is included here with this provisionality very much in mind. Fromm's body of work lacks a volume of theory that explicates radical humanism systematically and in full. Although his thinking is clearly intertwined with the philosophical and theoretical thought to which it adjoins, his overriding concern was not so much the penning of detailed philosophical treaties as the elucidation of the practical task and art of living (to which theory is an essential, though subsidiary, aspect). While this is the case, Fromm's writings, particularly from *Man for Himself* onward, display an impressive degree of coherence that can be said to rest on an underlying core position of great stability. Communicating this core position is the goal of this chapter. The fuller enunciation of radical humanism is the goal of the book, and will be achieved through discussion of a wider range of ideas and influences that, although constitutive of the fuller understanding of radical humanism as a social theory, are nevertheless always placed against the grounding of these initial and formative sources.

It is acknowledged that what follows is a somewhat idealized presentation, which, in chronological terms at least, implies an overly neat progression from aspect to aspect. My concern here, however, has not been to offer a purely chronological account of the development of Fromm's thought but rather to provide conceptual clarity on what can be said to be the roots of radical humanism as a system of thought taken in itself. My contention is that Fromm's late adoption of the label "radical humanism," although not wholly unproblematic for the categorization of his thought, is nevertheless far from a diversion or rupture in its pattern. While it is possible to read Fromm's work in stages, as Lawrence Wilde (2004a) has done,[1] it is not inconsistent to acknowledge the existence of these stages in broad terms and at the same time to hold to an underlying holistic understanding of Fromm's work which transcends this division—Wilde himself characterizes the underlying purpose of Fromm's thought as his "quest for solidarity" (Wilde, 2004). What Wilde describes as Fromm's social-psychological phase—running in essence from his dissertation to *Escape from Freedom*, and consisting of his exploratory work on the application of psychoanalysis to historical materialism and sociology—refers to the attempt to work through the methodological and epistemological issues involved in the fusion of Marxist and Freudian thought. Although it is true that during this period Fromm was to adopt the language of orthodox Freudianism (along with its view of religion as a childish illusion), at no point did this Freudianism rule alone; rather, it always existed alongside another philosophical position—initially a Judaic one, then a Marxian one, then a radical humanist one, each successive position being largely the extension of the previous influence. Reading Fromm's thought in retrospect, then, it is possible to say that he continued his Judaism in a secular manner in this methodological and epistemological social-psychological stage,[2] and that while there may be a tension between the more orthodox Freudianism of his early thought and his more rounded later philosophy (particularly with relation to the nature and role of religion), it is clear that the basic tenor of his thought is not affected. As such, the chapter may be said to reflect a relative order of primacy evident in Fromm's thought, considered as whole, and that, considered as such a whole, the connections outlined are real and significant.

Universalism, Prophetic Messianism, and the Solution to Creation

Fromm's radical humanism is most deeply and profoundly influenced by his understanding of the Judaic tradition. Certain of its central precepts, understood in radical humanist inversion, stand as axiomatic for his thought, effective well beyond his renunciation of theism—the first three clauses in particular (universalism, the capacity of man to develop his own powers and reach inner and outer harmony, and the goal of man as complete independence won through the penetration of fictions and illusions to full awareness of reality) can be said to gain their initial expression here. The first clause—the most foundational tenet of radical humanism, and its necessary premise—is the principle of universalism: the idea of the basic unity of the human race, or, in the older language of the Old Testament and its later tradition, the unity of man based on the assumption of a universal God. In spite of the undeniable tendency to nationalism evident in Jewish history—a tendency, which he attributed largely to the experience of exile and persecution central to that history (1966a: 82)—Fromm credited Judaic thought with one of the first historical expressions of the idea. He saw it as reaching its highest point in the prophetic writings (where it features as the assumed premise), but as being more clearly spelled out at a number of other occasions: firstly, in God's creation of only *one* woman and *one* man from whom every human descends (Genesis 1:27), and in the Pharisaic literature—particularly the Talmud—where it is taught that "the dust of the first man was gathered from all parts of the earth" (Sanhedrin 38a,b); secondly, in the Noachide Covenant (Genesis 9:11–16), in which God makes a pact with Noah and, by extension, the entire human race, whereby he promises never again to destroy life on earth (1966a: 26); thirdly, in the repeated injunction that Israel cannot hate or take advantage of the stranger (Deuteronomy 23:8); and finally, in the Talmudic idea that not only the Jews but the pious of every nation will share in salvation (1966a: 94). In each of these instances, Fromm sees the clear and (mostly) unambiguous statement of universalism.

This idea of universalism provides the impetus for the next crucial influence of Judaic thought on Fromm's radical humanism: namely, the idea of "Messianic Time." For Fromm, the messianic concept was rooted in the Creation Story of the Old Testament and in Adam's act of disobedience toward God in the eating of the forbidden fruit. Reading it as a humanistic allegory of the birth of man, Fromm interpreted Adam's act of disobedience as the beginning of human history, the act through which the "original pre-individualist harmony" of Paradise is torn asunder and replaced by conflict and struggle as man comes to experience "the split between himself as subject and the world as object" (1992 [1963]: 204). In contrast to the standard Christian interpretation of the Creation Story—as he understood it—in which Adam's disobedience toward God is characterized as the act of "original sin" through which concupiscence, weakness, and ignorance are transmitted to the entire human race, the interpretation Fromm held was of Adam's disobedience as the *first act of human freedom*, that is to say, the act through which the conditions for human self-awareness itself are historically created. On this reading, Adam's eating of the forbidden fruit represents an "awakening," "the beginning of man's rise," rather than a "Fall" (1966a: 71), his "sin" in disobeying God not resulting in a corruption of substance but, rather, the irreversible moment of human genesis, the creation of man as we know him, who, like God, knows good and evil and is possessed of the ability to choose between them. Whether it is hermeneutically legitimate to interpret it in this way is very much doubtful. Certainly most, if not all, of the Biblical literature interprets Adam's disobedience as in some sense a tragic act (Burston, 1991; Lundgren, 1998). In Fromm's defense—if it is a defense and not a further piece of damning evidence—he accepts that man is made "feeble and weak" (1966a: 77) but prefers to lay his stress on the fact that he can develop, evolve, and realize his "holy" essence (1966a: 65). Fromm takes as his basis for this interpretation Genesis 1:26–27, where it is said "Let us make man in our own image, after our likeness," Genesis 3:4–6, where the serpent tells Eve that she will not die by eating the forbidden fruit, but that her eyes will become opened and that she will be like God, knowing good and evil, and Genesis 3:22–23, where God acknowledges that the serpents prediction has come true: man did not die and is now *as* God knowing good and evil (1966a: 63–64).

The fact that the Old Testament and writings in the later prophetic tradition are comprised of selections from various authors from different time periods meant, for Fromm, that an interpretation can only occur by selecting "those elements that constitute *the* main stream, or at least *one* main stream, in the evolutionary process, weighing certain facts, selecting some as being more and others as being less representative" (1966a: 11). Working with such an interpretative principle, Fromm understands the Creation Story as a mythico-symbolic account of human genesis defined by its prior relationship to the prophetic idea of Messianic Time. In such an account, Adam's eating of the forbidden fruit stands at the beginning of a dialectical process in which man comes to experience himself as a stranger in the world, estranged from himself and from nature, but who, through this very estrangement, and through the subsequent development of his love and reason, can again become one with himself, with his fellow man, and with nature, returning to Paradise but on a new level of human individuation and independence (1992 [1963]: 207; 1966a: 123–124). His "sinning"— or disobedience—becomes justified historically, representing, as it does for Fromm, the beginning of the process that ends, in the form of the messianic idea, with the effective completion of human self-creation (1992: 207–208). On this understanding then, Messianic Time is not an accidental addendum to the history of biblical literature but "the inherent, logical answer to it" (1966a: 88–89) and, at that, the "historical answer to the existence of man" (1966a: 88). Using the Christian tradition as a counterpoint once more, Fromm contrasts the idea of salvation as a *metaphysical* phenomenon[3] made possible by the granting of God's mercy and grace through the personified figure of Jesus Christ, the messiah, with his own interpretation—which he takes as characteristic of the Judaic tradition—which sees it as a *historical* transformation in the material realm, the messiah acting as a *symbol* of man's own achievement. What is important is that, for Fromm, Messianic Time is not brought about through an act of grace but by man's effort. He points out that in the Old Testament God does not interfere in man's history, but, rather, paves the way for man's independence in the form of three acts: (1) showing man a new spiritual goal; (2) showing man the alternatives between which he has to choose; and (3) protesting against instances in which man strays from the path of salvation. It remains up to man to act, to find the path to salvation, and to reach a new harmony (1992 [1963]: 205). On such an understanding, salvation therefore refers to a process of intra- and inter-human development in which man comes to the full realization of his essence, his true human expression: namely, the potential for love, reason, and justice.

Whether Fromm is justified in counterposing this idea with the Christian understanding—or, indeed, whether Fromm's view is an accurate representation of the main thrust of the Judaic tradition itself—is doubtful. J. Stanley Glen has questioned Fromm's interpretation of the Gospel of Salvation by grace alone (*sola gratia*), suggesting that Fromm repeats "the popular misconception that the grace of God...can only mean an arbitrary omnipotence" (1966: 27). Glen says of Fromm that "he sees the action of the omnipotent God only as one of arbitrary force that compels man to submit and that reduces him to nothingness" (Glen, 1966: 54) and that he has "no appreciation of the substance of the doctrine of God the creator and particularly of it as an indication of the grace of God" (102). What can be said in the first instance is that Fromm's view of Christianity grew more charitable in later years, expressing admiration for Meister Eckhart, the Gospels, and even Augustine and Aquinas. In the writings quoted it is likely that Fromm was still influenced by the work of Leo Baeck and Joseph Klausner, both of whom read on messianism and both of whom stress the difference between the Jewish and Christian understanding of messianism to the same effect as Fromm. Fromm's account here certainly may be said to share the same idealizing tone found in these thinkers. As to the accuracy of his account of the Judaic tradition, it must be noted that Fromm explicitly acknowledges the fact that there are two interpretations of Messianic Time in Judaism: a humanistic version that accords with his position and a catastrophic, apocalyptical version that has clearly predominated at various points is history and always threatens to eclipse the former version. He insists—citing the same interpretative license as previously—that his version is the most consistent and representative of the later Jewish tradition (1996a; 2005: 141).

Fromm's understanding of prophetic messianism, as just outlined, forms an absolutely central pillar of his thought, providing, in either explicit or implied tone, the underlying basis to the utopian thread that runs throughout his work. Although an idea that is often expressed in translated Marxian or Freudian form (it is, however, also offered in its original vernacular at certain points), it is an understanding which in the first instance owes a debt to the thought of Hermann Cohen and, in particular, to his hermeneutical interpretation of the Old Testament in light of the later Jewish tradition.[4] Although Fromm's work lacks a detailed discussion of Cohen's ideas, which he came into contact with during his study under Rabbi Nehemiah Nobel, his dedication to Cohen in *You Shall Be as Gods* (1966a: 13) is testament to his influence. Crucially, just as Fromm saw it, Cohen understood prophetic messianism to be the "summit" of monotheism (Cohen, 1995: 21). He understood the prophets to be the "idealists of history" who, through their vision of the concept of history as "the being of the *future*," introduced utopianism as a formalized mode of thought to the world (Cohen, 1995: 261–262). Comparing the messianism of the prophets with the past-focused emphasis of classical Greek thought, the prophets stand as the revolutionary initiators of the concept of *world history* (1995: 246), the personal image of the messiah dissolved and overcome in the concept of the age and the idea of the "goal of history" (1995: 246, 249).

Cohen also—in a manner similar to Fromm—understood messianism to be the solution to the problem of creation:

> In monotheism the problem of creation is not exhausted in the creation of the world; in Greek philosophy the question concerns only the origin of the cosmos. Here in monotheism, however, *man* as the carrier of

reason and as the rational being of morality occupies a privileged position. Because of this, the problem of creation transfers its meaning from the realm of causality to the realm of teleology. (Cohen, 1995: 70)

Crucially, just as Fromm understood it, Cohen saw that the coming to pass of the serpent's prediction, of Adam and Eve's coming to know good and evil after eating the forbidden fruit, meant that "the question of creation, in the case of man, now concerns knowledge" (Cohen, 1995: 86). Considering the nature of knowledge as efficacious and tied to rationality, this means that to leave man in passivity would be a contradiction, or would at least make redundant the very attribution of a potential for knowledge. As such, the creation of man must mean the creation of his reason, which Cohen argues is oriented toward morality—the essence of man therefore as dependent upon on the "knowledge of morality" (Cohen, 1995: 86). The "carrier of reason"—the "rational being of morality" who "occupies a privileged position"—man is the object and vehicle of creation. His "unique being unfolds as the foundation for becoming, which in virtue of this being attains its foundation and its meaning" (Cohen, 1995: 88), the very fact that being stands as the presupposition of the foundation means that becoming—and, thus, man—is the presupposition of the unfolding of the foundation (Cohen, 1995: 88).

Indeed, following Kant, Cohen saw reason and, in particular, *moral reason* as the source of religion. The highest calling, and the faculty which brings us into contact with the divine, Cohen argued that morality is inextricably connected with religion such that religion without morality is not religion.[5] Just as Fromm was to see it, the focus in Cohen's religion of reason is not on God as transcendental, not on theological speculation as such but, rather, on the *imitatio Dei*, or, rather, *Halakah* ("the way"), the approximation of God's actions as the model for the purposive action of man (Cohen, 1995: 96). Cohen's, as with Fromm's, understanding has its roots in the *theologia negativa* of Maimonides, who contended that the unknowability of God's essence—as is necessitated by the incorporeal, unattributable Truth of God—is such that positive statements about God's nature are not statements of God's qualities but attributes of his acts.[6] Cohen, like Maimonides before him and Fromm after, understood that the fact that God revealed to Moses only the effects of his essence—or, rather, his actions—and not that essence itself (Exodus, 3:14), meant that "belief" in God involves the imitation of his actions and not knowledge *about* him (Cohen, 1995: 95; Maimonides, 1925: 75–76; Fromm, 1966a: 29). To "know" God, then, is to participate in the actions that define his essence ("right living"), in those attributes of action which communicate his being, namely, love and justice

(Cohen, 1995: 94). As such, a "correlation" (Cohen, 1995: 86) is seen to exist between man and God such that "man's spirit is based on God's spirit, not only as a living creature, or only as an intellectual creature, but insofar as his reason, which in an eminent way is moral reason, is also derived from God" (Cohen, 1995: 87).

These ideas—which are expressed in their own terms, but with unmistakable similarity, in *You Shall Be as Gods* (1966a: 65–70)—preface Fromm's interpretation of the Creation Story and Messianic Time and his focus on right living as the path to salvation—a focus which is clearly evidenced in Fromm's work in social-psychological and nontheistic radical humanist terms. The idea of reciprocal relation—or "correlation"—between man and God is a central facet of Fromm's understanding of Judaism, the stress on the qualities of love and justice (or love and reason, with justice implied, as it is found most commonly in Fromm) expressing the substantive import of this correlation. Crucially, the fact that the qualities of God are transformed into norms of right living—that, by "drawing near" (Cohen, 1995: 409) to God man approaches his own self-perfection, and that man's self-perfection therefore "amounts to the establishment of God's being on earth" (Cohen, 1995: 250)—means that God becomes the symbol of morality, the norm for human action embedded in humanity at the very center of its being and task.

Mysticism, Radical Autonomy, and the Absurdity of Theology

In addition to prophetic messianism and a Cohenian interpretation of the Old Testament, Fromm's radical humanism is also greatly indebted to the stress on experiential piety found in Hasidic thought. Fromm had been introduced to Hasidic thinking by Rabinkov while he was as a teenager, the central concerns and even the shape of his thinking seemingly influenced by this formative encounter. Although Fromm actually wrote very little on Hasidic thought and philosophy beyond his approving discussion of it in his doctoral dissertation and some extended sections in *You Shall Be as Gods*, it can be argued, much like his relationship to the thought of Cohen, that so deep does his connection with Hasidism run, and so many are the similarities between Hasidic thought and his own, that it seems that the relative lack of comment on the connection is testimony to its underlying pervasiveness.[7] A form of Jewish mysticism to which Martin Buber has given the ascription "mysticism...become ethos" (Buber, 1960: 198–199), Hasidism conceives the task of man as the direction of his whole inner purpose toward the restitution of the original harmony disturbed by the "Breaking of the Vessels"—the cataclysmic Kabbalistic understanding of the creation of the cosmos through which the world comes to be permeated by "divine sparks," or "clear lights," present in everything, which have sunk to the depths (Buber, 1960: 79; Weiss, 1985). In meditative and contemplative effort, through the inwardness of his soul's concentration, man comes into contact with the divine immanence in the world, God revealed in all things and in man (Buber, 1960: 125). Such an experiential piety expands and magnifies Cohen's correlation principle, placing a clear added stress on the intrapsychic effort of the individual in realizing communion with God.

This stress on intrapsychic effort is found to an even greater degree in Habad Hasidism, a form of Hasidism developed by Rabbi Shneur Zalman in the late eighteenth century in which the intellect plays an uncharacteristically prominent role (Habad being an acronym for *Hochmei Bina veda'at*, the wise men of insight and knowledge, or '*hochma Bina V'Da'at*, wisdom, insight, and knowledge). While studying with Rabinkov, Fromm became well-versed in the finer details of the central text of Habad Hasidism, Zalman's *Likkutei Amarim* (also known as *Tanya*). Based on a worldview taken primarily from the Talmud and Midrash, the works of Maimonides, the Zohar, and the Lurianic Kabbalah, Zalman's Hasidism stressed the importance of maintaining a continuous and powerful effort of will in the intense intellectual contemplation of God's greatness and unity; the central idea being that it is the intellect that gives birth to the emotions such that a mind engaged in contemplating sublime matters will eventually bring forth sublime emotions, ensuring by completely enveloping the emotion that it does not go astray (Foxbrunner, 1992: 100–102). In terms reminiscent of Fromm's later psychosociology, Zalman's Hasidism postulated a correlation between men of great compassion and minds with a tendency toward Habad, and, conversely, one between a love for petty, materialistic things and a weak or immature mind occupied with trivia (Foxbrunner, 1992: 102). Crucially, as part of the focus on the intellect in Habad, psychology itself is given a greater emphasis to the extent that Kabbalism—the ground from which Hasidism in general flows—acts as an instrument of psychological analysis and self-knowledge (Scholem, 1971: 341). In much the same way that Cohen's "correlation" between God and man works, Habad sees man as "God's corporealized reflection" (Foxbrunner, 1992: 199), and thus, by "descending into the depths of the self" through the "endless stages of the theosophical world," the secrets of the divine are presented in the guise of mystical psychology (Scholem, 1971: 341). What is important to understand here is that in Habad Hasidism theosophical concepts are explained in psychological terms, their corporeality infused with a godliness that is drawn to the ground and turned into a radical form of spiritual autonomy and self-sufficiency that goes beyond the reciprocal relation found in Cohen and in the prophets. It is this idea of spiritual autonomy and self-sufficiency that forms the central injunction of Fromm's radical humanism: the idea that man must "develop his own powers" and reach the goal of complete independence, "penetrating through fictions and illusions to full awareness of reality." This injunction, which prefaces the psychological appreciation of Fromm's entire mature work, is found here first, in the proto depth psychology of Hasidism, but expanded through his interest in Freud, Spinoza, Buddhism, and Meister Eckhart.

This sense of radical autonomy and self-sufficiency, although reaching an apex of sorts in Hasidic mysticism, was for Fromm a motif found in the wider Jewish tradition. Although noting that in the Old Testament God is generally conceived of as a supreme ruler and lawgiver, the King above Kings etc., Fromm saw a trend in Judaism that promised to "make man completely autonomous, even to the point where he will be free from God or, at least, where he can deal with God on terms of equality" (1966a: 77). The most dramatic expression of this trend, according to Fromm, is found in Abraham's argument with God (Genesis 18: 23–32) over the destruction of Sodom and Gomorrah—which Fromm suggests is understood in Talmudic tradition not as a result of homosexual practice but because the men of Sodom and Gomorrah strove to "keep strangers away in order to keep all the wealth for themselves" (1966a: 26–27). As Fromm notes:

> In courteous language, yet with the courage of a hero, Abraham challenges God to comply with the principles of justice. His is not the attitude of a meek supplicant but that of the proud man who has a right to demand that God uphold the principle of justice... With Abraham's challenge a new element has entered the biblical and later Jewish tradition. Precisely because God is bound by the norms of love and justice, man is no longer his slave. Man can challenge God—as God can challenge man—because above both are principles and norms. Adam and Eve challenged God, too, by disobedience; but they had to yield; Abraham challenges God not by disobedience but by accusing him of violating his own promises and principles. Abraham is not a rebellious Prometheus; he is a free man who has the right to demand, and God has no right to refuse. (1966a: 28)

Fromm offers various other instances as support for his central claim, one particularly illuminating instance being the following Hassidic story recounted in *Psychoanalysis and Religion*:

> A poor tailor came to a Chassidic rabbi the day after the Day of Atonement and said to him "Yesterday I had an argument with God. I told him, 'Oh God, you have committed sins and I have committed sins. But you have

committed grave sins and I have committed sins of no great importance. What have you done? You have separated mothers from their children and permitted people to starve. What have I done? I have sometimes failed to return a piece of cloth to a customer or have not been strict in the observance of the law. But I will tell you, God. I will forgive your sins and you forgive me mine. Thus we are even.'" Whereupon the Rabbi answered, "You fool! Why did you let him get away that easily? Yesterday you could have forced him to send the Messiah." (1950: 47–48)

The freedom of man illustrated in this attitude to God (challenging him on the basis of his own moral principles) was for Fromm the central motif of the Old Testament and later Jewish tradition. Seeing the Old Testament as a "revolutionary book" (1966a: 7) in which man is created as an open system with a capacity for evolution—the limit to which is not set but whose nature lies in the emergence from "incestuous ties to blood and soil, from the submission to idols, from slavery, from powerful masters, to freedom for the individual, for the nation, and for all mankind" (1966a: 7)—the aim of human action is therefore the constant process of liberating oneself from the shackles that bind us to the past, to nature, to the clan, and to idols in general. So central, in Fromm's view, was this idea to the Old Testament that idolatry—the alienation of essential human passions and qualities through the worship of false Gods—stands as the paramount sin in the Jewish faith, the fight against it considered as high, or higher, than the worship of God (1966a: 49). The negative precursor to *imitatio Dei* and *Halakah*, idolatry constitutes a fundamental human alienation, involving as it does the transferal of human powers and qualities to an object external to and separated from the individual, the very act of this transferal meaning that the individual comes to relate to its own externalized and separated powers and qualities through forms of submissive attachment that necessarily preclude freedom and independence.

The essence of what the prophets call "idolatry" is not that man worships many gods instead of only one. It is that the idols are the works of man's own hands—they are things, and man bows down and worships things; worships that which he has created himself. In so doing he transforms himself into a thing. He transfers to the things of his creation the attributes of his own life, and instead of experiencing himself as the creating person, he is in touch with himself only by the worship of the idol. He has become estranged from his own life forces, from the wealth of his own potentialities, and is in touch with himself only in the indirect way of submission to life frozen in the idols. (2004 [1961]: 37)

This inverse relationship between idolatry and freedom is one of the central themes of Fromm's radical humanist social analysis. Although found in the Marxian tradition via Hegel and Feuerbach in the form of the concept of estrangement or alienation, Fromm illustrates the precedence of the idea in the biblical tradition itself, and in Isaiah and the Psalms in particular (1966a: 44–46). Fromm notes that again and again that the prophets characterize idolatry as self-castigation and self-humiliation, and the worship of God as self-liberation and liberation from others. He notes too that in the Talmud it is said that "Whoever denies idolatry is as if he fulfilled the whole Torah" (Hullin 5a) and that the acknowledgment of God is fundamentally seen as consisting in the negation of all idols. What Fromm does with the concept is to rehabilitate it and transpose it into humanist rhetoric so that social analysis is focused on the material-hermeneutical analysis of the self and the human individual capable of authentic and productive action. That Fromm's social-analytical work is itself an attempt at this very "idology" illustrates its fundamental connection with the Judaic humanism from where it came—something clearly apparent from the following:

> Once idols were animals, trees, stars, figures of men and women. They were called Baal or Astarte and known by thousands of other names. Today they are called honor, flag, state, mother, fame, production, consumption, and many other names. But because the official object of worship is God, the idols of today are not recognized for what they are—the *real* objects of man's worship. Hence we need an "idology" that would examine the *effective* idols of any given period, the kind of worship they have been offered, the sacrifices man has brought them, how they have been syncretized with the worship of God, and how God himself has become one of the idols—in fact, often the highest idol who gives his blessing to the others. (1966a: 47–48)

From all of the concerns mentioned thus far—universalism; the ethical and moral foundations of religion, as opposed to "metaphysics," as the essence of religion; the establishment of reason and love in the world at hand; experiential humanism; radical freedom and autonomy; all interconnected with and permeable to each other—Fromm came to develop his own radical humanist interpretation of the Judaic tradition. It was also an interpretation that contained the seeds of his renunciation of the tradition itself and with it a move to explicitly nontheist terrain. Drawing on the negative theology of Maimonides—which itself connects with the very basis of Judaic monotheism in its opposition to idolatrous analogical thinking in the conveyance of the idea of God—Fromm sees contained in its logic the basis for the subversion of monotheism and for the establishment of a nontheistic humanism:

> If God has no name there is nothing to talk *about*. However, any talk about God—hence all theology—implies using God's name in vain; in fact, it brings one close to the danger of idolatry. (1966a: 47)

Thus

> the "negative theology" of Maimonides leads, in its ultimate consequence—though one not contemplated by Maimonides—to the end of theology. How can there be a "science of God" when there is nothing one can say or think *about* God? When God himself is the unthinkable, the "hidden," the "silent" God, the Nothing? (1966a: 37)[8]

Considered thus, negative theology—based on the prohibition of idolatry—leads to the forcing-out of the content of the theological idea of God and, as such, to "the absurdity of all theology" (1966a: 47).

Fromm finds further support for the de-theologizing of Judaism in the Talmudic concept of the "pious of the peoples of the world"—the idea that for its salvation, mankind ultimately does not need to worship God. All that is required—in Fromm's account at least—is not to blaspheme God and not to worship idols. Not even the worship of God is necessary (1966a: 51–52). Theology is thereby displaced as the essence of religion and religion comes to appear as an ethical form of nontheist experiential humanism. Whether or not this is accepted as an accurate or admissible interpretation of Judaic thought in the strictest sense, it is certainly expressive of definite humanistic trends within that tradition. What is more important for the issue at hand is that it is greatly illustrative of how Fromm conceived of his thought at its root. Although Fromm's renunciation of Judaism, which followed from his conclusion as to the "absurdity of all theology," was a significant rupture from his hitherto dominant worldview, he still regarded himself essentially as a Jew. As he suggests in a passage on the history of Jewish thought and on the history of Jews more generally,

> they [the Jews] developed their thought to the point where God ceases to be definable by any positive attributes of essence, and where the right way of living—for individuals and for nations—takes the place of theology. Although logically the next step in the Jewish development would be a system without "God," it is impossible for a theistic-religious system to take this step without losing its identity. Those who cannot accept

the concept of God find themselves outside the system of concepts that makes up the Jewish religion. They might, however, be quite close to the spirit of the Jewish tradition, provided that they make the task of "right living" the foremost goal of life, although this "right living" would not be the fulfillment of the rituals and of many specifically Jewish commandments, but acting in the spirit of justice and love within the frame of reference of modern life. (1966a: 53)

In these words we can see the undoubted resonance which the spirit of Judaism, as he understood it, continued to have for Fromm. So much does this spirit resonates in Fromm that it would not be a complete misrepresentation to say of his thought that it represents in large measure the nontheist development of the central ideas of the Judaic tradition as he understood it. But, as this development places him outside the bounds of Judaism proper, and therefore denying him much of its expository rubric, Fromm's thought was in strict need of a new framework within which to express the humanistic concerns maintained in its evolution. This he was largely to find in the thought of Karl Marx.

The Secular Messianism of Karl Marx

Fromm saw in the thought of Karl Marx the nontheistic continuation and extension of the messianic concerns of Judaism. In particular, he saw that messianic thinking had found "its latest and most complete expression" (2004 [1961]: 54) in Marx's concept of socialism,[9] representing as it does not only "the *genuine* resolution of the antagonism between man and nature, and between man and man" (Marx, 1977: 90), but also "the true realm of human freedom, the development of human powers as an end in itself" (Marx, 1991: 959). So conceived, Marx's is a messianism shorn of any theological referents; it is messianism come full circle, opened out in anthropological fullness to face a realm in which man is the measure of all things, where he has, as Marx says, becomes "his own true Sun" (Marx, 1970: 132) and not even God as the symbol of morality remains. But while Fromm had approached this position largely through his idiosyncratic interpretation of the Judaic tradition, Marx's path—to the extent it can be agreed he took such a path—was one that generally followed the trajectory of developments in or pertaining to German philosophy in the eighteenth and nineteenth centuries and, in particular, the debates that arose from the philosophies of Hegel and Feuerbach.[10]

As a thinker working in the lee of what Charles Taylor (2005) has called the "expressivist" tradition—that tradition of thinkers caught between

Enlightenment and Romantic thought among whom are Rousseau, Herder, Fichte, Schelling—Hegel was concerned with the task of healing the rift that had arisen in the wake of Kant's substantial philosophy between radical subjective freedom and unity with nature. He attempted to resolve the dichotomy through a synthesis in which the infinite, or Absolute, is posited as Spirit (*Geist*), which comes to realize itself through the struggle and self-awareness of finite spirit, that is, nature, or, rather, man as a natural entity. In what was in effect a pantheistic synthesis, the opposition between nature and autonomy is annulled: nature is seen as realizing itself in and through the self-knowledge of man and man as seeing himself in self-identification with nature. While this works for the second half of the equation, that is, unity with nature, it works less well for the first half. Despite the fact that Hegel describes *Geist*'s self-realization through finite spirit as a "*conscious, self-mediating* process" (Hegel, 1977: 492), finite spirit (man) ultimately acts as the *vehicle* of infinite spirit, and, as such, becomes subsumed in a view of history as an inevitable procession played out against the backdrop of cosmic time. It is thus a one-sided and therefore failed attempt at the solution to the expressivist dilemma.

Feuerbach—for whom atheism was the secret of religion (Feuerbach, 1957: xxxvi)—criticized what he saw as Hegel's "speculative doctrine," in which the same voiding of human powers as occurs in theology takes place once again (Feuerbach, 1958: 226). By setting up a system in which man's consciousness of *Geist* is the *self*-consciousness of *Geist* itself, Feuerbach argued that Hegel was perpetuating the divorce of man from true self-knowledge. "Only," he argued, "when we abandon a philosophy of religion, or a theology, which is distinct from psychology and anthropology, and recognize anthropology as itself theology, do we attain to a true, self-satisfying identity of the divine and human being, the identity of the human being with itself" (Feuerbach, 1958: 230–231). Marx praised Feuerbach's "*serious, critical* attitude" to the Hegelian dialectic, calling him the "true conqueror of the old philosophy" who saw clearly that such "philosophy is nothing else but religion rendered into thought and expounded by thought, i.e., another form and matter of existence of the estrangement of the essence of man" (Marx, 1977: 127). In his *Critique of Hegel's Philosophy of Right* Marx applies Feuerbach's approach to Hegel's philosophy, turning Hegel back on his feet, as the saying goes. While praising Hegel's philosophy for its "dialectic of negativity" (Marx, 1977: 132) and its uncovering of "the self-creation of man as a process" (Marx, 1977: 132)—a process which is itself an invocation of the Paradise-Fall-Redemption pattern found in the Judaeo-Christian tradition and in the philosophy of Fichte and Schelling— Marx saw that the ultimate rendering of his system was nothing more than the "self-objectification...of the *essence* of the philosophic mind," which is "nothing but the estranged mind of the world thinking within its self-estrangement—i.e., comprehending itself abstractly" (Marx, 1977: 129). As such, any retention of Hegel's thought required a conscious anthropological inversion. As Marx understood it in light of Feuerbach, the task of philosophy (and of history) had become "the establishment of *true materialism* and of *real science*, by making the social relationship of 'man to man' the basic principle of the theory" (Marx, 1977: 127). The fact that Hegel came to use his philosophy as a justification of capitalism and treated the bourgeois state as rational was merely further proof of the disingenuousness of his solution to the expressivist dichotomy and of the need to reconstitute the central referents of his thought.

But while Feuerbach's critique of Hegel was certainly damning, by failing to acknowledge man as a "natural, corporeal, sensuous, objective being" (Marx, 1977: 136), that is, by failing to "conceive of men...in their given social connection" (Marx, 2000a: 191), his anthropology remained stuck in the realm of theoretical abstraction which it purported to repudiate. Reproaching this failure to arrive at practical, human-sensuous activity, Marx took up where Feuerbach left off, establishing "really existing active men" (Marx, 2000a: 191) as the starting point of philosophy: "the premises from which we begin are not arbitrary ones, not dogmas, but the real premises from which abstraction can only be made in the imagination. They are real individuals, their activity and the material conditions under which they live, both those which they find already existing and those produced by their activity" (Marx, 2000a: 176). Such a starting-point, which overthrows the idealism that had for so long held sway over European philosophy, not only fulfills the radical humanist purpose of once and for all transposing thought firmly into its own realm, but also reaches out sociologically toward an understanding of this anthropology in action, to the recognition that "life is not determined by consciousness, but consciousness by life" (Marx, 2000a: 181) and that "the nature of individuals thus depends on the material conditions determining their production" (Marx, 2000a: 177).

Although these last two statements are justifiably recognized as oversimplifications, it is nevertheless here that we begin to appreciate the relevance of the fourth clause in Fromm's definition of radical humanism, discussed above. In line with the critique of theistic and idealist thought, radical humanism must, if it is to be a truly anthropological theory, engage with real, living individuals; and if it is to truly engage with real, living individuals then it must do so with meaningful reference to their modes and structures of living. In realizing this, Marx had laid the basis "for a new science of man and society which is empirical and at the same time filled with the spirit of the Western humanist tradition" (2006 [1962]: 7). For Fromm this was crucial: the science of man was to be a handmaiden for historical progress toward the prophetic goal. Marx—despite his sharp words for the utopians of his day—had made it clear that socialism (which can be seen as a secular form of the prophetic idea) is not an idle dream but a goal toward which individuals and societies can meaningfully strive. Radical humanism, therefore, is a materialist humanism.[11] Not only, however, is radical humanism a materialist humanism but materialist humanism is also a radical humanism. As Marx stated in his *Critique of Hegel's Philosophy of Right*, "it is the task of history, therefore, once the other-world of truth has vanished, to establish the truth of this world. It is above all the task of philosophy, which is in the service of history, to unmask human self-alienation in its secular forms" (Marx, 1970: 132). The focus of materialist humanism on the phenomena of self-alienation, that is, a form of alienation in the material realm, belies its religious origin ("religion" here understood in Fromm's more encompassing sense). It is, as was seen in the previous discussion of idolatry, the transposition of the fundamental religious concern: man's relinquishment of God within himself or, in radical humanist terms, of his own powers, which are projected outward onto external "idols." As Marx's writes in the preface to *The German Ideology*:

> Hitherto men have constantly made up for themselves false conceptions about themselves, about what they are and what they ought to be. They have arranged their relationships according to their ideas of God, of normal man, etc. The phantoms of their brains have got out of their hands. They, the creators, have bowed down before their creations. Let us liberate them from the chimeras, the ideas, dogmas, imaginary beings under the yoke of which they are pining away. Let us revolt against the rule of thoughts. Let us teach men, says one, to exchange these imaginations for thoughts which correspond to the essence of man; says the second, to take up a critical attitude to them; says the third, to knock them out of their heads; and—existing reality will collapse. (Marx, 2000a: 175–176)

For Fromm, then, Marx was fundamentally a radical humanist truth seeker whose account of the obfuscatory workings of capital—of alienation as it occurred in the labor process itself and in our relationship to the products of labor—placed his thought alongside the penetrating visions provided by Copernicus, Darwin, and Freud in their respective fields. His account of the dehumanization of the worker in the capitalist mode of production (estranged labor), with its appropriated Hegelian themes, and his later idea that we live in general ignorance of the conditions by which our material existence is sustained (the fetishism of commodities), were great spurs for Fromm's developing radical humanism. Although he was to broaden the range of the concepts considerably, expanded on the basis of further psychological insights, the Marxian tropes of the degradation of humanity, reification, mechanization, and the perversion of values feature centrally in his social analysis.

Similarly important to Fromm was Marx's notion of human self-realization, and, in particular, self-realization as achieved through active relation to the world. Based on the Hegelian idea—found in his "master-slave" or "lord-bondsman" dialectic—that man strives for an external embodiment in the world which expresses his humanity, it features in Marx as the positive counterpoint to the alienation of estranged labor. In a materialistic extension of Hegel, Marx posits work, or labor, as the anthropological category through which man achieves genuine self-expression, what Marx describes as the *objectification of man's species life* (Marx, 1977: 69). The act of man's self-creation through labor is the basis for the realization of his own essence: namely, free, conscious life-activity. Although Fromm recognized the importance of labor in phylogenetic and ontogenetic self-realization, it was for him a facet of a broader concern with what can be called psychological or "existential" *productiveness*; in other words, "the physical, mental, emotional, and sensory responses to others, to oneself, and to things" (Fromm and Maccoby, 1996 [1970]: 71). This idea can in fact be found underdeveloped in Marx's *Economic and Philosophic Manuscripts*, but is given greater expression in Fromm where it is developed with aid of the thought of the likes of Spinoza, Goethe, and Meister Eckhart.

As well as this (and, in fact, implied in it), Marx's thought offered further corroboration of the principle of universalism that Fromm had seen expressed in the writings of the Judaic tradition. In defiance of the widespread "epistemological break" interpretation (and the separation of Marx's thought into an earlier "ideological" and a later "scientific" phases) proffered by Louis Althusser in the mid-1960s, Fromm argued for a fundamental continuity in Marx's thought based on what he identified as the retained notion of an essential humanity. Still a largely contentious assertion today, Fromm nevertheless draws the steadfast conclusion that "that which is universally human, and which is realized in the process of history by man through his productive activity" (2004 [1961]: 29) is the absolute grounding-point of Marx's thought. He argues that, in addition to it being impossible for Marx to sustain his "criticism of capitalism as developed in his later years, except on the basis of the concept of man which he developed in his early writings" (2004 [1961]: 64), Marx in fact pays explicit reference to this concept on a number of occasions in those very texts which have been taken as examples of his antiessentialism. In *Marx's Concept of Man* Fromm quotes a famous passage from *Capital*: "To know what is useful for a dog one must investigate the nature of dogs. This nature is not itself deducible from the principle of utility. Applying this to man, he that would criticize all human acts, movements, relations, etc., by the principle of utility, *must first deal with human nature in general, and then with human nature as modified in each historical epoch*" (Marx in Fromm, 2004 [1961]: 23). Fromm also points out the clearly essentialistic nature of Marx's discussion at certain points of *Capital*, including his use of expressions such as "fully developed human beings," "the full development of the human race," "man's necessity to develop himself," and the description of the individual under capitalist production relations as being a "deformed monstrosity" (2004 [1961]: 62).

Fromm traces part of what he sees as the genesis of the erroneous "epistemological break" interpretation of Marx to a misunderstanding of a pivotal passage in the *Theses on Feuerbach*. With particular reference to Daniel Bell's discussion of Marx's concept of alienation (Bell, 1959), Fromm contends that it is mistaken to suggest that Marx says in the sixth thesis that there is "no human nature inherent in each separate individual." What Marx actually says, as Fromm points out, is that "the essence man is no *abstraction* inherent in each single individual" (Fromm, 2004 [1961]: 63); this, as Fromm notes, is the essential point of Marx's materialism against Hegel's idealism. The fact that Marx became increasingly wary of terms connected with the nonanthropological, idealist philosophy he was trying to escape ought not to, Fromm argued, prejudice the fact that his work was fundamentally the materialist extension of Hegel's concept of human self-realization and, therefore, necessarily makes reference to some form of essentialism, that is to say, some conception of what it is to be human and of what counts as characteristic human powers and capacities.

While this account of Marx as a consistent humanist centrally reliant on a conception of human nature has gained much greater traction in the past 40 years, it is still considered questionable in many quarters. What is certainly the case is that, broadly convincing though it is, the certainty in Fromm's account of Marx's retention of the notion of an essential humanity belies a more complex and contested picture. First of all, there are serious hermeneutical and exegetical issues involved in the comprehension of Marx's position here, said issues compounded by the sheer complexity and scope of Marx's thought. As a result of this—and of the ideological motivations that underpin the use of Marx's work in a variety of traditions of thought— there are numerous, often directly conflicting interpretations. A conclusive discussion of the issues involved here is well beyond the scope of the present book. What can be said, however, is that the discussion centrally reduces to a debate over the fundamental nature of Marx's thinking: is it humanist and moral or historical and scientific—or does it comprise combinations of these aspects? What seems certain is that, in addition to being influenced by Hegel and Feuerbach, Marx was influenced by ancient Greek thought, particularly that of Aristotle. This fact has become fairly well established since Ernst Bloch spoke of the "left Aristotelian" connection in *Avicenna und die Aristotelische Linke* (Bloch, 1952).[12] Although it is debatable precisely how much of Aristotle's thought Marx appropriated, it seems fairly evident that he appropriated certain central conceptual aspects, including a form of essentialism in which man is understood as a fundamentally *zoon politikon*, or "political animal" (Aristotle, 1995: 10).[13] While this is so, there is an extant and seemingly intractable debate as to whether Marx's understanding of man as a political animal might still be said to be relativist or not and, if so, what *degree* of relativism can be said to be involved.

What is undoubtedly the case is that Marx's thought is strongly historical, formulated through an immersion in Hegel's thinking and in opposition to the rationalist and static thought of certain Enlightenment thinkers. Whether or not it is as historic*ist* as some would argue it is, is not so clear. Certainly Fromm, as we have seen, made reference to the distinction Marx makes in *Capital* between human nature *in general* and human nature as *historically modified* (Marx, 1990: 758–759n). But there are other passages in which Marx clearly criticizes the idea of an abstract human nature, and probably the majority of Marxists would interpret Marx primarily as a historicist thinker. While this is so, these thinkers have to explain the compatibility of their reading of Marx and the moments—such as the one mentioned above—where he speaks in terms that imply the existence of aspects of human existence not thoroughly historicized.[14] As far as Fromm was concerned, it is clear that Marx was opposed to both absolute essentialism and to absolute historicism, but that "he never arrived at the full development of his own theory concerning the nature of man...hence he left himself open to various and contradictory interpretations" (2006 [1962]: 22). Fromm himself followed Marx in opposing the unhistorical essentialism of the political economists and idealists of the time as well as the blank slate relativism that had grown increasingly popular since Marx's day, but, unlike Marx, he explicitly tried to resolve the issue of the relative weight of the essential and historical aspects. Fromm traces part of the problem in Marx's account with what he sees as the insufficiency of the *zoon politikon* definition itself. While he acknowledges that although the definition can hardly be denied, so clearly does it describe part of the fundamental existence of human life, it is rather general and tells us very little about this life. This, as will be demonstrated in chapter 3, is what Fromm tries to fill out in his account of what he termed "the human situation" and the psychosocial existential "questions" that stem from it.

Returning to the issue at hand, however, it should be stressed that Fromm proffers a humanist, moral, *and* historical reading of Marx (not sharing Althusser's hyperbolic "science/ideology" separation, Fromm also sees Marx as scientific—although I will not try to defend this contention here). Like Marcuse, Fromm takes the influence of Hegel on Marx—which is often seen as leading Marx to a strongly historic*ist* position—to be manifested in a concern with the realization of the potentials of the human essence in the process of existence, that is to say, the realization of potentials that have developed in history but are also inherent and thus stem from a relatively constant and universal basis. Quoting Marcuse's explication of Hegel's thinking in *Reason and Revolution*, Fromm explicitly endorses that idea that "the essence is...as much historical as it is ontological" (2004 [1961]: 25). The essence is as much historical as it is ontological in that it is in history, that is, in existence, that the essence manifests itself; but the precondition of something manifesting itself in history is that the thing itself exists. Norman Geras, who takes a similar position to Fromm here, argues acutely for the salience of this interpretation (Geras, 1983). What Fromm and Geras affirm is the old-fashioned idea that there *is* a human nature or essence and that its realization is always a bounded modification of those essential characteristics, an idea that Marx sometimes seems to hold but which at others he seems to apparently disavow. Although many Marxists would themselves disavow Fromm's essentialist reading of Marx, there is definite (if a little ambiguous) textual support for it.

Nevertheless, there *is* an evident qualitative difference between Marx's earlier and later works—something that Fromm himself acknowledged. Despite this acknowledgement, it is clear that Fromm's account of Marx relies rather heavily on his earlier works and, in particular, on the *Economic and Philosophic Manuscripts*, with almost no account of the dense economic analyses that characterize *Capital, Grundrisse,* or *A Critique of Political Economy*. This being so, Fromm has been criticized for depicting Marx as an "idealistic materialist" (Knapp, 1993: 113), or for being no Marxist at all (O'Brien, 1997: 25). While it is certainly true that Fromm focuses particularly on Marx's philosophical and prophetic aspects, he does so less in ignorance of the economic aspects than in protest at the insufficient understanding of what Fromm felt were how Marx's economic analyses stem from his underlying philosophical position. In assessing the merit of Fromm's account of Marx it is important to consider the time at, and purpose for, which he was writing. *Marx's Concept of Man* (which contained an early translation of the *Manuscripts*) and *Beyond the Chains of Illusion* played important roles, particularly in America, in popularizing the philosophical, humanist side of Marx, rescuing his thought from the Stalinist interpretation that predominated. The themes of these books also chimed with the thrust of Fromm's own methodological focus, which was generally centered on the addition of a deep psychological dimension to Marxian thought and on developing his own radical humanism.

What Fromm was most concerned with in Marx's thought taken in itself was the positing of a *true* individualism, as opposed to the false, egoistic version offered by bourgeois thought (his account of this positing was specifically opposed to idealism). While it is true that he pointed to alignments between Marx and existentialist philosophy in respect of their shared protest at man's alienation, this ought not to be considered without cognizance of his general criticism of existentialism, which he advances at various points in his works. In the very work taken as an example of his apparently idealistic account, Fromm gives explicit stress to the fact that Marx, in contrast to Kierkegaard, sees man in his full concreteness as a member of a given society and a given class, aided and at the same time held captive in his development by society (2004 [1961]: v–vi). Marx, for Fromm, was "the first thinker who saw that the realization of the universally and fully awakened man can occur only together with social changes which lead to a new and truly human economic and social organization of mankind" (2006 [1962]: 86). He identified with Marx's idea of self-realization precisely *because* it sought to traverse the line between idealism and mechanical materialism that prevents philosophy from completing its task.

Rather than slipping into idealism, Fromm in fact critiques Marx for an inadequate materialism; and he does so partly because he thinks Marx overestimates economic concerns. Fromm criticized Marx's evidently erroneous prediction of imminent revolution as resting on a grave underestimation of the ability of the capitalist mode of production to modify and satisfy the economic needs of an unprecedented number of the population (2004 [1961]: vii–viii). He criticized his faith in revolution and belief in the proletariat as the agent of change (identifications stemming from his bourgeois and Hegelian backgrounds, respectively) as naïve and the cause of his failure to foresee the authoritarian systems that would envelop most if not all of the socialistic revolutions. He was also critical of what he took to be Marx's failure to foresee the affluent alienation that came to characterize advanced capitalism in the latter half of the twentieth century, and the fact that alienation spreads beyond the productive labor relationship (although, in fact, in Marx and Engels (1956: 51–52) are clear that alienation is *not* confined solely to the proletariat). But, ultimately—and despite that fact that he saw some important psychological observations contained in Marx's thought—Fromm was critical of Marx's failure to see the true importance of the psychological as a semiautonomous causal realm in the social process:

> He did not recognize the irrational forces in man which make him afraid of freedom, and which produce his lust for power and his destructiveness. On the contrary, underlying his concept of man was the implicit assumption of man's natural goodness, which would assert itself as soon as the crippling economic shackles were released. The famous statement at the end of the Communist Manifesto that the workers "have nothing to lose but their chains," contains a profound psychological error. With their chains they have also to lose all those irrational needs and satisfactions which were originated while they were wearing the chains. In this respect, Marx and Engels never transcended the naïve optimism of the eighteenth century. (2002 [1955]: 257)

Fromm was to find a more adequate appreciation of those "irrational needs and satisfactions," whose constitutional power was relatively unseen by Marx, in the thought of Sigmund Freud.

Sigmund Freud and the Truth that Shall Make us Free

Although it would be inappropriate to unproblematically declare it "radical humanist," Fromm found in the thought of Sigmund Freud a definite means of pushing still further his extension of radicalized religiosity into secular terrain. Well aware of his description of religion as a "childish" fixation aimed at making helplessness tolerable (Freud, 2001a,b), Fromm nevertheless saw a clear religious underpinning to Freud's thought, revealed particularly in its concern with the furthering of man's capacity for independence and freedom. So much did Fromm believe this to be the case that he suggests that psychoanalysis—literally "cure of the soul"—cannot be expressed more adequately than by John's statement in the Gospels: "And the truth shall make you free" (1982 [1980]: vii). Such an understanding will no doubt prove hard to accept at face value, Freud's Schopenhauerian pessimism and Hobbesian fatalism preceding him—statements such as the following springing to mind: "In reality there is no such thing as 'eradicating' evil" (Freud, 1991a: 68); "If you want to endure life, prepare yourself for death" (Freud, 1991a: 89); "The intention that man should be 'happy' is not contained in the plan of 'Creation'"(Freud, 2001c:76); "The aim of life is death" (Freud, 1984a: 311). For someone who believed in *homo homini lupus est* (that man is a wolf to other men), and who held that civilization was built on coercion and renunciation of instinct (Freud, 2001c: 7–8), messianism hardly seems to fit. But while a clear pessimism is evident, it alone does not account for the full complexity of Freud's thinking.

The ambiguous nature of Freud's thought is tellingly expressed in his choice of epigraph for his first work, *The Interpretation of Dreams*. Here Freud inscribes as a preface a line from Virgil: *Flectere si nequeo Superos, Acheronta movebo* [If I cannot deflect the will of Heaven, I shall move Hell]. While not an example of a full-fledged messianism, identification with such sentiment is a clear testament to a Promethean bent that colors his otherwise fatalistic aspects. In fact, it was Fromm's contention that underneath Freud's exterior of rationalistic humbleness ran a strong desire to transform the world. In true psychoanalytic fashion, Fromm adduces support for such a view by reference to what he contended was Freud's unconscious wish to realize his old dream "to be the Moses who showed the human race the promised land, the conquest of the Id by the Ego, and the way to this conquest" (1959: 94).[15] His Promethean slogan, "Where id is, there shall ego be," a declaration to "move hell," implied for Fromm a fundamental religious-ethical principle—"the conquest of passion by reason" (1959: 93)—developed by Protestantism, Enlightenment philosophy, and the "religion of reason," but which "assumed its specific form in Freud's concept" (1959: 93). Attacking, as he did, "the last fortress that had been left untouched—man's consciousness as the ultimate datum of psychic experience" (Fromm, 1970: 5)—Freud proffered a robust challenge to philosophical idealism and traditional psychology. The "last great representative of rationalism" (1959: 114), imbued with the Enlightenment spirit *Sapere Aude* [Dare to Know], but at the same time "an heir of romanticism," he had, in his concept of the *unconscious*, struck "a fatal blow against rationalism" (1959: 115). Although not the first to have posited the existence of unconscious mental processes, it was nevertheless in the thought of Freud that they came for the first time to occupy an epistemologically central position. The functional application of the idea of the unconscious in Freud was such that the straightforward rationalist view of man as transparent to himself was fundamentally shattered, replaced by a radical epistemic uncertainty: despite all appearances to the contrary, man lived in a world of convoluted self-deception characterized by an integral discrepancy between thought and reality, doubt placed at the center of self-understanding. Rather than a romantic turn to the irrational for the sake of the irrational, Freud's unveiling of the hidden forces of personality was carried out in the physician-patient relationship with the purposive Enlightenment goal of conquering the irrational. Building from his experience in the use of posthypnotic suggestion in the treatment of hysterical patients, Freud devised a brilliantly detailed exploratory system that purported to map and explain the operation of unconscious processes and to enable their manipulation for the purposes of therapeutic transformation. Through the minute observation and analysis of dreams, fantasies, slips of the tongue, and other aspects of daily life, together with the introduction of a whole realm of lexical creation constructed to map out the workings of the mind, Freud had created what Fromm considered to be a "science of the irrational" (1970: 5).

Aside from procedural therapeutic considerations—about which he said very little in print—three epistemological principles of this "science of the irrational," pertaining to the conscious/unconscious duality, stand out as of great and lasting importance to Fromm's thought. The concepts of *character*, *repression*, and *transference*, of all of Freud's "discoveries," were for Fromm the foundations of a new basis for critical thought. Although Fromm's understanding of these concepts is altered in certain crucial respects—and particularly so after 1937—they nevertheless functioned for him as *radical humanist conceptual instruments* that furthered the materialization of thought. In the concept of character, for instance, while Fromm came to abandon the psychosexual etiological schema and semimonistic mechanicism that underpinned Freud's account, the thrust of the theory nevertheless represented significant progress in relation to the explanation of how it is that "the way a person acts, feels, and thinks is to a large extent determined by the specificity of his character and is not merely the result of rational responses to realistic situations" (1969 [1941]: 41). In the case of the concept of repression too, while Fromm could not accept the exclusive identification with infantile libidinal cathexes, the concept was nevertheless a fundamental advance toward the explanation of the phenomenon of self-alienation, suggesting how it was that "unconscious forces have gone underground and determine man's actions behind his back" (2006 [1962]: 72). As for the concept of transference, while Fromm criticized Freud's construction of the concept as something to be understood exclusively in line with his psychosexual etiology, as well as criticizing his limited application of it to the analytic encounter, it nevertheless stood as a fundamental leap forward in the clarification of the distorted nature of thought processes, illustrating the human reality of the projection of expectations, desires, and anxieties on to others.

All of this represented for Fromm a crucial extension of the radical humanist groundings of his own thought, paralleling as it does his concern with self-determination and the need to challenge the idolatrous projection of human powers and qualities. In a manner analogous to Marx's unveiling in the economic realm, Freud had pointed to forces—of which we are largely unaware—operating behind our back and which determine our behavior to a greater or lesser degree. What was important in Freud's account for Fromm was not so much the accuracy of the overall explanation but the *basic principles* that it laid down for the development of the historically efficacious "science of man." Freud had, Fromm thought, demonstrated in empirical terms the efficacy of a curative process for psychoneurosis based on gaining insight into, and the affective challenging of, one's own mental structure. While this is so, substantive disagreements with Freud—particularly from 1937 onward—can be found throughout Fromm's writings. A "prisoner of the feelings and thought habits of his society" (1982 [1980]: 122), Fromm saw Freud's thought as permeated by a patriarchal-bourgeois bias, which caused him to interpret the nature and possibility of psychoanalysis in the comparatively restricted way that he did. His famously chauvinistic picture of women was merely a "grotesque" representation of the dominant patriarchalism of his day, whereas his stress on the therapeutic goal of adaptation to the liberal-bourgeois status quo effectively aligned political radicalism with neurosis (1982 [1980]: 7–8, 134). Fromm's adoption of psychoanalysis, in contrast, accentuates the Promethean-humanistic elements without any of the ambiguity of purpose that was evident in Freud. Whereas Freud's pessimistic rationalism only allowed him (in terms of explicit statements at least) modest faith in the power of psychoanalysis (and at that, faith only in social adjustment), for Fromm it was *transtherapeutic*: "Psychoanalysis is not only a therapy, but an instrument for self-understanding. That is to say, an instrument of self-liberation, an instrument for the art of living" (1994: 46).

Fromm also found fault with what he saw as Freud's failure to acknowledge the true extent and depth of the social connection (he did not, however, argue that Freud failed to take the social connection into consideration at all, merely that he insufficiently conceptualized it). Despite some statements to the contrary, Fromm saw that Freud's thought tended to universalize the bourgeois psychic structure, failing to follow its own logic and stress the constitutional importance of society. For Fromm, the separation of personal from social analysis is impossible:

> I do believe that one cannot understand a person, an individual, unless one is critical and understands the forces of society which have molded this person, which have made this person what he or she is. To stop at the story of the family is not enough. For the full understanding of the patient it is not enough either. He will also only be fully aware of who he is if he is aware of the whole social situation in which he lives, all the pressures and all the factors which have their impact on him. (1994: 102)

As such, individual psychology is simultaneously social psychology, and the extrapolation of the critical function of individual psychoanalysis in the form of a psychoanalytic social psychology which sought to extend the basic insights of Freud on the basis of Marxian thought is possible. Psychoanalysis can, then, lay the basis of a critical social analysis. In addition to—and, in fact, stemming from—this, Fromm sought to replace the "mechanistic" philosophical underpinnings of Freud's thought with a radical humanist philosophy constructed along socio-anthropological and existential-phenomenological lines.[16]

Interestingly, despite breaking with what are generally seen as fundamental aspects of Freudian psychoanalysis, Fromm nevertheless proclaimed fidelity to what he took to be the essence of Freud's ideas, disclaiming the suggestion that he had "revised" Freud (revised understood here in the pejorative sense) and calling himself a "pupil and translator of Freud... attempting to bring out his most important discoveries in order to enrich and to deepen them by liberating them from the somewhat narrow libido theory" (1966b: 59). Depending on one's position as to what the essence of Freud's ideas is, this claim is certainly questionable. The idea that Fromm could be seen as modifying but not abandoning the essence of Freud's thinking certainly goes against the expressed belief of a number of Fromm's contemporaries—not only his Instut ex-colleagues, but also practicing psychoanalysts such as Fenichel. Generally, this criticism is centered round the contention that in rejecting libido theory Fromm is simultaneously rejecting the explanatory basis of psychoanalysis and, therefore, "abandon[ing] psychoanalysis altogether" (Fenichel, 1944: 152). As such, Fromm's revisions (as they surely are—however much they are carried out in the spirit of development) elicited accusations of "common-sense psychology," "culturalism," "moralism," "idealism," and were criticized for merely rehashing the apostasy of Jung, Rank, and particularly Adler.

What must be stressed here is that Fromm's revisions clearly bear, if not direct correspondence, then certainly a definite degree of similarity to the revisions of Freudian thought carried out by these thinkers—each thinker taking issue, in their own way, with Freud's seemingly all-pervasive stress on the thoroughly sexualized nature of libido—although Fromm generally neglected to acknowledge these similarities. While this is so, there are clear differences. A thorough description of the respective accounts is not possible here,[17] but something can be said. What is important to note is that, of the three thinkers, it is with Jung that Fromm shares the greatest similarity. First of all, Jung's reconceptualization of the concept of libido from one of *sexual* energy to *general* psychic energy clearly parallels Fromm's own revision—although Jung's conceptualization did not connect it to the sociobiological function of character as did Fromm's. Like Fromm, Jung saw the unconscious as positive and as a bridge to universal humanity, suggesting in the process structural aspects of the human psyche that can be generally applied—although, again, there are differences, particularly the fact that Fromm sought to avoid what is seen as the unwarranted mysticism found in Jung. Jung also, like Fromm, regarded the aim of therapy as more than symptom alleviation, and made reference to moral and religious sources in his explanations and hypotheses as to the nature of mental life. In addition to these points, there are number of striking clinical similarities between Fromm and Jung, such as the positing of the struggle to emancipate oneself from the regressive lure of symbiotic fusion with the mother as the first and most momentous problem of human development (Jung calls this tendency "incestuous libido"—the idea of trying to reinstate intrauterine existence—an idea which is clearly manifest in Fromm's writings). While this was so, Fromm ultimately saw Jung as a "conservative romantic" (1970: 7) and thus lacking the radical humanist spirit that animated his own thinking.

Fromm's similarities to Rank and Adler are less pronounced. In the case of Rank there is again the similarity of challenging Freud's apparent reduction of all emotional experience to libido. Rank, who drew on the work of Bachofen, also challenged the primary importance of the Oedipus complex and stressed the importance of the problem of separation from the mother, both central aspects to Fromm's own psychoanalytic position (although Fromm did not place the same stress as did Rank of the "birth trauma"). Rank also (as with Ferenczi, whom Fromm was not shy of proclaiming a debt to) thought that the analyst should not be emotionless and that establishing a human connection could assist in the curing of neuroses. But, while Fromm praised Rank for developing original views, he was strongly critical of what he saw as Rank's "close kinship with the elements of Fascist philosophy"—as evidenced in his relativistic theory of will that disclaims any search for an objective truth and his adoption of "the sadomasochistic Weltanschauung" that separates the world into the powerful and powerless (1939b). For a radical humanist truth seeker, this was tantamount to a molestation of the humanistic potential in Freud. As for Adler, who was the first to break away from the Freudian orthodoxy, it can be said that there are similarities in the manner in which they both sought to account for the influence of society on mental life and in which they both drew on Bachofen's theory of matriarchy to suggest positive features of femininity as well as linking aspects of female psychopathology to their historical subordination. In addition to this, both shared a view of the individual as an indivisible whole and held to underlying socialist positions that attracted disapproval from many in their profession. Despite these similarities, Fromm disagreed with Adler's doubt over the centrality of repression and was wholly opposed to his Nietzschean stress on the strivings for power, prestige, and possession, and on the importance of "adjustment."

These similarities noted, then, it is clear that Fromm did revise aspects of Freud's theory; as to whether they are revisions that pulled him away from the essence of Freud's thinking is more debatable, and will be discussed in chapter 3. Either way, what is important to stress here is that the psychoanalytic theory that resulted from Fromm's revisions, with its rejection of the constitutional role of libido and stress on the social-psychological, which bears a distinct resemblance to the kind of relational and intersubjective theory that predominates in psychotherapeutic thought today. Burston lists a number of prominent psychoanalysts who work with an approximate rejection of central role of libido—W. R. D. Fairbairn, Harry Guntrip, John Sutherland, John Bowlby, Charles Rycroft, Peter Lomas, R. D. Laing, Jacques Lacan, Heinz Kohut, Roy Schafer, Donald Spence, Edgar Levenson, and Morris Eagle—and suggests that Fromm played a largely under-recognized mediating role in the transformation of mainstream psychoanalytic orthodoxy (Burston, 1991: 218, 4). Fromm's distinction resides in the fact that he is humanist, socialist, moral, and sociological all at once, and develops his thought in a committedly radical humanist direction. Whether or not Fromm's claim of fidelity to Freud is taken to be legitimate, it is clear that Freud provides in many respects the working language of Fromm's thought: his writing style can be said to mirror that of Freud's in its lucidity and clarity in conveying complex conceptual and empirical issues; there are also profound structural and thematic similarities that will be obvious to the student of Freud, with many ideas often conceived in opposition to, or with direct impetus from, aspects of Freud's corpus (Fromm, in fact, claimed that whenever he came to analyze a particular issue his first task was to consult Freud's position on the matter and work his theorizing from there, revising and correcting wherever appropriate). In the final analysis, however, what I want to argue is that Freud's influence to Fromm is subservient to the more constitutional influences of Judaism and Marx. As such, the issue of whether Fromm was a Freudian or not is something of a moot point for the present discussion. What is important is to recognize is that the persistence of the religio-philosophical influence in particular, from the renunciation of Judaism through its inversion and reconceptualization set on the logic of the inversion, as he saw it through Marx and then Freud, is the characterizing basis of Fromm's radical humanism. The furthering of this religio-philosophical influence through Marx and Freud was a progressive step (or, in fact, a lifelong iterative process) in the humanization and materialization of Fromm's thought, taken so as to be able to better understand the reality and fundamental nature of human existence.

CHAPTER 3

Radical Humanist Psychoanalysis

In the earliest part of Fromm's career, the time from which he cofounded the Frankfurt Psychoanalytic Institute to his emigration to the United States along with the *Institut für Sozialforschung*, his work had focused primarily on the development of a psychoanalytic social psychology, which could be used in historical materialist analysis. All throughout this period, it is clear that he adhered to what was a more or less orthodox Freudian position characterized by the understanding of the individual as driven by "libido," "libidinal strivings," "instincts," etc. His works during this period were invariably concerned with the social application of psychoanalysis and with the conceptual preparation necessary for this application to occur. What was increasingly clear in these writings is that, through his repeated drawing out of the implicit and explicit constructions of Freudian theory that allow, and even demand the social extension that he proposes, the logic of Fromm's own argument seemed to point ever more clearly at the insufficiency of that theory itself.[1] By the time of the publication of *Escape from Freedom*, Freud's failure to, as Fromm saw it, adequately acknowledge the importance of social relations, social structure, and wider society beyond the family, narrowly conceived, is taken as one facet of a deeper failure: namely, the inadequate conception of relatedness per se. In particular, Fromm took issue with what he saw as Freud's relatively denuded account of human motivation and its base in the flawed philosophical and physiological theories of his teachers. Reductively mechanical and bourgeois, Fromm came to see that Freud's theory wrongly interpreted the phylogenetic and ontogenetic realities, giving a causal role to sexuality which greatly exaggerated its actual influence. In opposition to this, Fromm developed his own account of what it means to be human—what can be termed "existential" anthropology—and his own account of the psychoanalytic concept of character. Together, these are the crucial conceptual revisions that frame Fromm's thought, helping to lay the basis for his own radical humanist psychoanalytic theory.

In the course of working through his points of contention with Freud, Fromm was to take himself beyond the bounds of psychoanalytic orthodoxy and to estrange himself from the other members of the Institut, who maintained something of a quasi-orthodox opposition to his revision. Increasingly important for Fromm was what he would later term the "creative renewal of psychoanalysis," the modernization of psychoanalysis, and its reversion to a "critical and challenging theory" that was relevant to the contemporary environment (1970: 29). The conflict that ensued between Fromm and his erstwhile colleagues exposed divergent views of the nature of psychoanalysis and social theory, allowing relatively unencumbered insight into the material and dialectical status of the respective accounts. Despite the fact that the conflict has served Fromm poorly in reputational terms, it is argued here that this has more to do with assertion than assessment, and that Fromm's position, fairly appraised, is the more promising of the two conflicting interpretations, providing as it does the basis for a genuinely materialist account of the biological core which is not reductively tied to modifications of the sexual instinct.

An Insufficient Account of Relatedness

Reconstructed from the bottom upwards, Freud's thought can be said to rest first and foremost on the reductive mechanical materialism of Ernst Brücke, whose 1876 Lectures on Physiology he attended as a young medical student. Greatly influenced by these lectures, in which Brücke advanced a physical-mathematical position, the central point of which was the contention that all psychic phenomena can be sufficiently explained by reference to the physiological processes that underlie them, Freud's nascent thought was stamped with the desire "to investigate what form the theory of mental functioning assumes if one introduces the quantitative point of view, a sort of economics of nerve forces" (Freud in Gay, 2006: 78). Although Freud was later to demur from this quantitative natural-scientific task—which he referred to as his "Psychology for Neurologists"—and explore the more qualitative and esoteric realm of the unconscious, his residual and underlying debt was nevertheless to the mechanical materialism of Brücke, which informs even his psychoanalytic work. Ever the student of Brücke, it was imperative for Freud that his new psychoanalytic theory identify a physiological substrate for the drives—a substrate that he was to find located in the impulse toward *sexuality*. Although his first work, *On Aphasia: A Critical Study*, argued for the recognition of the importance of the functional conditions of language over neurological explanations in relation to aphasia, his experience of hysterical patients had convinced him of the structural role that sexuality plays. Encouraged by the sexual exceptionalism of Paul Ehrlich, by *Three Essays on the Theory of Sexuality*, Freud had come to view psychoneurosis as based on sexual instinctual forces (Freud, 2000: 29). In this work, in which he starts out from the analysis of "aberrations of the sexual instinct" (Freud, 2000: 97), Freud goes on to infer a view of "normal" functioning to which the sexual instinct contributes the most important and constant source of energy (Freud, 2000: 29). Conceived as "an endosomatic, continuously flowing source of stimulation," the aim of the sexual instinct (libido) consists in the removal of the organic stimulus set into motion through the excitation of the organ (Freud, 2000: 34).

This hydraulic idea of the buildup and removal of stimulus is similarly active in his account of the psychic structure. Mirroring his earlier idea of an economics of nerve function, in this account Freud posits the general tendency of the mental apparatus as being geared toward the principle of limiting expenditure of energy (Freud, 1984b: 39). As outlined in "Instincts and Their Vicissitudes," Freud's view of man is of a being driven by two fundamental biological forces—the ego, or self-preservative instincts, and the sexual instincts, or libido (Freud, 1984c: 120). Corresponding to these two biological instincts are two psychical principles—the reality principle and the pleasure principle—which form part of a psychical apparatus, whose primary function is the reduction of stimuli to the lowest, or at least the most stable level possible (known as the "principle of constancy") (Freud, 1984c: 116; 1984b). In this schema, mental events are seen as precipitated by the libido and its concomitant psychical correlate, the pleasure principle, imposing a constant, quantitatively similar pressure—or "unpleasurable tension," as it is described later in *Beyond the Pleasure Principle*—which it is the task of the mental apparatus to reduce (1984c: 118–120; 1984a: 275). Faced with the demands of the external world, however, the pleasure principle is frequently replaced by the reality principle and the temporary deferral of gratifications in the pursuit of long-term, world-consistent pleasure. From this there ensues a general developmental battle between the drive to instinctual gratification and the mastery of the ego, with inevitably conflictual results.

Governed by what he calls the "three great polarities that dominate mental life"—activity-passivity, ego-external world, and pleasure-unpleasure—the instincts may follow different paths in attaining the aim of gratification through tension reduction (Freud, 1984c: 138). At times inhibited or deflected, they will gain partial satisfaction; at other times they may be found to have "various nearer or intermediate aims, which are combined or interchanged with one another" (Freud, 1984c: 119). Freud lists four such instinctual vicissitudes: (1) reversal into its opposite; (2) turning round upon the subject's own self; (3) repression; and (4) sublimation (Freud, 1984c: 123).

In the case of reversal into its opposite, two different processes are involved: a change from activity to passivity, and a reversal of content (Freud, 1984c: 124). In relation to the first instance, Freud offers the examples of sadism-masochism and scopophilia-exhibitionism (reversal of aim), stressing that the reversal here never involves the whole quota of instinctual impulse (Freud 1984c: 127–128). In relation to the second instance, he stresses that there is only one example: namely, the transformation of love into hate (Freud 1984c: 130). In the case of turning upon the subject's own self, Freud cites the psychoanalytic observation that masochism and exhibitionism are reversals of their opposites considered from the point of the view of the self. Repression and sublimation relate, respectively, to the withdrawing of the pleasure principle from reality and the directing of the instinct toward an aim other than, and remote from, that of sexual satisfaction.

For Fromm this was an unduly mechanistic picture.[2] Although it does, through the discussion of the vicissitudes of the instincts, recognize conflict and dissention in the mental apparatus during ego development and, therefore, a sense of differentiated struggle, the picture, according to Fromm, remains a denuded one based essentially on the forces and cathexes of nineteenth-century physics and chemistry. Conceived as a defense against the instincts, the vicissitudes—under which almost every kind of human action other than direct instinctual gratification is denoted—remain fundamentally tied to and implicated in the drive to organ-pleasure. As such, man under Freud is a "physiologically driven and motivated *homme machine*" (1970: 31) incapable of "all categories of spontaneity, such as love, tenderness, joy, and even sexual pleasure as far as it is more than relief from tension" (letter to Robert Lynd, March 1, 1939, quoted in Funk, 2000: 93). The ascendency of the motive of tension reduction in Freud's account, Fromm argues, "could hardly be squared with the wealth of data showing that man, at all ages, seeks excitation, stimulation, relations of love and friendship, is eager to increase his relatedness to the world; in short, man seems to be motivated just as much by the principle of tension increase as by that of tension reduction" (1997 [1973]: 630).

To hold this position is not to claim that Freud was unaware of the existence and power of these forms of relationship to the world; it is, rather, to claim that his conception of them stems from an underlying mechanical philosophy, which reduces the complexity of human life to an economistic semi-monism. While it is true that in the theory of libido Freud clearly states that, alongside the biological and physiological influence of the instincts, the social environment acts as a crucial modifying factor upon these very instincts, the essence of his view of man is nevertheless of a relatively closed, self-sufficient system, primarily isolated and unrelated and only secondarily forced or "seduced" into relations with others (1970: 31). The relationship between the individual and society is thus essentially static in nature: "the individual remains virtually the same and becomes changed only insofar as society exercises greater pressure on his natural drives (and thus enforces more sublimation) or allows more satisfaction (and thus sacrifices culture)" (1969 [1941]: 9). Such a view of man as relatively self-sufficient fits well with the bourgeois view of the self-sufficient individual as the ever lone competitor eternally seeking his own power or gain—a form of Hobbesianism in which society features only as a constraint on the gratification needs of the individual. The fact that the gratification is conceived in primarily sexual terms does not invalidate the thrust of the characterization—in fact, as Fromm notes, Freud's *homo sexualis* can be seen as a direct variant of the classical *homo economicus*: in each theory "persons essentially remain strangers to each other, related only by the common aim of drive satisfaction" (1970: 31; 1959: 100). In *Escape from Freedom*, Fromm stresses that, although Freud always perceives the individual in relation to others, these relations are formed on the basis of the economic relations of capital: "an exchange of satisfaction of biologically given needs, in which the relation to the other individual is always a means to an end but never an end in itself" (1969 [1941]: 10).

Freud's thought on the matter of instincts did, however, undergo significant change later in his life. In "Beyond the Pleasure Principle", the work in which he announces that "the aim of all life is death" (Freud, 1984a: 310), Freud replaces the duality of the self-preservative and the libido instincts with a new duality centered around the opposition of Eros and the death instinct. In a highly speculative enunciation—even for Freud—he now holds that an instinct is "an urge inherent in life to restore an earlier state of things" (Freud, 1984a: 308), and in particular, to restore inorganic existence—by which is meant nonexistence or death. The idea of the conservative nature of the psychic apparatus (reduction of tension) has been transferred here to the biological realm and inverted such that, in the words of Schopenhauer, "death is the true result and to that extent the purpose of life" (Freud, 1984a: 322). The specious justification that Freud gives for this drastic reconceptualization amounts, the words of Schopenhauer aside, to allusions to the morphological process of cellular and multicellular life forms and circular inferential assumptions based on the idea that death is the purpose of life. While this new conceptualization is a clear outgrowth of the pleasure principle's tendency toward stability, it also marks a fundamental departure from the view outlined above. Freud now draws a sharp distinction between the "ego-instincts" and sexual ones, saying that the former exert a pressure toward death and the latter toward prolongation of life (Freud, 1984a: 316). No longer are the instincts solely and ultimately in existence to ensure libidinal self-preservation; they now serve the opposite function: namely, annihilation. Despite Eros being functionally concerned with the prolongation of life—concerned as it is with the unification and integration of all cells and, beyond that, aggregation of individuals, communities, and nations (Freud, 2001c: 122)—the prolongation it seeks is one that will ensure that the organism can follow its natural path to death and not succumb to any extraneous one.

For Fromm, this theory was a partial improvement on its predecessor, despite what he saw as its overall implausibility. In the first instance, it can be seen as a change from a materialistic-mechanistic to a "biological, vitalistic oriented concept" (1970: 34). With this change the whole nature of the instincts are altered: whereas before the libido was located in the erogenous zones, now the instincts are "active in every particle of living substance" (Freud, 1984d: 381); similarly, whereas before the instincts function by nature of a hydraulic mechanism, now they operate without any special stimulation at all (1970: 33). In both respects Freud can be said to have transcended his initial mechanical psychologism. In addition to this, the introduction of Eros makes the theory more relational in that it represents man as related to other men as a result of a concern for union with others, not just pleasure (1997 [1973]: 590). But while it does this, it also posits a tragic struggle at the very center of human existence. While Eros is given the function of promoting unity and civilization, the death instinct opposes this and the struggle between Eros and death as motivating factors becomes the struggle of the human species. What is more, "cruel aggressiveness" is posited as innate, a "primary mutual hostility" and "inclination to aggression'" which seeks an outlet in order to guard against the internalization of its destructive qualities (Freud, 2001c: 111–114).[3] As if to prove the hollowness of this apparently more relational approach, Freud's grim conclusion is that "it really seems as though it is necessary for us to destroy some other thing or person in order not to destroy ourselves, in order to guard against the impulse to self-destruction" (Freud, 1964: 131).

So while this is an improved conception in certain respects, its overall effect is in fact the magnification of the antisocial Hobbesian aspects of the previous theory. Freud, the arch tragedian, introduces Eros, the preserver of life, and sets it with the task of creating unity and greater civilization, only to undercut its efficacy by positing a cruel and aggressive destructiveness behind its efforts. This was a picture that Fromm could not accept. Besides the fact that it was problematic taken in itself (laden as it is with internal inconsistencies which Freud never resolved[4]), it was also a poor construction more generally, failing to distinguish between aggressiveness, destructiveness, mastery, will for power and other similarly qualitatively distinct psychological phenomena (1997 [1973]: 620). The idea of the death instinct became a cover-all concept, which, in fact, served to occlude detailed psychological investigation of the problem of destructiveness. As Fromm notes, "destructiveness varies enormously among individuals, and by no means in such a way that the variation is only one between the respective outward- and inward-directed manifestations of the death instinct" (1980 [1964]: 49–50). The vitalism that had pulled Freud away from his initial mechanicism itself led him to an excessively rigid biological materialism, which comes to mirror the inversely proportional mechanical relationship of the earlier theory.

Existential Anthropology

In marked distinction to the manifest Hobbesianism of Freud, Fromm proposed a conception of what it means to be human in which relatedness is posited as foundational, a non-optional primary need stemming from the very conditions of human existence. Whereas Freud's essential principle is of man largely as a closed, self-sufficient system, Fromm understands the human individual in terms of its relations to the world, to other human beings, to nature and to itself (1969 [1941]: 287–288). "Man," for Fromm, is therefore "*primarily* a social being, and not, as he contends that Freud assumes, primarily self-sufficient and only secondarily in need of others in order to satisfy his instinctual needs" (1969 [1941]: 288). Fromm arrives at this position through a philosophical anthropological rereading of Freud, which dispenses with both his mechanical-materialist and vitalistic-instinctual philosophical frameworks, replacing them with what he calls a "sociobiological and historical" conception (1997 [1973]: 27). Following the logic of *radical* humanism by "returning to the roots," Fromm's conception draws on an evolutionary view of the human species as a biological type placed among, but differentiated from, other species. Rather than seeing the human being as preeminently structured by instinct, Fromm, in fact, conceives of relative *freedom* from instinct as the definitional feature of the human species. Human existence begins, says Fromm, "when the lack of fixation of action by instincts exceeds a certain point; when the adaptation to nature loses its coercive character; when the way to act is no longer fixed by hereditary given mechanisms" (1969 [1941]: 31). The product of a unique "break" in the evolutionary process, we stand *in* nature yet also *transcend* it; in respect of our body and physiological functions we belong to the animal kingdom and are determined by instincts (specific action patterns, which are, in turn, developed by inherited neurological structures), but, to the degree that human action is no longer fixed by hereditary given mechanisms, we have broken with the general trend of nature and are thus, in a sense, "out of nature." Considered thus, man is a "freak of nature" (1970 [1968]: 60), a biological oddity inhabiting an anomalous ontological position vis-à-vis the rest of the natural world.

Central to Fromm's understanding of the nature of what it is to be human is the idea that the "harmony" of animal existence has been shattered. The possessors of reason and self-awareness, enhanced by our capacity for complex symbolic and linguistic manipulation, the human species is characterized by the move from *autoplastic* to *alloplastic* behavior, that is, from behavior characterized by the attempt to change the internal environment (or entity) to behavior characterized by the attempt to change the external environment. With this move a dilemma arises: "Man's life cannot 'be lived' by repeating the pattern of his species; *he* must live" (2003 [1947]: 29). Human existence for Fromm, then, is inherently dichotomous, the capacity for reason effectively cleaving man in two:

> He is set apart while being a part; he is homeless yet chained to the home he shares with all creatures. Cast into this world at an accidental place and time, he is forced out of it, again accidentally. Being aware of himself, he realizes his powerlessness and the limitations of his existence. He visualizes his own end: death. Never is he free from the dichotomy of his existence... Reason, man's blessing, is also his curse; it forces him to cope everlastingly with the task of solving an insoluble dichotomy. (2003 [1947]: 29)

The "essence" of man for Fromm then lies not in a given quality or substance, but in the "contradiction inherent in human existence" (1980 [1964]: 116). This view has certain obvious parallels to existentialist thought, although it is more accurately conceived as growing out of the common ground that it shares with existentialism: namely, the classical religio-philosophical view of man as "both body and soul, angel and animal, belonging to two worlds in conflict with each other" (1980 [1964]: 117).[5]

As was shown in chapter 2, Fromm's thought owes a lasting debt to the Judaic tradition. His account of the human situation, particularly from *Psychoanalysis and Religion* onward, is often presented heuristically, with reference to the biblical idea of man's expulsion from paradise. As utilized by Fromm, the biblical myth acts as a telling representation of the existential dichotomy of missing instincts and self-awareness (1997 [1973]: 304), the notion of Adam's "Fall" providing an appropriate analogy for man's fundamental alienation. Fromm makes a distinction between what he calls *existential* and *historical* dichotomies—the former ineradicable, the latter eradicable in principle (2003 [1947]: 30–31). The contradiction at the basis of man's being constitutes, Fromm contends, a fundamental existential dichotomy that impels man to react in order to find a solution: the conflict is therefore *dynamic*. Our dichotomous existential position, and the disequilibrium it generates, pose fundamental *questions* for human existence, the answers to which represent the myriad manifestations of human nature—it is the questions, then, and not the answers that are man's "essence" (Fromm and Xirau, 1979 [1968]: 9). The many dichotomies which appear that are extraneous to the existential dichotomy are "historical," not existential, in nature—they are "accidental" or man-made and resolvable in principle. Confusion over the respective designation of certain given historical dichotomies as existential is often the precursor or accompaniment to unnecessary suffering and inequality (historical dichotomies often being passed off as existential dichotomies, thus having the effect of naturalizing historical and social contradictions).

It is important to note here that Fromm wants to make a distinction between complete malleability and the fact that there are some aspects of what it is to be human, which are relatively fixed—and that, in the process, he is clearly assenting to a form of essentialism. The general reaction to this kind of thinking in academic thought today, particularly in the social sciences and humanities, veers between disdain and disbelief. But this is the point that Fromm wants to make, and it is the challenge his thought poses.

In Fromm's account, man must overcome the split at the center of human existence, the basic imperatives set in motion by the split itself generating a series of what he terms "existential needs," so named in respect of the fact they are rooted in the human species' very existence. Fromm's discussion of these needs—which can be seen as putative "structural preconditions" (Funk, 2005) that lie at the root of all human psychic dynamism—suffers from what is, considering the supposed centrality and scope of application, a somewhat circuitous and imprecise elucidation. That this is so can be explained in part by reference to the fact that Fromm never intended that his account of these needs be a conclusive summation but, rather, an exploratory exercise in line with his elucidation of psychoanalytic issues, understood as a general philosophical anthropological prompt to further discussion. Fromm, in fact, stressed that his account of the existential needs amounted less to a final list than a suggestive projection of some central issues. As he was to explain it in an interview with Huston Smith in 1960, they were merely things in his own thinking that "struck him as the most important"; he was "sure there [was] nothing final about it" (2011 [1960]). The underlying position from which the needs stem—the need to transcend the disharmony brought about by the rupture with "paradisiacal" nature that characterizes the basic human situation—is the central point; the overlapping extrapolations and partial restatements that occur in Fromm's writings all reduce to it.

Although Fromm first speaks in explicit terms of "existential needs" in *The Sane Society*, the idea is clearly apparent as far back as *Escape from Freedom*. In fact, Fromm's account of the human predicament in this work is an important preparatory elucidation that is summarized here prior to discussing his later statement of the existential needs themselves. In a chapter titled "The Rise of the Individual and the Emergence of Freedom," Fromm provides an outline of a dialectical process with ontogenetic and phylogenetic correlates, which he terms *individuation*. Not to be confused with Jung's concept of the same name, although with certain definite similarities, the process of individuation in Fromm represents the growing sense of self-strength but also of aloneness in the human being as it matures from infanthood toward adulthood, and in the human race as it evolves from "primitive" and medieval cultures to modern, secular societies. (The unfortunate comparison here cannot be escaped, although it should be kept in mind that Fromm makes this kind of distinction from a value position in which the transcendence of theological or mythical thought is seen as representing, in potential at least, the greater realization of human powers recognized as such, and that, therefore, the distinction only holds to the degree to which any given society has been able to conceive a world without these idolatrous elements.)[6]

Fromm depicts this process as the giving up of the "primary ties" that connect child with mother, the member of "primitive community" with clan and nature, and medieval man with church and caste (1969 [1941]: 24)— processes, which although exhibiting similar aspects, surely cannot be seen as fully analogous. (The assumption here has to be that Fromm sees full individuation as impossible in all but our post-Reformation and post-Renaissance world, with its apparently increased potential for the realization of reason and love, and that when he speaks of child and mother he is referring to the societies that are heirs to these periods and to the child in terms of its *potential*, this potential being more fully realized in a secular and "democratic" environment.) The idea behind this account is that once this stage of individuation is reached, and the individual is free from primary ties, it is confronted with the new task of orienting and rooting itself in the world, finding security on the terms of individuated existence (1969 [1941]: 24). Considering the fact that the descriptors "orienting" and "rooting" foreshadow Fromm's later statement of the existential needs, as will be seen, conceptual clarity would be gained here by understanding this central task as *relating*, which corresponds directly with what Fromm names as the preeminent existential need, namely, *relatedness*. (Although Fromm in fact lists eight existential needs over the course of his work, in the discussion that follows I will use as my basis the account he gives in *The Sane Society*, where they are discussed in most detail, making note of any additional needs as and when the occasion arises.)

The need for relatedness, Fromm argues, is what lies behind the human desire for association and partnership and a whole range of other forms of interaction, many of which are dealt with in the subsequent discussion of

Fromm's account of the character orientations. The need for relatedness, crucially, does not refer solely to physical contact and socialization but also to ideas and values—"moral aloneness," therefore, is as much a problem as physical loneliness (1969 [1941]: 17–18). For Fromm, in fact, it is fundamental to the human predicament that we find unrelatedness in both these senses intolerable. It was not possible, Fromm held, to exist without relatedness and avoid serious negative psychological consequences. To be alone and therefore unrelated, is unbearable.

The next existential need that Fromm stresses, which is closely associated with the need for relatedness, is the need for *transcendence*. In his account of the human situation, and therefore as a consequence of the anomalous ontological situation we inhabit, Fromm contends that it is an imperative for a member of the human species to want to "transcend the role of the creature, the accidentalness and passivity of his existence, by becoming a 'creator'" (2002 [1955]: 35). Transcendence, thus understood, is possible in a variety of ways that are, however, broadly separated into creative and destructive responses. In *The Anatomy of Human Destructiveness* Fromm fails to list transcendence as an existential need but does, nevertheless, speak of *effectiveness*—"the proof that one is," the fact that "I am because I effect" (1997 [1973]: 316)—which largely mirrors his discussion of transcendence but with the benefit of appearing less theologically oriented. Either way— and this is the salient point—both demonstrate the urge to overcome the sense of impotence that is part of the dialectical process of individuation.

The need for *rootedness* is the third existential need that Fromm discusses. Yet a further refraction from the fact of our fundamentally dichotomous existential position, this need receives extended treatment in *The Sane Society* and a rather more attenuated discussion in *The Anatomy of Human Destructiveness*. The central issue involved in both discussions is what Fromm sees as a deep craving for roots. In the former instance, Fromm indulges in a discussion of Bachofen as part of a rereading of Freud's idea of the Oedipus complex in which the child's longing for motherly love (in figurative language: its longing to return to the womb) is the primary affective reality and not the rationalistically conceived sexual desire for the mother, as it is in Freud. In Fromm's account the idea of "incestuousness" is retained but reinterpreted in "existential" rather than sexual terms as a regressive phylogenetic fixation, other variants of which are ties to nature, blood, family, clan, state, nation, church, etc. In each of these fixations the individual leans on, feels rooted in, and achieves a sense of identity as a part of identification with, these surrogates for individuality (2002 [1955]: 39). The choice, as Fromm conceives of it, is between developing through *brotherly love* (understood in the biblical sense) or remaining fixated on the mother or other incestuous objects. In the discussion in *The Anatomy of Human Destructiveness,* much of this detail is spared but the issue of "leaving the womb" remains. The implication is that without strong affective ties to the world, man would "suffer from utter isolation and loneliness" (1997 [1973]: 313).

The fourth existential need Fromm discusses is the need for a *sense of identity.* In the process of individuation, as the person is faced with the need to emerge from the primary ties (or bonds) with mother and nature, that person comes to develop a sense of identity reflective of the level of self-awareness that has been attained. Positive achievement in this process consists in experiencing the world as separate and different, thereby enabling the understanding of oneself as a distinct being. At basis, this is the need to say "I am I" because I am not *lived,* but *live* (2002 [1955]: 59).[7] Specific discussion of this need appears only in *The Sane Society* but it is, to all intents and purposes, a close extrapolation of the need for transcendence and effectiveness (which are themselves close extrapolations of each other) as well as the need for rootedness, and is clearly apparent in the majority of Fromm's sociopsychoanalytical discussions.

The need for a *frame of orientation and devotion* is the final need that Fromm discusses.[8] To have a frame of orientation and devotion gives meaning to life, elevating the individual beyond otherwise isolated existence. The demand of this need is that we find a cohesive picture of the world and of our place in it. This picture can be illusory or can approximate reality, but failure to adopt a frame leads to insanity. The greater the development of objectivity the more man is in touch with reality, the more he matures, the better he can create a human world in which to live (reason, therefore, is important here, and the difference between necessary and sufficient levels of realization). In *The Anatomy of Human Destructiveness,* Fromm stresses a biological aspect to this need: animals have instincts which provide both a map and goals; humans broadly lack these instincts, and therefore, a frame of orientation and object of devotion can help integrate human energies in one direction.

What is important in the discussion of these needs is the cognizance of Fromm's "existential" position. While retaining the Freudian idea of a dichotomy at the heart of human existence, Fromm conceives of this dichotomy as existential rather than instinctual (although it refers to instincts, it does so with reference to their relative absence). Man's passions, then, are not the result of frustrated or sublimated physiological needs; they are his "attempt to make sense out of life and to experience the optimum of intensity and strength he can (or believes he can) achieve under the given circumstances" (1997 [1973]: 31). In this sense, Fromm's thinking here extends from his radical humanist groundings into what can be called an "existential anthropology," that is to say, a *biopsychosocial* account of the general human condition in abstraction, which can, together with the corresponding social analysis, act as a baseline for further inquiry. In this anthropology is contained the central theme of Fromm's mature writings: a binary division rooted in an *alternativism*, which holds that there are better and worse means of human satisfaction and therefore better and worse answers to the questions posed by existence. The fact that the descriptions Fromm offers are untidy and imprecise naturally detracts from the strength of his account. That this is so, however, is not a fatal blow to his wider radical humanism. As was seen earlier, Fromm did not claim to be conclusive in this regard. What is important is his *willingness to attempt* to map out some fundamental human motivations in explicit terms, without Freud's mechanical materialist baggage and in opposition to the relativist disavowal that would oppose him. Issues stemming from Fromm's position in this section—such as his potential ethno- and anthropo-centrism—are discussed in chapters 5 and 6.

Character and Characterology

The main conceptual tool of Fromm's work is the psychoanalytic idea of *character*. Successively developed by Freud in the *Three Essays on the Theory of Sexuality*, "Character and Anal Eroticism," "The Disposition to Obsessional Neurosis," and "The Infantile Genital Organization of the Libido," and extended by Karl Abraham, Ernest Jones, and Otto Fenichel, character is the dynamic, conative "system of strivings which underlie, but are not identical with, behavior" (2003 [1947]: 39). Alongside temperament and constitution, character forms the basis of the human personality, providing the generally unconscious motivation that is crucial in the shaping of thought and action. It can be seen as the psychological subsystem, developed through life experience, that permits consistency in action and relief from constant conscious decision, structuring the passions into "an integrated system which has its own logic and order" (Fromm and Maccoby, 1996 [1970]: 13). But whereas Freud interpreted the dynamic nature of character as an expression, through sublimation or reaction formation, of its libidinous source, Fromm sees the fundamental basis of character as deriving from the specific kinds of relatedness to the world gained in the process of living. As opposed to the relatively closed and instinctually determined forms of relatedness posited by Freud, the forms of relatedness in Fromm are open and highly interactive, varying both individually and culturally.[9]

In Fromm's account, character acts as man's "second nature" (1997 [1973]: 26), the human substitute for the instinctive animal apparatus that was lost in the rupture with nature that defines human existence.

The functional-adaptive, *socio-biological* requirement of the human species, Fromm defines character as the "relatively permanent structure of [the] passions" (1982 [1980]: 54), or more revealingly as "the relatively permanent system of all non-instinctual strivings through which man relates himself to the human and natural world" (1997 [1973]: 305). In a reconfiguring of Freud's developmental schema, Fromm posits character as the result of psychic development in two fundamental processes—the process of *assimilation* (the acquiring and assimilating of things encountered in the external world) and the process of *socialization* (relating to oneself and others) (2003 [1947]: 42)—during which *orientations* of character form. The orientations that arise in these two processes represent what can be considered the core of character, the analysis of which Fromm describes as "characterology."

Fromm's own character typology—the formalized account of the responses to the existential needs—is interspersed across his mature writings, representing a fairly consistent whole. Making explicit the implicit normative assumptions of Freud, Fromm separates his typology into *productive* and *nonproductive* orientations, the respective designations to be understood in terms of the *quality* of relatedness they offer. In the process of assimilation, the following nonproductive orientations are discussed: receptive, exploitative, hoarding, marketing, and necrophilous-destructive. Fromm outlines the first four orientations in *Man for Himself*, the fifth being introduced as a distinct orientation in *The Heart of Man*, and subsequently developed in *The Anatomy of Human Destructiveness*.[10] What Fromm does in his discussion of these orientations is to replace and extend Freud's existing typology, largely by accounting for it in libido-free language and in line with his own observations. The essential thrust of Freud's clinical description is broadly accepted, but the sexual etiology is rejected as a reversal of the actual causal relationship. It is replaced by an understanding that sees the so-called libidinous aspects less as fixations at psycho-sexual stages than expressions of the underlying assimilative relationship to the world, therefore stressing the *quality of relationship to the world* as the causal factor.

Whereas, as was shown, Freud assumed the child experiences pleasure at erogenous zones (the mouth and anus) in connection with process of feeding and defecation, and argued that these zones retain their libidinous character in later years, Fromm saw one's character as primarily developing through experiences with others. The desire to *receive* everything, for instance, represented for Fromm a passionate dynamism in which receiving from others is felt as being the only way in which a person can realize his or her wishes in relation to the external world. Fromm contends that the fact that such people often have dreams and fantasies of being fed, nursed etc., is due to fact that the mouth, more than any other organ, lends itself to expression of this receptive attitude. The oral sensation, therefore, is not the *cause* of this attitude, but rather "the expression of an attitude toward the word in the language of the body" (1969 [1941]: 290). The certain pleasurable sensations that are experienced by child in connection with feeding and defecation do not assume importance for character development unless they represent—on the psychical level—attitudes that are rooted in the whole character structure.

In the *receptive orientation*, the individual is said to perceive the source of all good as residing in the external world: if something is desired it is to be passively received rather than actively gotten. Corresponding to Freud's oral-receptive character, people characterized by this orientation are said to have a fondness for eating, drinking, smoking, etc., but not as a direct effect of an oral "fixation" so much as an orientation to the world in which receiving is the primary affective mode (2003 [1947]: 45–46). In the *exploitative orientation*, in which the source of all good is also seen as residing externally, oral receptiveness is transformed into a tendency to take by cunning rather than receiving—an affective mode in which suspicion, cynicism, envy, and jealousy predominate (2003 [1947]: 46–47). In the case of the *hoarding orientation*, anal retentiveness is reconfigured as a lack of faith in anything that might be gained from the external world. Security features as a primary concern, a facet of which is a characteristic orderliness motivated by the desire to master the outside world and remove it as a threat (2003 [1947]: 47–49).

The remaining two orientations are broadly additions to the transfigured Freudian schema. The *marketing orientation* is said to represent a relatively new phenomenon, applicable particularly to contemporary industrial-capitalist societies. (Note that the very fact that Fromm introduces this new orientation makes it explicit that he understands character as a fundamentally social and contextual construction, that is to say, a specific historical response to the fundamental dilemma that he sees as definitive of human existence.) Posited as the experience of oneself as a commodity and of one's own value as exchange value, the marketing orientation reflects the dominance and subterranean reach of the market, the extent to which its principles and values have become submerged and embedded in the very functioning of the psychological system (2003 [1947]: 50). Self-esteem is said to suffer as market value, rather than primary human qualities, become the criterion against which appraisal occurs—a situation exacerbated by the fact that one must constantly seek success judged on this very criterion (2003 [1947]: 52–53). This idea of the marketing character is a self-acknowledged anomaly in Fromm's system, in the sense that no specific and permanent kind of relatedness is developed, but, rather, a *protean impermanence of attitude*. The premise of the orientation is in fact "emptiness, the lack of any specific quality which could not be subject to change, since any persistent trait of character might conflict some day with requirements of the market" (2003 [1947]: 57).

The *necrophilous-destructive orientation*, while not a direct transposition of Freudian categories, is, unlike the marketing orientation, partly based on them (it shares certain aspects with Freud's delineation of anal character—in particular the interest and affinity to feces—as well as those outlined in his idea of the death instinct). The origins of the idea can be traced not only to Freud but also to the Spanish philosopher, Miguel Unamuno, who Fromm credits with coining the term "necrophilous" in response to Falangist General Millán Astray's infamous Civil War motto: "Viva la muerte!" [Long live death!].[11] In characterological terms, necrophilia can be described as "the passionate attraction to all that is dead, decayed, putrid, sickly; it is the passion to transform that which is alive into something unalive; to destroy for the sake of destruction; the exclusive interest in all that is mechanical. It is the passion to tear apart living structures" (1997 [1973]: 441). So considered, it is less of an anomaly than a perversion; an "attraction to death," it is in fact "the true perversion," an example of "the one answer to life which is in complete opposition to it" (1980 [1964]: 45). Necrophilous characters are said to prefer to live in the past, to be drawn to violence, force, control, and to all that is mechanical. They are said to be cold, distant devotees of law and order with a craving for certainty.

The *productive* orientation in the process of assimilation can be said to formally parallel Freud's concept of the genital character, referring as it does to a norm of human development (albeit, a less socially restricted and sexually defined norm). It is not to be confused with the modern idea of "productivity," with its connotations of measurement of production of goods and services, but rather to be seen as "the free activity of the self [which] implies, psychologically, what the Latin root of the word 'sponte' means literally: of one's free will" (1969 [1941]: 35). In *Man for Himself*, this is translated so as to designate the experience of the world "through the spontaneous activity of one's own mental and emotional powers" (2003 [1947]: 88). Fromm's discussion of the productive orientation in the process of assimilation in *Man for Himself* seems to go beyond the realm of assimilation and into the realm of socialization: "The 'productive orientation' of personality," he says, "refers to a fundamental attitude, a *mode of relatedness* in all realms of human experience. It covers mental, emotional, and sensory responses to others, to oneself, and to things" (2003 [1947]: 61). As will be seen, this is a facet of the excessive porosity and insufficient incisiveness that tends to mar Fromm's descriptive account.

Fromm's account of the development of the orientations in the process of socialization first appears in *Escape from Freedom*, with significant additions occurring in his subsequent works. Whereas in the process of assimilation what was delineated was assimilative relatedness to the world, in the process of socialization it is relatedness to others that is under consideration (although, as was noted above, Fromm is not always completely precise in upholding these boundaries). Fromm's account of the nonproductive orientations in this process is divided into two broad categories: *symbiotic relatedness* and *withdrawal*.[12] In the case of symbiotic relatedness, what is essentially involved is "the tendency to fuse one's self with somebody or something outside of oneself in order to acquire the strength which the individual self is lacking" (1969 [1941]: 140). Fromm separates this tendency into three aspects: the striving for domination, for submission (*sadism* and *masochism*, respectively), and for what he terms "incestuous symbiosis." A clear refraction of Fromm's account of the human situation, as discussed, the passion of the sadist is said to consist in the gaining of absolute control over another living being and, thereby, the transformation of his or her impotence into the experience of omnipotence (1997 [1973]: 386). The goal is not necessarily the infliction of pain but, rather, the transformation of a human being into a thing, or of something animate into something inanimate (1980 [1964]: 32). The passion of the masochist is, in a certain sense, the opposite of the sadist. Rather than inflating him or herself to omnipotence, the masochist is concerned with the reduction of the self to nothing, to lose the self and thereby eradicate the burden of freedom (1969 [1941]: 151). In both sadism and masochism, freedom is given up and a negatively individuated dependency is adopted.

Although informally discussed as far back as *Escape from Freedom*, Fromm formally introduces incestuous symbiosis as a character orientation in *The Heart of Man*. Understood in existential-phylogenetic rather than psycho-sexual terms, incestuous symbiosis refers to the dependency on the mothering figure and/or substitutes. Inasmuch as this is the case—and considered in light of Fromm's account of the human condition—incestuous symbiosis constitutes a failure to develop to independence and to supplant the primary natural ties with mature human ones. As a form of relatedness, then, incestuous symbiosis develops as a counter to the tendency to grow, leading to the distortion of reason and the lack of an experience of another as a fully human being. Whereas symbiotic relatedness constitutes a fusing with someone or something else, withdrawal represents a *distancing* from others and the world as threats. It is, therefore, a form of *negative relating* (Fromm and Maccoby, 1996 [1970]: 74). The three main forms of withdrawal Fromm discusses are: *indifference, necrophilous-destructiveness,* and *narcissism*. The case of withdrawal through indifference is yet another example of the loss of individual autonomy. In *Escape from Freedom*, Fromm speaks of "automaton conformity," the deep-rooted adoption by the personality of the dominant cultural patterns. In this form of relatedness, a merging with the world occurs such that the discrepancy between "I" and the world disappears, aloneness and anxiety receding together with the loss of the self (1969 [1941]: 184). The counterpoint of the marketing orientation in the process of assimilation, the indifferent orientation can be said to entail a submission to the anonymous authorities that govern contemporary industrial capitalist society, the internalization of this authority resulting in the creation of a pseudo-self, which leaves the individual in an intense state of insecurity, characteristic of which is the need to continuously gain approval in order to avoid deeper insecurity and doubt at this loss of self (1969 [1941]: 203).

The necrophilous-destructive orientation in the process of socialization can be seen as the extreme form of withdrawal. To understand this orientation, Fromm's distinction between various forms of destructiveness—reactive or defensive aggression, sadistic-cruel destructiveness, and necrophilous-destructiveness—is helpful. Whereas the first form can be said to have a rational, biologically induced function for the human organism, the latter two are irrational.[13] Necrophilous-destructiveness differs from the sadistic-cruel form, aside from its extremity, by the fact that it is an active form of withdrawal—Fromm, in fact, conceives of it as a form of negative transcendence: the desperate attempt to save oneself by crushing the world and all objects with which the individual has to compare itself (1969 [1941]: 177). In Fromm's conception, it can be seen as the answer to question of life when life is otherwise thwarted (1969 [1941]: 179), and thus as the "outcome of unlived life" (1969 [1941]: 182). As Burston (1991: ix, 75) has noted, Fromm's account of destructiveness undergoes an unsatisfactory change later in his career. In *The Heart of Man* he speculates that necrophilia represents a morbid intensification of anal trends issuing in a regressive reactivation of a previous phyletic stage, the so-called anal-olfactory-hating orientation. Here I am focusing on Fromm's preferable, earlier formation.[14] Burston describes this lapse as emblematic of Fromm's whole posture toward Freud and the psychoanalytic movement namely, "a desperate, last-minute attempt to authenticate his claim to be following in Freud's footsteps" (Burston, 1991: ix). Whether this is accepted or not, it certainly seems a regression from his previous theory in which it is the result of "the blockage of spontaneity of growth and expression of man's sensuous, emotional, and intellectual capacities" (1969 [1941]: 182).

In the narcissistic orientation, a greater degree of withdrawal takes place than is found in the others. In fact, of all of the nonproductive orientations in the process of socialization, the narcissistic orientation is the least effective, characterized as it is by the fact that "the narcissistic person cannot perceive the reality within another person as distinct from his own" (1980 [1964]: 68). Through the self-inflation of the narcissistic personality, and the consequent undervaluing of the external world insofar as it is not an echo of him or herself, the narcissist attempts to quell the sense of aloneness and fright: "If he *is* the world, there is nothing outside which can frighten him; if he is everything, he is not alone" (1980 [1964]: 75). Although primary narcissism is recognized by Fromm as an important biological function, its characterological form is problematic, leading to the distortion of rational and moral judgment and often to psychosis.

Fromm's account of the productive orientation in the process of assimilation is clearly conceived in opposition to the submissive "escapes" from freedom found in the negative orientations. Whereas in these escapes independent and spontaneous human relations are lacking, the productive orientation is founded on "the active and creative relatedness of man to man, to himself, and to nature" (2003 [1947]: 31). As opposed to being controlled by irrational passions, as is the case in the nonproductive orientations, the productive orientation is said to represent the achievement of interpersonal relations based on the qualities of love and reason. Love in this context is understood as "the achievement of interpersonal union" (1956a: 17) on the basis of integrity and autonomy of self ("union" understood here inasmuch as "care, responsibility, knowledge and respect" presuppose it; "autonomy of self," in that these qualities can be truly actualized *only* on the basis of an autonomous self). Just as love can be seen as the breaking through the surface of the other, reason can be conceived as the breaking through of the surface of world, grasping at essence and actively relating and reacting to the things that surround us (2003 [1947]: 72). In saying this, it must be noted that reason, as it is discussed here, seems to be more strictly associated with the assimilative process, with the way in which we grasp the world, and therefore acts as the *precondition* for relating to others in a productive fashion, as well as being a facet of this form of relatedness. Despite this porosity, the main point remains: interpersonal union is possible *because* of the fact the person is related to world through reason and love.

Any appraisal of Fromm's account of the character orientations must be based on cognizance of the ideal-typical nature of his discussion. His presentation of the orientations is deliberately didactic, including only a limited number of traits that follow immediately from the underlying orientation so as to be rendered useful for incorporation into his social-psychological analysis; he stressed that a number of other traits could be dealt with similarly (2003 [1947]: 42). The reality, Fromm contends, is that any given person will represent a *blend* of the various orientations. What matters in the characterization of a given person is the relative *weight* of each orientation, and, therefore, which orientation is *dominant* and which is secondary (2003 [1947]: 84). This *weight/dominance* criterion applies not only in relation to the orientation as a whole but also to the material, emotional, and intellectual spheres of activity considered in themselves (2003 [1947]: 86). It is also necessary to differentiate between the blend of nonproductive orientations among themselves and that of the nonproductive with the productive orientations, the crucial factor being the *degree* of productiveness present. In a character in which productiveness is dominant, for instance, the nonproductive orientations do not have their negative meaning but, rather, a positive or "constructive" one (2003 [1947]: 84).

Narrowing down the variability somewhat, Fromm posits a series of *affinities* between certain orientations in the process of assimilation and process of socialization. Fromm captures these affinities in the following diagram, transplanted from *Man for Himself*:

	ASSIMILATION		SOCIALIZATION	
I	**Nonproductive orientation**			
	a) Receiving (Accepting)	....	Masochistic (Loyalty)	⎤ Symbiosis
	b) Exploiting (Taking)	....	Sadistic (Authority)	⎦
	c) Hoarding (Preserving)	....	Destructive (Assertiveness)	⎤ Withdrawal
	d) Marketing (Exchanging)	....	Indifferent (Fairness)	⎦
II	**Productive orientation**			
	Working	....	Loving, Reasoning	

The affinities outlined here ought to be seen as the obvious preconditions for the existence of blends, certain orientations in the process of assimilation clearly implying different types of interpersonal relations and vice versa. The consequence of these affinities within and between the orientations and processes is the formation of *syndromes* of character development—the *syndrome of growth* and the *syndrome of decay*—which represent what Fromm, in *The Heart of Man*, calls the most fundamental distinction between men, namely, *biophilia* and *necrophilia*. Conceived along the normative lines of Fromm's theory as already outlined, and with clear correlation to his idea of productiveness and nonproductiveness, biophilia, the "love of life," is understood by Fromm as the tendency of life to preserve itself and to integrate and unite (1980 [1964]: 45); and necrophilia, the "love of death," following on from its characterological representations, is conceived as the love of everything that is dead and does not grow, everything inorganic, thing-like, and mechanical (1980 [1964]: 39). (Fromm's choice of "love" as the adjective to describe the antithetical syndrome is poor—although he has little choice in the matter, having coined the syndrome "necro*philia*." This choice of adjective surely connotes entirely the wrong sentiment for describing the actions of a person incapable of love: if "love" means what Fromm says it means elsewhere, then, by definition, it cannot apply here, as a description of something that is diametrically opposed to loving.)

Characteristic of these syndromes, building on the affinities between orientations and processes, is what Fromm identifies as the tendency toward *convergence* and *correlation*. Narrowing down the variability in characterological analysis even further, Fromm argues that the more malignant the nonproductive components (and therefore the deeper the level of regression) the more readily they converge, and vice versa with the productive components; and the more markedly they converge the more they exclude the other (an inverse proportionality in which tendencies of action become deeply ingrained as a part of character). In the case of the productive passions, Fromm stresses love, solidarity, justice, reason, as interrelated manifestations of the growth or, "life-furthering syndrome" (1997 [1973]: 341). This is the "natural," "biological" path of organic life.[15] In the case of the nonproductive passions, Fromm stresses the presence of narcissism and incestuous symbiosis as greatly inclining toward the decay syndrome. On this account, decay is understood as the result of the thwarting of growth, and, therefore, as a *malignant* phenomenon (1980 [1964]: 50)—narcissism preventing productive relatedness and incestuous ties preventing development toward independence.

A further distinction Fromm draws, which is pertinent here, is that between *having* and *being* as fundamental modes of existence. An extrapolation of sorts from the binary divisions so far outlined, Fromm understood this distinction, together with the biophilia/necrophilia distinction, as representing "the most crucial problem of human existence" (2009 [1976]: 14)—although, as was seen, Fromm had hitherto accorded the biophilia-necrophilia distinction the most fundamental place. Inspired by the central teachings of the great world religions, the mystic movements at their margins, and secular thinkers such as Marx, Fromm posited the distinction as applying in a most elementary sense to the *nature* of our relationship to the world. Those orientated in the having mode of existence, for instance, are seen as functioning in a proprietary mode of relatedness to things, people, and to themselves. What matters in this mode of existence is that my relationship to things, people, myself, is fundamentally governed by the fact of *having*: I *have* this, I *have* that, I *have*... in the process of this or that. "If my *self* is constituted by what I *have*, then I am immortal if the things I have are indestructible" (2009 [1976]: 67).

In contrast, the being mode is characterized by that fact that one has given up one's egocentricity and selfishness and is instead oriented to loving, sharing, giving, and even to sacrifice (the insistence on this last orientation to sacrifice, which seemingly runs counter to the dictum of productive self-fulfillment, threatening to tip Fromm into contraction here). Fromm understands being as orientated to the specific conditions of human existence and the inherent need to overcome one's isolation by achieving oneness with others. This does not equate to an ascetic selflessness, however. The fundamental characteristic of being is what Fromm terms "activity," or "productive activeness" (conceived in terms of inner activity, as is consistent with the criteria stipulated in the earlier discussion of the various "escapes from freedom"), which involves giving expression to one's faculties and talents and is premised on individuality, independence, and the presence of critical reason (2009 [1976]: 72–74). The contrast between having and being, therefore, is the contrast between *passivity* (determined, controlled, idolatrous living) and *activity* (spontaneous, free, self-formational living). Again, this should be understood as an ideal-typical distinction. As was the case with the character orientations and syndromes, Fromm insisted that in the analysis of any existing case one should consider these modes as being "more" or "less" dominant rather than absolutely so.

Fromm's introduction of the having and being modes of existence is an untidy late addition to his schema, which leaves the connections (and overlap) between this distinction and his previous distinctions relatively unexplained. Had he devoted more time to the explicit construction of radical humanism as a distinct theory, he would have been faced with this issue. As it is, his account of the character orientations (which in real life are blends) spirals from the orientations in the process of assimilation and socialization, where affinities exists between each process, to syndromes of these orientations, and then to the modes of having and being. It has to be noted that, overall, and notwithstanding recognition of its value as a deep discussion of progressive and regressive aspects of human personality, Fromm's account of the character orientations (including the syndromes, and the having and being modes of existence), is rather messy and unnecessarily porous, essentially consisting of the delineation of what appear to be different modalities and aspects of the same phenomenon. What seems to be the simplest and most accurate resolution of this issue is to take *productiveness/nonproductiveness* as the ultimate distinction and to view the *biophilia/necrophilia* and *having/being* distinctions as particular analytical manifestations of this distinction considered in relation to the sociocultural sphere. What is most important is Fromm's framing of the whole characterological discussion in terms of the fundamental existential dichotomy underlying human existence, and the conclusions that he draws from it. To live productively, that is to say, to be actively related to the world and to others, to be free from neurotic passions and the compulsions of greed and egotism, to love life and experience it through being rather than having, is to respond to the dichotomy in the optimal way (or, in other words, to *flourish* as the beings that we are capable of being). The point of psychoanalysis as a practical activity, then, is to assist in this quest for human flourishing, to help achieve full awareness, to encourage the emergence of self as the integrating subject of authentic experience.

Obviously, there is much more to say on this matter. Further discussion—including discussion of particular aspects of Fromm's characterology—will take place in the subsequent chapters. What will take place presently is an attempt to clarify some points pertaining to the status of his account relative to Freud and to his Institut ex-colleagues.

Creative Renewal and Dialectical Revision

To consider Fromm's psychoanalytic theory as a whole is to see both its affinity to and divergence from orthodox Freudian theory. The affinity should be clear by now. The main divergence, which should be similarly clear, centers on the issue of how to interpret the fundamental nature of human existence and the fashioning of this interpretation into an appropriate analytical schema which makes possible a more complete understanding of lived experience. For Fromm, psychoanalysis is essentially "a theory of unconscious strivings, of resistance, of falsification of reality according to one's subjective needs and expectations ("transference"), of character, and of conflicts between passionate strivings embodied in character traits and the demands for self-preservation" (1997 [1973]: 126). As such, psychic structures and neurotic conflicts are seen to stem primarily from one's actual experience of connecting with outer and inner realities rather than as reductively sexually derived phenomena, as in Freud (this is not to say that sexuality plays no role, only that the overwhelming centrality accorded it in the orthodox Freudian schema is exaggerated to the point of obscuring the actual psychological processes). This alteration of the underlying core of Freud's system alienated Fromm from the psychoanalytic establishment. That this is so is hardly surprising. That it alienated him from his colleagues at the Institut is much more surprising, and requires some explanation.

Despite the fact that Fromm was originally brought to the Institut to work on the connections between psychoanalysis and historical materialism, and had developed his revision of Freud as a direct consequence of this work (and in line with the central stipulations of historical materialist thought), by the time he had made his first full statement of opposition to Freudian orthodoxy he found himself opposed at almost every step by Horkheimer, his once eager collaborator, and by the others working at the Institut, particularly Adorno and Marcuse. Following his departure from the Institut in 1939, Fromm was repeatedly labeled a "revisionist" or "neo-Freudian revisionist" by his erstwhile colleagues, who generally proffered a rehashed version of the Freudian critique of the Adlerian apostasy. The central point of the criticism, considered in clinical or psychoanalytic terms, was the contention that, by rejecting libido theory, Fromm, a la Adler, was spurning the biological materialist core, and thereby the radical elements, of psychoanalytic thought (Wiggershaus, 1994: 271). Variously presented by Horkheimer, Adorno, and Marcuse, and echoed by people like Jacoby, this central criticism is refracted into a series of subsidiary criticisms pertaining to the respective assessment of Freud and to what can be said to be the most suitable account of the relationship obtaining between the individual and society. Characteristic of these criticisms—and in fact underlying the central criticism—is the proffering of a *nonidentity* philosophy based on the common insistence on the nonidentity between subject and object, appearance and essence, particular and universal in advanced capitalist society. Identity thinking in such a society, following the patterns of classical idealist metaphysics by identifying the subject by its object (for instance, by identifying human freedom on the basis of its bastardized current form as propounded by bourgeois thought), is seen as representing a premature foreclosure of possibility and the chances of realizing a "true" or "real" humanism. In breaking with libido theory, Fromm, as Adler before him, was charged with returning to "common-sense psychology," "rejecting the most daring hypotheses," and "flattening out" the depth dimension that

Freud had uncovered. For Horkheimer, Adorno, and Marcuse, Freud's idea of libido furnished materialism with an autonomous realm of human existence outside of the control of social forces, acknowledgment of which was crucial in maintaining the nonidentity of man in contemporary society. In response to Fromm's criticism of Freud's account of relatedness, they argued that Freud's account was *already* sociological. Whereas Fromm criticized what he saw as Freud's patriarchal and bourgeois aspects, these very aspects were taken by his ex-colleagues as evidence of Freud's superior grounding in the manifest historical situation, even his death instinct theory seen as incisive commentary on the destruction of individuality evident in mass war and in contemporary society more generally. Fromm, on the contrary, by rejecting Freud's libido and death instinct theories, was seen as guilty of identity (or "positive") thinking, idealistically taking society as his ready-made environment, and of a sociologism that denied the relations between culture and repression.

Dealing with the main issue at hand, it must be stressed (contrary to what Horkheimer, Adorno, and Marcuse, as well as thinkers such as Fenichel and Jacoby claimed) that Fromm did not quarrel with the fact that Freud made recourse to biology in his explanation of the human drives; his issue was only with Freud's *specific* biological interpretation. Despite his socio-existential revision, Fromm's thought retains the idea of a causative "natural" element in the human situation, as is clear from this passage from *Escape from Freedom*: "Human nature is neither a biologically fixed and innate sum of total drives, nor is it a lifeless shadow of cultural patterns to which it adapts itself smoothly; it is the product of human evolution, but it also has certain inherent mechanisms and laws" (1969 [1941]: 20). Fromm's account of the human being therefore clearly retains some idea of a biological materialist core, functioning in contrast to theories that assume a completely fixed biological essence but also in contrast to the voluntarism of existentialist philosophy and a whole variety of constructivist systems extant today. Admittedly, Fromm could have said more as to precisely what this biological materialist core is—something he gave more consideration to in his later works, especially *The Anatomy of Human Destructiveness*, where he makes a concerted effort to ground this account in contemporary evolutionary biology, and thereby to arrive at a more precise account of this core. What is important in his account relative to that of Freud is that it constitutes an improvement on Freud in the sense that it frees his theory of its mechanical elements and lays the basis for a more accurate materialist account of the biological core. As such, the veracity of the claim that Fromm *spurns* the biological materialist core of Freudian thought turns out itself to be especially contingent on the respective assessment of what is the most accurate account of the biological core; the claim only becomes a valid criticism of Fromm's account of this core (or an account developed from its basic position) if it can be said to be demonstrably poorer than that of Freud. Either way, what surely must be recognized in relation to the orthodox defense of Freud (whether in Adorno, Marcuse, or Fenichel—although it is surely best expressed in Fenichel), is that it reduces to an extreme and unwarranted inflexibility over what is and what is not materialist. For, on such an account, materialism in relation to the psychic structure equates to a central stress on the sexual instincts, and any deviation from that is held to be idealist per se; thus, any attempt to question the centrality of the sexual instincts as the primary motivating factor of life is a priori set up as a form of idealist revisionism. As such, one becomes caught in a trap. Again, while Fromm does not develop his thought far enough in terms of isolating the biological or neurological specifics of this true materialist core, he did prepare the ground for such a specification, and even made productive suggestions toward how to go about specifying it.

As for the accusation of "flattening out" the depth dimension, it must be stressed that while Fromm dispenses with certain central Freudian ideas he does so in light of what he saw as their mechanistic account of human functioning. In addition to his rejection of Freud's libido, death instinct, and Oedipus complex theories, Fromm also rejected the Freudian ideas of *repetition compulsion*—the idea that early traumatic experiences and the responses to them are invariably relived throughout the life history of a person—and *sublimation*—the idea that libido energy is routinely transformed into socially useful activity. Although Fromm was of the belief that much of great importance does occur in the first five years of life, he held that these early events do not determine us, for there is much that takes place later in life that is equally important and that may counteract the earlier influences (1994: 56–57). As such, what matters is to "arrive at an insight into the unconscious processes which the patient has right now," not historical research per se, which may risk the construction of false events and memories (1994: 57–58). In the case of sublimation, Fromm simply found the concept untenable, arguing instead for the more or less direct expression of passions (at least in the forms adequate to the given historical and personal circumstances). To be able to say that this is the "flattening out" of the depth dimension in psychoanalysis depends on how depth in this instance is defined. In Fromm's account, unconscious processes are still very much central; there is, due to the relative de-eroticization, a natural change in how these processes are conceived, but this does not represent the reduction to an ego psychology nor to a strictly hermeneutical or phenomenological psychology. Fromm, in fact, was explicitly critical of ego psychology, much of the language he employed in discussing it markedly similar, as it happens, to that utilized in the criticism of his own work by his Institut ex-colleagues (accusations of a loss of critical, dialectical aspects, and capitulation to conformist tendencies, etc.). The idea of the unconscious—a *quality* of certain mental states not identical with any particular content—and therefore resistance, repression, transference, and rationalization remain central, and remain so alongside a revived account of symbolism and dreams with parallels to that of Bachofen and Jung. The fact that ego, hermeneutical, and phenomenological elements are given more central emphasis—something characteristic of Freud's later writings in any case—does not flatten depth or untangle complexity, although it does temper the tendency toward fantastical constructions so characteristic of Freud.

The question that has to be asked is, rather, of Horkheimer, Adorno, and Marcuse: by rejecting Fromm's account and praising Freud's above it, are they not in effect assenting to the mechanical materialism in Freud that Fromm found so inadequate? What has to be noted in this respect is that neither Horkheimer, Adorno, nor Marcuse were practicing psychoanalysts and, other than in the case of Marcuse, detailed psychoanalytic discussion is notably absent from their writings.[16] In fact, other than Marcuse—who is far from unequivocal on this point[17]—their work is characterized by a decidedly restricted view of psychoanalysis, a view that can be said to stem from their underlying nonidentity philosophical position. This is particularly so in the case of Adorno, the most consistent and pronounced nonidentity theorist. For Adorno, psychoanalysis is effectively impossible. Clinging to the individualist façade of contemporary society, as he sees it, psychoanalysis is futile and is necessarily restricted to the negative function of affirming the destruction wrought upon the individual by capitalist society (Adorno, 1968). Its attempt to speak positively, especially in revisionist form, is merely a form of propagandistic conformism. Horkheimer, who initially saw psychoanalysis as an essential component of his social-philosophical project and who had approved of Fromm's early work on psychoanalytic social psychology, had, by the *Dialectic of Enlightenment* at least, effectively come to concur with Adorno's restrictive position. But, it must be asked, what kind of picture of mental life can be extracted from this position other than one in which dynamism and struggle (a dynamism and struggle which, incidentally, was integral to Freud's understanding of mental functioning) have disappeared? By ruling out struggle within the individual and thereby any conceivable sense of agency this theory is even more mechanistic and, therefore, less deep than Freud's.

The case of Marcuse bears a curious relation to that of Adorno and Horkheimer. At once more reliant on psychoanalytic concepts, and thus not as restrictive (although he appears to contradict himself at times—the consequence of an inconsistent reliance on aspects of Adorno's identity critique), Marcuse nevertheless ends with a similarly shallow mechanicism. What is characteristic of Marcuse's account is the fact that, despite his criticism of Fromm for revising Freud's theory (in his *Dissent* articles and in *Eros and Civilization*, he carried out the most extended and public criticism of Fromm[18]), Marcuse himself offers a strangely unorthodox account of Freudian theory. While Fromm pulled away from the central stress on libido, Marcuse, in *Eros and Civilization* in particular, parallels Reich's pan-sexualism in focusing preeminently on the free expression of libidinous needs. He goes beyond Reich, however, in seeking a utopian integration of Freud and Marx based on a return to the polymorphous perverse pleasure of the childhood ego—a return in effect to primary narcissism and, therefore, the elevation of "a narcissistic relation to reality as the height of ego development" (Chodorow, 1985: 285).[19]

Marcuse, by his own admission, suffered from a "lack of competence" in practical psychoanalytic matters (Marcuse, 1966 [1955]: 245). He, in fact, proclaimed himself only interested in theoretical psychoanalysis which, as Fromm points out, goes against the basic position of Freud, who always mixed theoretical and empirical speculation based on observation and analysis. For Fromm, this was inexcusable and led to Marcuse's painting a misleading picture of Freud which was then disseminated to his many readers. Fromm criticized Marcuse (and by extension Horkheimer and Adorno) for an inadequate materialism, which was worse, in fact, than Freud's. "It was," Fromm argued, "the great achievement of Freud to have taken up a number of problems so far only dealt with abstractly by philosophy and to transform them into the subject matter of empirical investigation. Marcuse seems to be undoing this achievement by retransforming Freud's empirical concepts into the subject matter of philosophical speculation—and a rather muddy speculation, at that" (1970: 20). Fromm, like Freud, offers a mixture of empirical observations and speculation (in fact, Fromm praises this mixture as the basis of the scientific mindset). As was noted above, Fromm could not accept the etiological postulates of Freud's libido theory. Although he found the account implausible in itself, he also found it lacking in empirical accuracy. From his own experience as a practicing psychoanalyst Fromm observed that the idea that various impulses—such as parsimony, greed, orderliness, etc.—were to be understood as the sublimation of pleasure derived from the retention of feces was untenable (2010: 38):

> Attempting "to interpret" parsimony as a sublimation of pleasure in withholding the feces usually resulted not only in no change in behavior, but also no great deepening of the understanding of the phenomenon. Even if

it could be assumed or guessed that the pleasure in holding back the feces was developed early on the grounds of defiant outside influences, the basis for explaining a trait as significant for the entire personality as parsimony was extremely small; furthermore, this explanation was incapable of encompassing the trait in its connection with the whole personality structure and as an expression of it. In many other cases there was no such connection at all. A strong, driving parsimony was found, but early childhood experiences in regard to bowel movements were absolutely normal. In other cases it could be seen that a certain pleasure in retarding the bowel movement may have existed in fact, but when the amount of this pleasure was compared with that in other cases where no greed developed, the quantitative difference seemed in no [way] commensurate with the assumed end result in character of early childhood experiences. The same observation held not only for attributes of the anal character, but even more for attributes such as ambition, whose alleged causal connection with urethral eroticism almost never appeared, even as a vague speculation. (2010: 38–39)

The consequences of Freud's implied sociology and social psychology were similarly untenable:

Thus, for instance, character traits designated by Freud as anal are found to a pronounced and, in relation to the rest of society, to a markedly greater degree in the European lower middle-classes. According to Freud's theory, the assumption would have to be made that prevalence of the anal character structure in the European lower middle-classes stems either from a special constitutionally determined excitation of the anal zone, or that certain experiences in toilet training are common to all lower middle-class people, which are responsible for the pleasure in withholding the feces or the fixation on the anal level. (2010: 40)

In these empirico-clinical and empirico-social-psychological discernments Fromm illustrates his grasp of the problems facing Freud's theory; and it is in their wake that he proceeds to develop his own account. As such—and in contradiction to Fenichel's accusation that he abandons psychoanalysis—Fromm can be seen as trying to modify Freudian theory so as to make it more consistent theoretically as well as in its application.

What was important for Fromm was the "dialectic revision" of psychoanalysis which "revises the 'classic' formulations, with the aim of preserving their spirit" (1970: 26). It was not—as he felt was the case in ego psychology—the revision of the essence of the theory, but the preservation of this essence through a "creative renewal" (1970: 29) in which its underlying categories were actively translated into ones more suitable to a historical materialist and radical humanist framework. As thinkers who proclaimed at least some kind of central fidelity to Marxian thought, it is strange that Fromm's ex-colleagues did not concur with at least the first aspect of this approach. That they did not is due, at least in part, to their adoption of a similarly pessimistic outlook to that of (the later) Freud and to the development of a nonidentity philosophy that pulled them firmly away from the second aspect. It is also surely down to that fact that their appraisal of Fromm in itself was insufficient (this is as true of Adorno and Marcuse as it is of Jacoby, who seems to repeat with a more strained rhetoric flourish the central criticism of the former thinkers). Characteristic of their accounts of Fromm is the continual conflation of Fromm with Horney and Sullivan, all three lumped together without any significant differentiation as "neo-Freudian revisionists" and "culturalists." While Fromm learnt much from, and had definite similarities with, Horney and Sullivan, he felt closer to Freud than they did and saw them ultimately as insufficiently essentialist in their relativistic emphasis on "culture." In contradistinction, Fromm stresses that "more emphasis should be placed on social structure, class structure, economic structure, the impact these elements have on the development of the individual, and the practice of life which follows from each of these" (1966b: 58).

Even if this distinction were to be assented to, with all that follows from it, it might still be objected that Fromm was guilty of his own, related form of revisionism. Trying to separate the pejorative strands, it must be asked: what is wrong with revising a theory? Surely it is characteristic of all sciences that they undergo processes of revision—a science that does not undergo such a process is, by definition, no longer a science but a dogma. Jacoby, however, denounces revisionism for involving "a decline of theory per se" and "a refusal or inability to conceptualize," before moving on in a confusing and counterproductive remark to caution against the false opposition between orthodoxy and revisionism (Jacoby, 1977: 11–12). Speaking in terms reminiscent of Fromm's own description of this work (albeit speaking of "dialectical orthodoxy" rather than dialectical revision), Jacoby proclaims: "If revisionism is marked by a decline of theory, dialectical orthodoxy reworks and rethinks...not by thoughtless repetition but by reworking" (Jacoby, 1977: 12–13). What needs to be stressed once more here is the fact that, as was shown above, unconscious processes remain central to Fromm's account of psychic life, as does the idea of a dynamic, conative character structure, as does the phenomena of transference and repression. All that is altered is the fact that Fromm understands them without recourse to the mechanistic reductionism, which underpins Freud's libido theory, and thus is able to accord more due to the social and cultural influences on the individual in the process of dealing with the fundamental existential dichotomies of life. Fromm himself explains dialectical revision: "Such a revision tries to preserve the essence of the original teaching by liberating it from time-conditioned, restricting theoretical assumptions; it tries to resolve contradictions within the classic theory in a dialectical fashion and to modify the theory in the process of applying it to new problems and experiences" (1970: 26). That Fromm was criticized for a "decline of theory," is surely unjust—although the fact he never published a prospective volume on clinical practice[20] and generally avoided reproducing procedural deliberations in print, no doubt made it easier for such criticisms to stick.

As for the idea that Freud was *already* sociological, his account of the death instinct acting as some kind of historical materialist recognition of the destruction of man under capitalism, is surely wrong. Freud was clearly not merely passing comment, in Marxian fashion, on the unnecessary destruction wrought on the individual by bourgeois civilization. He was attempting, as the bourgeois scientist he was, to discover the fundamental phylo- and onto-genetic laws of the human species (he also believed in a correlation between repression and civilization, and therefore openly approved of bourgeois social arrangements). Fromm's assessment gets it the right way round. Whereas his former colleagues take Freud's death instinct theory less as a universalistic attribution than a historico-specific observation, Fromm recognizes Freud's theory as involving an unintentional and illicit universalization. This was the initial point of rupture Fromm had with Freud, and is evident before his 1937 essay, rejected by Horkheimer, in which Fromm criticized Freud for "ignoring the determining social derivations" (2010: 27). The fact that Fromm introduces moral and ethical aspects into his explanation of psychic life is surely not a threat to his otherwise quite stringent sociological statements: where else are moral and ethical concerns played out than in social life? The supposed presence of "moralism" in Fromm then (along with an apparent culturalism—the presence of which surely ought to place the imputation of moralism into severe doubt) seems to serve as a convenient hook for Horkheimer, Adorno, Marcuse, and Jacoby, to pin their rehashed criticism of the Adlerian apostasy onto Fromm without dealing with the full substance of his thinking.

Interestingly, Fromm's revised radical humanist account of Freud bears closer relation in many respects to the thought of Jürgen Habermas than to Horkheimer, Adorno, or Marcuse.[21] Although Habermas was not a practicing psychoanalyst, and did not devote his career to developing an explicitly psychoanalytically informed social theory, he did, particularly in *Knowledge and Human Interests*, discuss the importance of psychoanalysis as an example of a critical social science. As with Fromm, Habermas's account of psycho-analytic theory breaks with Freudian orthodoxy in apportioning a reduced role to the instincts—although Habermas can be said to lean further toward ego psychology than Fromm in this regard, drawing directly on the thought of Heinz Hartmann as well as George Herbert Mead and Wilhelm Dilthey. Crucially, as is the case in Fromm, Habermas emphasizes the transcendental goal of psychoanalysis, what he describes as the "emancipatory power of the reflection that the subject experiences in itself to the extent that it becomes transparent to itself in the history of its genesis" (Habermas, 1987: 197). But while representing an improvement on Fromm in terms of his analysis of the structural sphere, unlike Fromm, Habermas "criticises elements of Freud's thesis without providing a systematic critique of the assumptions that underpin it" (Willmott and Knights, 1982: 213). In addition to this, although mounting a qualified defense of the Enlightenment, Habermas ultimately rejects the traditional philosophy of the subject and its paradigm of consciousness, something which for Fromm is essential to radical human-ist psychoanalysis, in spite of the qualifications his sociological appreciation brings. The importance of this last fact—Fromm's reliance on a qualified philosophy of the subject—will be drawn out and built upon in the chapters that follow.

CHAPTER 4

Psychoanalytic Social Psychology

As developed by Fromm, psychoanalytic social psychology[1] represents a synthesis of the thought of Marx and Freud. In particular, it is the recognition of Marx's demonstration of our enmeshment in socioeconomic conditions and Freud's demonstration of our enmeshment in psychological needs (and the enmeshment of the one with the other). As such, it concerns the adding of an extra dimension to Marxian analysis in the form of the understanding of the human psyche as a determinant of social development alongside external factors, while at the same time grounding the claims of psychoanalysis on a more accurate sociological footing. As Fromm explains in a letter to Adam Schaff (dated March 18, 1965), it was "an attempt to concretize the empirical Marxist statement that it is man's social existence that determines consciousness. I believe that I can show that Freud's discovery makes full sense only if one looks at it from the standpoint of Marx, and that Marx's statement becomes open to empirical study only if one uses the empirical method of studying the unconscious."

This Marx-Freud synthesis can be said to have its roots in the critique of mechanical Marxism emerging in the early decades of the twentieth century, being most notably expressed in the thought of Wilhelm Reich during the late 1920s and early 1930s and in the research program of the Institut for Social Research. What is distinct about Fromm's account is that it is advanced on the basis of revised accounts of the theories in question—particularly so in the case of Freud—which enables him, better than others, to bring together what are generally assumed to be two antagonistic bodies of work. The goal of the synthesis, as Fromm was to state some years later, was "to understand the laws that govern the life of the individual man, and the laws of society—that is, of men in their social existence" (2006 [1962]: 5) and, in particular, to try to understand the extent to which the psychic structure is a sociologically relevant factor in the social process. In Fromm's account, this amounts to the reinstating of the historical, social principle that he thought had been effectively overlooked in Freud and, thus, the dialectical revision of Freud, and the attempted integration into a Marxian or historical materialist framework. The central product of this synthesis is the concept of *social character*—the idea of a core character structure common to every group, class, or society—which rests on the concept of the *social unconscious*—the core areas of repression common to every group, class, or society.

Not only was this synthesis conceived in conceptual terms, it was also applied in a number of intriguing historical and empirical case studies. Despite certain flaws, and their overall underutilization by subsequent thinkers, these analyses represent truly groundbreaking studies that have much to offer contemporary sociology and social psychology. In them, Fromm forges a path toward a psychoanalytic Marxism and to the early study of taste and emotions, as well as introducing the interpretative questionnaire to social-psychological inquiry, thereby opening up the ground for the empirical meeting of psychoanalysis and sociology. While ultimately, perhaps, rather dated, and failing to live up to his own standards at certain crucial points, Fromm's work here illustrates the importance of the adequate recognition of the psychological dimension and of the application of humanist analytical categories in relation to social analysis.

Psychoanalysis and Historical Materialism

From the very outset of his career, Fromm was preoccupied with social psychology. This can be seen in the choice of subject matter for his doctoral dissertation, prior to his interest in psychoanalysis, and in his early articles after becoming a psychoanalyst. His position at the Frankfurt Psychoanalytic Institute was concerned primarily with the relationship between sociology and psychoanalysis, and his first monograph, *The Dogma of Christ*, was a sociopsychoanalytical study of the Christological dogma and the early Christian sects. When Fromm accepted a tenured position at the *Institut für Sozialforschung*, he did so in order to take charge of the Institut's interdisciplinary sociopsychoanalytical program. This early part of his career, culminating in *Escape from Freedom*, was a particularly productive period, during which the vast majority of the epistemological and methodological work necessary for this synthesis was carried out. The ideas laid out at this time stand as absolutely pivotal for Fromm's later applied social-psychological work, pulling his thought away from the orthodox Freudian standpoint and providing the ground for his radical humanist social analyses. It was also a period in which he wrote exclusively in his native German and with a broadly academic audience in mind. Fromm's was not the first attempt to fuse Marx and Freud, however. This synthesis can be said to have its roots in the critique of mechanical Marxism inaugurated by Karl Korsch and Georg Lukács in the late 1910s and early 1920s, following the failure of the German proletariat to realize the transition from capitalism to socialism in the aftermath of the First World War.[2] Korsch had seen that this failure could be attributed to the social-psychological ill-preparedness of the workers for revolution (Korsch, 1974: 128) and Lukács had seen the general need for Marxism to deepen its shallow empirical understanding of the subjective experience of the working class (Lukács, 1971). But while this was so, neither Korsch nor Lukács were to follow up on the substance of their realizations with detailed investigation of the psychological dimension that seemed to be centrally implicated in this political failure[3]—something that was not to happen until Siegfried Bernfeld and, later, Wilhelm Reich and Fromm himself, took up the issue explicitly.

Bernfeld, an educational psychologist whom Fromm knew from his time in Berlin, can be said to have prepared the ground for the translation of the critique of mechanical Marxism into distinctively psychological territory. His "Psychoanalysis and Socialism," which originally appeared in 1925, stands as the crucial introduction to the synthesis. This was followed in 1929 by Reich's *Dialectical Materialism and Psychoanalysis*. In the same year, Fromm gave a short paper on "Psychoanalysis and Sociology" at the inauguration of the Psychoanalytic Institute, and, a few years later, in 1932, "The Method and Function of an Analytic Social Psychology" was published in the *Zeitschrift*, exhibiting numerous points of connection with Bernfeld's and, particularly, Reich's essay. What was central to Fromm's account, as with those of Bernfeld and Reich, was the realization that "historical materialism... calls for a psychology—i.e., a science of man's psychic structure" and the contention that "psychoanalysis is the first discipline to provide a psychology that historical materialism can really use" (1970: 127). Echoing the central premise of the critique of mechanical Marxism, Fromm stresses the role of the human psychic apparatus as a determinant of social development alongside technological, economic, financial, and cultural factors (1989 [1929]; 1970). Although Fromm saw Marx's work as full of psychological concepts (the "essence of man," the "crippled" man, "alienation," "consciousness," "passionate strivings," "independence," etc.), they existed in Marx without a detailed or developed psychological system by means of which they might have achieved systematic expression.[4]

In the case of Freudian thought, conversely—and as was touched on in the preceding chapter—Fromm saw clear suggestions of the possibility of a greater social orientation. As Freud puts it in "Group Psychology and the Analysis of the Ego": "In the individual's mental life someone else is invariably involved, as a model, as an object, as a helper, as an opponent; and so from the very first, individual psychology, in this extended but entirely justifiable sense of the words, is at the same time social psychology as well" (Freud, 1991b: 95). Psychoanalysis, then, from the very outset, "does away with the false distinction between social psychology and individual psychology" (1992 [1963]: 3). But while this is undoubtedly true in terms of the positing of the theory, in the application of psychoanalytic thought to social analysis, Freud and the early psychoanalytic researchers failed to realize the full substance of this connection, committing what was in effect a psychologistic reduction. For Fromm this boiled down to a failure to use the analytic method in the correct way:

> Since they did not concern themselves with the variety of life experiences, the socio-economic structure of other types of society, and therefore did not try to explain their psychic structure as determined by their social structure, they necessarily began to *analogize* instead of *analyzing*. They treated mankind or a given society as an individual, transposed the specific mechanisms found in contemporary individuals to every possible type of society, and "explained" the psychic structure of these societies by analogy with certain phenomena (usually of a neurotic sort) typical of human beings in their own society. (1970: 119)

Allied to and implied in this failure to adequately develop the social aspect in the extension of the theory was what Fromm saw as the absolutizing of bourgeois-capitalist society, its naturalization and installation as society per se—a manifestly false sociological starting point that had to be transcended.

What was important then was the bringing into conjunction of two positions: (1) the recognition that "society, in reality consists of individuals, and it is these human beings, rather than abstract society as such, whose actions, thoughts, and feelings are the object of sociological research" (1989 [1929]: 37); and (2) the understanding that we need to transcend the realm of individual psychology and study the given socioeconomic conditions. A Freudian point to Marxists, and a Marxian point to the Freudians. In other words, Fromm was concerned with the dual recognition of the fact that "'society'...consists of living individuals, who must be subject to the same psychological laws that psychoanalysis discovered in the individual"

(1970: 114) and of the importance of avoiding "psychoanalytical answers where economic, technological, or political facts provide the real and sufficient explanation of sociological questions" (1989 [1929]: 37). Fromm expressed this in his pivotal 1937 essay:

> Social psychology is pointed in two directions. On the one hand, it deals with the problem of the extent to which the personality structure of the individual is determined by social factors and on the other hand, with the extent to which psychological factors themselves influence and alter the social process. The two sides of the problem are indissolubly bound together. The personality structure, which we can recognize as affecting the social process, is itself the product of this process and whether we observe the one side or the other, the question is only which aspect of the whole problem is the center of interest at the time. (2010: 17)

In arguing this, Fromm is transposing the social principle of Marx into psychological territory and extending the psychological principle of Freud into sociological territory. Inasmuch as this is the case, his account is fundamentally in line with other similar attempts, particularly that of Reich. Fromm and Reich differed, however, in their opinions as to the applicability of psychoanalysis to social analysis (as well as, later, in their view of the heart of Freudian theory). Despite otherwise praising Reich, Fromm, in his 1932 article, criticizes his dictum that psychoanalysis was to be restricted to the sphere of individual psychology.[5] For Fromm, although traditional psychoanalytic research was concerned primarily with neurotic individuals, the development of the concept of character, which applies to both neurotic and "healthy" individuals, meant that sociopsychological research based on psychoanalytic principles could be conducted with groups of "normal" people. This difference, Fromm argued, was essentially a quantitative one:

> Individual psychology takes into account all determinants that have affected the lot of the individual, and in this way arrives at a maximally complete picture of the individual's psychic structure. The more we extend the sphere of psychological investigation—that is, the greater the number of men whose common traits permit them to be grouped—the more we must reduce the extent of our examination of the total psychic structure of the individual members of the group... [therefore]... social-psychological investigation can study only the character matrix common to all members of the group, and does not take into account the total character structure of a particular individual. The latter can never be the task of social psychology, and is possible only if an extensive knowledge

of the individual's development is available... The value of social-psychological investigation, therefore, cannot lie in the fact that we acquire from
it a full insight into the psychic peculiarities of the individual members,
but only in the fact that we can establish those common psychic tendencies that play a decisive role in their social development. (1992 [1963]:
5–6)

The role of psychoanalysis in social psychology for Fromm then, as the
culmination of his early attempts to fuse Marx and Freud, was to help discern the psychic traits common to the members of a group, and to explain
their unconscious roots in terms of shared life experiences (1970: 116, 121).
As noted, because of the Marxian basis to this synthesis—the stress on
the individual's manner of life as largely determined by society—there is,
Fromm contended, no difference in principle between social and individual
psychoanalysis. They are implied in each other and cannot be properly separated. What psychoanalytic social psychology aims to do, therefore, is to
"investigate how certain psychic attitudes common to members of a group
are related to their common life experiences" (1992 [1963]: 9). The general
method is, then, essentially the same as in individual psychoanalysis, only
focusing on the detailed knowledge of the common life pattern instead of
the individual emotional constellation.[6] The challenge implied by such a
view, of course, is that of adequately relating the individual to the social, and
of understanding the relationship between these aspects. It is in this light
that Fromm's theory of social character should primarily be seen.

Social Character and the Social Unconscious

Fromm's theory of social character is the culmination of his early social-psychological work and a central analytical tool in his radical humanist social
analyses. A clear extrapolation from the idea of individual character, Fromm
understands social character as "the essential nucleus of the character structure of most members of a group which has developed as the result of the
basic experience and mode of life common to that group" (1969 [1941]: 276).
Based on the idea that "the differences in the manner of production and
life of various societies or classes lead to the development of different character structures typical of the particular society" (Fromm, 2010: 58), it is
the conceptual construction that is meant to make possible the Marx-Freud
synthesis and realize the promise of psychoanalytic historical materialism.
The practical intention of the theory, therefore, is to show the connection
between the economic conditions and prevailing character traits, as well to
as explain why it is that a particular class should have a specific kind of social

character. The conceptual ground this covers is clearly implied in his early work, as seen above, provisionally captured here with proximate terminology such as "common-life fate," "psychic surfaces," "the libidinous structure of society," etc. Fromm's first use of the term "social character" dates to his essay in *Studies on Authority and the Family* (Wiggershaus, 1994: 153). After this, in his pivotal essay, he speaks of the "socially typical character" in 1937, and much later, in *Social Character in Mexican Village*, refers to the "character matrix," but social character is the term that generally holds from 1941 onward.

As with the account of individual character, considered in relation to the individual, social character should be considered as distinguishing "certain fundamental traits" that, considered "in their dynamic nature and their weight, are of decisive importance for all individuals of this society" (Fromm, 2010: 59). While this is perhaps a fairly general delineation, for Fromm it is an essential one, giving due recognition to the fact that an individual's character is never sufficiently explained without reference to the society in which they live and their place in that particular social order. In addition to this, the theory helps us to understand that the specific character orientations, shared by most members of a culture or class, "represent powerful emotional forces the operation of which we must know in order to understand the functioning of society" (2003 [1947]: 57). Extending his functional-adaptive account of individual character, Fromm argues that it is the function of the social character to "mold and channel human energy within a given society for the purpose of the continued functioning of this society" (2002 [1955: 77). In other words, "the social character internalizes external necessities and thus harnesses human energy for the task of a given economic and social system," creating an "inner compulsion" to do what is necessary (1969 [1941]: 282). As such, the social character carries a double implication: "if an individual's character more or less closely conforms with the social character, the dominant drives in his personality lead him to do what is necessary and desirable under the specific social conditions of his culture" (1969 [1941]: 280), which leads to a profound psychological satisfaction, or gratification, resultant of the functional-adaptive process of acting in accordance to what is necessary in social-practical terms.[7]

Crucially, the social character shapes the energies of members of society so that it is not a matter of straightforwardly conscious decision as to whether or not they follow the social pattern: "Social stability depends relatively little upon the use of external force. It depends for the most part upon the fact that men find themselves in a psychic condition that roots them inwardly in an existing social situation" (1992 [1963]: 14). The idea here is that, generally, at some pre-reflective level, individuals in any given society can be said to be predisposed to act as they have to act. This need not imply complete functional alignment, only that a certain critical mass of active, creative agents in a society, class, or status group are internally motivated to fulfill the roles necessary to the society of which they are part; neither does it imply the impossibility of a distinct mismatch between the socially necessary roles and desires of agents. Social character is therefore a psychological force "cementing" the social structure and ensuring the survival of the individual in any given society (1969 [1941]: 282). If the majority are adapted to the objective tasks individuals are required to perform in that society, or in the group or class to which they are a member, the energies of people are molded in ways that make them productive forces indispensible for the functioning of that society, group, or class (1969 [1941]: 281).

A serf, a free peasant, and independent entrepreneur of the 19th century and an industrial manager of the 20th century have different functions to fill. Furthermore, the different social context demands that they relate themselves in different ways to equals, superiors, and inferiors. To give specific examples: the industrial worker has to be disciplined and punctual; the 19th-century bourgeois had to be parsimonious, individualistic, and self-reliant; today, members of all classes, except the poor, have to work in teams, and they must wish to spend and to consume new products. (Fromm and Maccoby, 1996 [1970]: 17–18)

Just as in the case of individual character, Fromm is not suggesting a simple correlation or lack of complexity here, but making a general judgment based on the dynamic psychological preconditions that must obtain for a society to function. This does not involve a directly passive and mechanical transmission from the social forces and does not result in the forced harmony of an identical social character for all members of any given society. It is clear that the peculiarities of parents, differences in social environment, temperamental differences, differences in individual character, etc., will have the effect of ensuring that there will always be deviations and different degrees to which the common character in each particular social grouping can be said to hold. Such variety and complexity is, of course, already implicit in Fromm's very proposition of a plural set of character types. In case this needed stressing further, Fromm and Maccoby make it clear in *Social Character in a Mexican Village* that, "asides from the extreme deviants who form a small minority, there are much larger minorities whose social character is different from that of the majority, but not enough so to make them unable to function in their society" (1996 [1970]: 232–233), and even some for whom social needs do not mold character at all.

As to how this functional-adaptive process works, Fromm in fact stresses that the genesis of social character is not understandable by reference to any one single cause but, rather, consists in the interaction of economic, socio-logical, and ideological factors (1949: 6). He says that "the formation of the social character is mediated by the influence of the 'total culture': the meth-ods of raising children, of education in terms of schooling, literature, art, religion, customs; in short, the whole cultural fabric guarantees its stability" (Fromm and Maccoby, 1996 [1970]: 18).[8] Following the dominant Marxian strain in his synthesis, Fromm accords the economic factors "a certain pre-dominance" in this interplay—the need to produce, secure a minimum of food and shelter, as well as the lesser modifiability of economic reality all featuring here—but recognizes that though the mode of production arising from survival determines the mode and practice of life (the social relations, etc.), religious, political, and philosophical ideas also "determine, system-atize and stabilize the social character" (2002 [1955]: 79). As such, Fromm saw the concept of social character as capable of completing the Marxian idea of the interdependence between the economic base of a given society and its ideological superstructure by showing *how* it was that the one was translated into the other. Fromm's conception was of the social character as the "transmission belt" (2006 [1962]: 62) between the two realms, insofar as they can be separated:

Economic basis

↓ ↑

Social character

↓ ↑

Ideas and ideals

In this rather rudimentary schema, each position is seen to possess a definitive causative function, which, although accorded its own degree of autonomy, is also implied in part by the previous phase: the economic base influences a particular social character, which influences particular ideas, which in turn influences the social character, which then influences the socioeconomic structure. (The circular configuration of this process is con-sistent with Fromm's evolutionary account of the development of character as the replacement for instinctual guidance, and ought to face no greater initial opposition than the evolutionary biological account of the genesis of species in which hereditary and environmental factors are seen as possessing a similar independent-but-interlinked logic of development.)

On this account, social structures are considered to be relatively fixed at any given historical period, other than during revolutions or periods of acute disintegration. As long as the "objective conditions" of a culture remain stable, the social character is seen to exercise a predominantly stabilizing function. If these objective conditions change, so that they no longer fit with the social character, a *lag* is said to arise:

> The social character is formed by socioeconomic conditions which have existed over centuries and have resulted in the formulation of ideologies, customs, and methods of child rearing. This cultural tradition determines the character of parents, so that even though traditional culture no longer fits changed economic conditions, the children—through the mediation of the traditional social character of their parents and the old educational methods, ideologies, and values—are still determined by the past. Even if they acquire the *knowledge* necessary to be effective in a changed economy through a selected system, their traditional character stands in the way. (Fromm and Maccoby, 1996 [1970]: 235)

In certain cases, this results in the social character acting as an element of disintegration, turning into "dynamite instead of social mortar" (2002 [1955]: 79). Fromm contends that the failure to understand this characterologically conditioned lag is one of the factors which Marxist theory has overlooked and which led to the naïve view that altered social conditions would immediately and straightforwardly produce changed human beings. The psychoanalytic view that Fromm adopted holds that character is relatively stable and capable of outlasting alterations in the social context. In *Social Character in a Mexican Village*, Fromm notes that the general principle of a "lag" needs an important qualification, asking why it was that the hoarding character of European and US middle-class, prevalent until 1930s, changed drastically into a consumer character within one generation. Fromm attributes this occurrence as, in the main, down to "the unprecedented possibility of influencing man's character through the new communications media" (Fromm and Maccoby, 1996 [1970]: 236). In particular, he contends that the fact the new communications media was controlled by private enterprise and, as he saw it, offered not intellectual but almost hypnotic engagement, meant it was possible to affect people of all ages as never before.

To stress again, Fromm's conception here should not be seen as restricted to a dead circularity. Beyond the interaction of economic base, with character, and ideology, which was sketched above, basic human needs or strivings—such as for love, happiness, belonging, freedom, either biologically inherent or instilled in historical evolution—feature in the social process, often acting as the spur to revolutionary struggle or civic unrest, as a population (or individuals within that population) attempts to change the social order so that it accords more directly with these needs.

> The relation between social change and economic change is not only the one which Marx emphasized, namely, the interests of new classes in changed social and political conditions, but that social changes are at the same time determined by the fundamental human needs which make use, as it were, of favorable circumstances for their realization. The middle class which won the French revolution wanted freedom for their economic pursuits from the fetters of the old order. But they were also driven by a genuine wish for human freedom inherent in them as human beings. While most were satisfied with a narrow concept of freedom after the revolution had won, the very best spirits of the bourgeoisie became aware of the limitation of bourgeois freedom and, in their search for a more satisfactory answer to man's needs, arrived at a concept which considered freedom to the be the condition for the unfolding of the total man. (2006 [1962]: 64–65)

Yet, in analytical terms, the ascendance and popularity of an idea can only be understood historically by reference to the social character(s) of a given society. Fromm is clear: "Ideas can become powerful forces, but only to the extent to which they are answers to specific human needs prominent in a given social character" (1969 [1941]: 279).

Fromm's theory of the social character is underpinned by a concept he formally introduced relatively late in his career in *Beyond the Chains of Illusion*, but which is implied in the very possibility of psychoanalytic social psychology namely, the theory of *the social unconscious*. Exactly as with the extension of the principles of individual character to the level of the social character, Fromm simply extends the principles of repression here from the level of the individual to that of society. Just as every society possesses a core character structure that is functionally conducive to the stability of that society, so every society tends to repress certain core experiences that are functionally counter-conducive to the stability of that society. This is essentially the same process as Freud has shown to occur in relation to the more confined individual case, only that the phenomenon is socially patterned and aggregative rather than peculiar and fortuitous. This is not to deny that the socially patterned repression is also an individual phenomenon; it is of course something that happens to individuals and individuals only and that affects each individual in ultimately unique ways. The point is that is it not fortuitous, and that it serves a functional purpose in relation to the society.

Fromm's discussion of the social unconscious is offered not as an oblique and mysterious positing, but as connected with and expressed in the responses to a series of historical and cultural questions that practically shape social understanding at any given historical moment. He acknowledges that to be aware of any potential experience that experience must itself be comprehensible in terms of the organizational categories that function in a given system: "Every society, by its own practice of living and by the mode of relatedness, of feeling and perceiving, develops a system, or categories, which determines the forms of awareness. This system works, as it were, like a *socially conditioned filter*: experience cannot enter awareness unless it can penetrate this filter" (2006 [1962]: 87). In his discussion of the ways in which a given society or culture mediates what can and cannot penetrate into consciousness, Fromm discusses three such socially conditioned filters—namely, *language, logic,* and *social taboos*.

In the case of language, Fromm points out the fact that the ability of certain, generally subtle, affective experiences to enter into consciousness is dependent on the degree to which a particular language can accommodate the potential experience (while this is clearly not absolutely true, it is surely true to a certain extent, and certainly to the extent to which these experiences can be fully integrated into consciousness). Not only this, the whole structure of language, its grammar, syntax, etc., act as a kind of boundary for aspects of experience. As Fromm puts it, "the whole language contains an attitude of life, is a frozen expression of experiencing life in a certain way... Language, by its words, its grammar, its syntax, by the whole spirit which is frozen in it, determines which experiences penetrate to our awareness" (2006 [1962]: 89)—which, of course, does not necessarily rule out our being unconsciously aware. In the case of the logic of a culture, Fromm stresses that in the same way that we assume that our language is "natural" and that other languages only use different words for same thing, we also tend to assume that the rules of logic are natural and universal—despite the fact that different cultures (historically and temporally) have varying standards and conceptions of what logic is (whether they call it "logic" or not) (2006 [1962]: 89–90). Fromm takes as a case in point the differences between Aristotelian logic (based on law of identity—A=A—and law of noncontradiction—A cannot be A *and* non-A, neither A *nor* non-A), which predominates in "Western" societies, and paradoxical logic (based on the assumption that A and non-A do not exclude each other as predicates of X), which he claims is historically predominant in Chinese and Indian thinking. Finally, and significantly, in the case of social taboos, Fromm stresses the role such taboos play in declaring certain ideas and feelings to be improper, forbidden, dangerous, preventing them from reaching consciousness (and tending to expel them if they have already done so) (2006 [1962]: 90). In connection with this point Fromm cites a series of hypothetical cases, examples including that of a member of a warrior-tribe who represses his revulsion at killing and robbing, and that of an urban shopkeeper who represses his impulse to give for free a suit of clothes to a customer who badly needs one but who is unable to afford it.

The conclusion that Fromm is proffering an overly functionalist account is harder to avoid in this last instance, making, as he does, the steadfast and seemingly exclusive assumption that these experiences are repressed because they are not compatible with objective societal needs. Read in the context of his wider writings, however, it is clear that Fromm is more sophisticated than this: while he maintains that "the irrationalities of any given society result in the necessity for its members to repress the awareness of many of their own feelings and observations" (2006 [1962]: 92), he stresses that this repression of awareness "is, and must be, supplemented by [the] acceptance of many fictions," fictions impressed since childhood (by parents, schools, churches, movies, television, newspapers, etc.), which "take hold of men's minds as if they were the result of the men's own thinking or observation" (2006 [1962]: 93). Despite this caveat, it may still be objected that Fromm's approach is guilty of an excessive functionalism. The main point, however, is that Fromm was concerned to think, in practical and historical terms, about how individual and social character aligned, and about the mechanisms that shaped this alignment. As a psychoanalyst, Fromm stressed the idea that what we often take to be central to our self-understanding (as represented in systems of language or logic) can function in ways that impede as well as enable such self-understanding. These issues, and others mentioned earlier, are discussed later in the chapter.

Social Character Applied

Fromm's idea of the social character was an applied concept from the very start. His first monograph, *The Dogma of Christ*, written while still an orthodox Freudian, is his first full-length attempt at sociopsychoanalytical analysis, and can be seen as the first example of character analysis (although "social character" is not explicitly spoken of here, the underpinning ideas are clearly in evidence in basic form, acting as an early practical template for his sociopsychoanalytic project). Conceived in opposition to Theodore Reik's *Dogma and Compulsion*, which had emphasized the traditional psychoanalytic method and therefore, Fromm argued, attempted to understand individuals based on their ideas and ideology, *The Dogma of Christ* consists of an analysis of the morphology of Christian Dogma in which the ideas conveyed, relative to the particular stage of their morphology, are understood as expressions of the socioeconomic situation and psychic attitude of its followers, particularly of the psychic attitude as conditioned by the socioeconomic situation. In particular, Fromm was concerned with "the motives conditioning the evolution of concepts about the relationship of God the Father to Jesus from the beginning of Christianity to the formulation of the Nicene Creed in the fourth century" (1992 [1963]: 9–10). Through analysis of such motives, Fromm sought "to show what influence social reality had in a specific situation upon a specific group of men, and how emotional trends found expression in certain dogmas, in collective fantasies, and to show further what psychic change was brought about by a change in the social situation" (1992 [1963]: 20–21).

Although *The Dogma of Christ* is not fully representative of Fromm's thought as it later developed, it remains an important document in the history of social psychology, being described by Franz Borkenau in the first issue of *Zeitschrift* as the first concrete example of the integration of Freud and Marx (Jay, 1996: 91). For despite its shortcomings as an academic document—particularly its somewhat cavalier attempt to render simple the complicated issues of Christology and exegesis—the work does make an attempt to describe the socioeconomic situation of the social class from which the early Christian faith originated and to understand the meaning of this faith in terms of the psychic situation of those to which it applied. Naturally, such an undertaking faces many barriers—the most central of which is the problem of deep-historical attributions of psychic states—said barriers leaving the conclusion inherently speculative (although notably less speculative than some of Freud's conclusions, even considering Fromm's reliance on Oedipal explanatory themes).

Escape from Freedom, published some 11 years after *The Dogma of Christ*, sought to continue this sociopsychoanalytical development, this time applying Fromm's sociopsychoanalytical principles to the rise of Fascism. In particular, it sought "to analyze those dynamic factors in the character structure of modern man, which made him want to give up freedom in Fascist countries and which so widely prevail in millions of our own people" (1969 [1941]: 4). Fromm's argument extended historically, advancing the contention that the growing individualism, fostered by developments associated with the Renaissance and the Reformation, actually led to a retreat into dependency, initially as submission to what he saw as the anti-humanist doctrinal authoritarianism of Lutheranism and Calvinism and latterly as submission to the racist-demagogic authoritarianism of Hitler. In both instances, Fromm advances an argument based on the attribution of the characterological appeal of the respective ideologies to what he contends was the pivotal position of the Protestant middle class.

In the case of Lutheranism and Calvinism, Fromm argues that their Reformation doctrines gave articulate expression to (and actually increased) the new and uneasy (uneasy because it was coupled with the release of intense feelings of powerlessness) sense of independence brought about by social and economic change occurring in the sixteenth century. Of particular importance in the case of Lutheranism was the fact that Luther's stress on the helplessness of man in relation to God mirrored the urban middle class's position in relation to the new economic forces, threatened as they were by revolutionary movements and the resentment of the lower classes as well as by the new wealth of the capitalist entrepreneurs.[9] Crucially, Fromm argues that Luther's doctrines provided a solution to this helplessness: "By not only accepting his own insignificance but by humiliating himself to the utmost, by giving up every vestige of individual will etc., by renouncing and denouncing his individual strength, the individual could hope to gain acceptance from God" (1969 [1941]: 81). Fromm, in fact, stressed the fact that Luther's theology emphasized a relationship to God as "complete submission" as well as the nothingness of the individual. From here, Fromm argues that "once the individual had lost his sense of pride and dignity, he was psychologically prepared to lose the feeling which had been characteristic of medieval thinking, namely, that man, his spiritual salvation, and his spiritual aims were the purpose of life; he was prepared to accept a role in which life has become a means to a purpose outside himself" (1969 [1941]: 83).

In Calvinism, which Fromm saw as mirroring Lutheranism in its effect and appeal to middle classes, the submissive element was even more prominent, although in this instance Fromm attributes the appeal to the conservative middle class, artisans, and small businessmen. Fromm focuses here on the idea of self-humiliation and the destruction of human pride as the *leitmotif* of Calvin's whole thinking: "Only he who despises this world can devote himself to the preparation for the future world" (1969 [1941]: 84). According to Fromm, who quotes Calvin on the matter, the individual should not feel its own master, and should avoid striving for virtue for its own sake. Fromm concludes that Calvin's God "has all the features of a tyrant without any quality of love and justice" (1969 [1941]: 88). As was the case with Luther, Fromm argues that in terms of psychological significance, Calvin's theology expresses and enhances the feeling of individual powerlessness and insignificance at the same time as silencing irrational doubt.

Fromm singles out Calvin's "doctrine of predestination" for particular attention. What is crucial in psychological terms about the doctrine of predestination is not just that it involves the selection of some as predestined for grace and others as predestined for eternal damnation (a judgment that sets up the principle of the basic inequality between men), but that, as a result of this distinction (and its inscrutable certainty), unceasing effort, and success because of this effort, becomes a sign of salvation. For Fromm, this was crucial in that it appears to directly contradict the doctrine that human effort plays no part in man's salvation. Anxiety, powerlessness, and fear therefore return—the former compulsorily set off against the latter two in order to keep them at bay.

In line with what has been said above, Fromm concludes "that these doctrines intensified and stabilized the characterological changes; and that the character traits that thus developed then became productive forces in the development of capitalism which in itself resulted from economic and political changes" (1969 [1941]: 294). It is clear that Fromm's account exhibits many points of connection with that of Weber in *The Protestant Ethic and the Spirit of Capitalism*. But what Fromm particularly argues is that it was the *characterological* aspects that explained the high degree of receptivity of these ideas. "In both instances," Fromm argues, "we see that when a certain class is threatened by new economic tendencies it reacts to this threat psychologically and ideologically; and that the psychological changes brought about by this reaction further the development of economic forces even if those contradict the economic interests of that class" (1969 [1941]: 295).

What Fromm says about Luther and Calvin can also be applied in relation to his account of the rise of Hitler. In this case, Fromm argues that certain socioeconomic changes, particularly the decline of the traditional middle class and the rising power of monopolistic capitalism, had a deep psychical effect, helping to prepare this class for the psychological acceptance of Hitler's ideology. Fromm argues that the young of the lower middle class, in particular, consciously thought of their fate in terms of the nation—national defeat in the First World War and Treaty of Versailles functioning as symbols for actual frustrations, and nationalistic resentment acting as a rationalization, which projected social inferiority to national inferiority (1969 [1941]: 215). In addition to this, Fromm contends that Hitler's demand for the renunciation of the individual's right to a personal opinion, and therefore their submission to the authority of the Thou, played directly into the deep feelings of powerlessness, fear, and anxiety already existent in this segment of the population. Being addressed to people who, on account of similar character structures, felt attracted to and excited by these teachings and who thus became ardent followers, the Nazi ideology therefore appealed to and intensified the preexisting character traits, which now became effective forces in supporting the rise of Hitler. In addition to this, Fromm argues that the political *practice* of the Nazis actively realized their ideology: a hierarchy was created in which each person had somebody above them to submit to and somebody beneath them to feel power over. "Thus," Fromm concludes, "the Nazi ideology and practice satisfied the desire springing from the character structure of one part of the population and gives direction and orientation to those who, though not enjoying domination and submission, were resigned and had given up faith in life, in their own decisions, in everything" (1969 [1941]: 236).

As with *The Dogma of Christ*, the analysis in *Escape from Freedom* is far from conclusive, suffering from some questionable inferences at certain crucial points. In particular, it proffers an idealized account of the Middle Ages and the Renaissance, reliant on Burckhardt, Tawney, Lamprecht, and Shapiro, as well as a largely one-sided representation of the Reformation (although Fromm does at least acknowledge this latter point). In particular, Fromm can be seen as offering a hasty and arguably unrepresentative account of the theology and personalities of Luther and Calvin as well as failing to consider the role of Catholicism and the Renaissance in rise of capitalism—points that have been fairly forcefully argued by J. Stanley Glen (1966). Although Fromm does acknowledge the role of Renaissance in the rise of the individual, it is true that his account lacks an explanation of the role of Catholicism in the rise of capitalism; and though Fromm does offer some evidence for his psychoanalytical characterizations of Luther and Calvin, they are not pitched at the same level as those offered, for instance, by Erikson in his *Young Man Luther*. What Glen can be said to miss in his criticism, however, is the fact that Fromm's stress here is less on the Luther and Calvin's *theological doctrines* and more on the *psychological consequences* of these doctrines (Lundgren, 1998: 54), and that, as such, strict theological accuracy is not quite the point. Despite this caveat, its is clear that both criticisms do have a degree of weight to them, something that is not without consequence for Fromm's account.

Fromm has also been criticized for his account of the rise of Hitler. McLaughlin (1996) points out that Fromm's account of the rise of Hitler offers fairly scant evidence to support his claims, and that current evidence in fact suggests that the role Fromm ascribes to the urban lower middle class is questionable.[10] McLaughlin also argues that *Escape from Freedom* ultimately rests on an outdated class model and leans too heavily on Weber's account in *The Protestant Ethic and the Spirit of Capitalism*, where an organizational analysis of the role of religions in political life would be more illuminating (McLaughlin, 1996: 259). A further criticism worthy of note here is that of Wilde, who notes that Fromm's analysis of Nazism in *Escape from Freedom* ignores the role of economic recovery in consolidating national sentiment—a strange oversight given Fromm's stated adherence to the Marxist stress on the primary role of the economic factors in shaping historical outcomes (Wilde, 2004a: 27).

Despite all of this, however, *Escape from Freedom* is an important part of the development of Fromm's thought, representing an innovative attempt to analyze the sociopsychological phenomenon of groups and leaders and the relationship of class position, psychic character, and ideology. In this regard, Fromm saw himself as building on Freud and Weber by adding a Marxian level to their analysis. His critique of Protestantism, although one-sided, does highlight its connections with Fascism, thereby challenging its stereotypical correlation with liberal and democratic movements (McLaughlin, 1996: 253). And, as Martin Jay notes, Fromm's demonstration of the relationship of rationality, possessiveness, and Puritanism to anal repression and orderliness, was novel at the time, even if his description of Freud's genital character as associated with freedom was also to be found in Reich (Jay, 1996: 94).

As well as these historical analyses, Fromm was centrally involved with two notable but largely ignored empirical studies of social character. The first of these, implemented in the early 1930s but only published posthumously in 1980 as *Arbiter ind Angestellte am Vorabend des Dritten Reiches. Eine sozialpsychologische Untersuchung* (*The Working Class in Weimar Germany*), was coordinated by Fromm in his position of director of social psychology at the *Institut für Sozialforschung*. An innovative sociopsychoanalytical project with direct thematic connections to Korsch's critique of mechanical Marxism, the study was concerned with eliciting the attitudes and psyche of German manual and white-collar workers with the purpose of discovering the relationships that exist between character structure and political allegiances. In particular, the study pursued the assumption that there are many reasons for declaring oneself a socialist, many degrees of commitment to socialist ideas and, therefore, greater and lesser degrees of commitment to these ideals when faced with a program such as that offered by the National Socialists. In light of this, the central premise of the study was as an extension of the psychological maxim that, in spite of subjective honesty, an individual's statement about his or her thoughts and feelings cannot be taken literally but must instead be interpreted so as to try to unearth their deeper psychological motivation. The practical method chosen to enable this was what Fromm was to call the "interpretative questionnaire": a method which sought to facilitate the psychoanalytical analysis of data gleaned from an open-ended questionnaire in such a way so as to elicit a picture of the kinds of lifestyles the interviewees lived, the opinions they held, the books they read, how they furnished their homes, etc. The hope in using such a method was that it would thereby enable the researchers to bypass cultural clichés and the veneer of appropriateness to get at the dynamic forces that constitute character.

As with the other studies already discussed, the Weimar study suffers from insufficiencies compared to more contemporary accounts. The low response rate of 33 percent detracts from the strength of the conclusions drawn, as does the potential accusation that Fromm reads these conclusions into the study. But, as with the other studies, the Weimar study was a genuinely groundbreaking piece of work, forming a significant early step in the empirical mapping of taste and character that has been realized to a significant degree in the sociology of Pierre Bourdieu, particularly so in his *Distinction*. The study's use of a largely open-ended questionnaire distinguishes it sharply from *The Authoritarian Personality*, which, although appearing in print a few decades prior to the Weimar study, was, in fact, preceded by the latter by close to 20 years. Crucially, the study's conclusion was particularly unsettling, considering that, as Bonss describes it, "the majority of respondents associated themselves with the (usually left-wing) slogans of their party, but...their degree of radicalism was considerably reduced in more subtle, seemingly unpolitical questions" (1984: 28). This suggested that there was a profound complexity to political commitment, the conclusion itself uncannily foreshadowing the reality of what was to occur during Hitler's regime.

In the late 1950s, Fromm started work on a follow-up to the Weimar study. Published in 1970 as *Social Character in a Mexican Village*, the study sought to determine what happened to the *campesino* (Mexican peasant class) after the Mexican revolution in the 1920s. In particular, the study was interested in *why* it was that, despite being given land as a consequence of the revolution, levels of violence and alcoholism, for instance, rose among the campesinos. The work, which was coauthored by Michael Maccoby and which was based on the fieldwork data gathered by a team of anthropologists and psychoanalysts, was a continuation of the Weimar study based on the conceptual stipulations that Fromm had honed in the intervening years. Vexed by criticism over the "unempirical" nature of his theorizations in the field of social character, Fromm hoped the study would offer proof of his contention that specific social structures promote and are sustained by specific personality types.[11] To this end, Fromm arranged the incorporation of the use of statistical methods in the analysis of the data and a far greater level of collation and analysis of socioeconomic data and ethnographic material than was the case in the Weimar study (in addition to this, Fromm ensured a concerted effort to interact with the villagers over the course of a number of years, to enable the strongest ethnographic encounter). Fromm heralded the resulting work as a confirmation of the social character theory, demonstrating as it did the general correspondence of certain character types to certain socioeconomic conditions. In particular, the study showed the existence of three main village character types and their statistically significant correspondence to certain socioeconomic conditions: the *nonproductive-receptive* character, corresponding with the landless day laborer; the *productive-hoarding* character, corresponding with the free landowner; and *productive-exploitative* character, corresponding with the new entrepreneur. In line with Fromm's social character theory, these correlations are explained in terms of the *adaptation* of personality to distinct historical socioeconomic conditions, character featuring as a causative factor in the socioeconomic situation of each group.

In a particularly important conclusion to the study, explaining empirically what is a routine sociological assumption, Fromm and Maccoby argue that their findings show that "those individuals whose character coincides with their class role tend to be more successful, provided that their class role objectivity allows the possibility of economic success" and that, therefore, "when the economic situation of a class does not provide the basis for economic success...only exceptional individuals whose character differs from the social character of their class can escape from a level of extreme poverty and dependence" (Fromm and Maccoby, 1996 [1970]: 230). In the context of the study—although clearly extendable beyond this context—Fromm and Maccoby show that an understanding of character can help us account for the increasing gap between poorer and richer villagers. Character, which was shown to be clearly correlated with economic activity (even down to the type of crops that were planted—the receptive-hoarding characters choosing to plant less time-consuming, but poorer yielding, crops) and to cases of alcoholism, appears to be an empirically facilitating/confounding factor in daily life and also, therefore, in political and social change. To help these connections, and to specifically address the issue of social change, Fromm and Maccoby introduce the idea of *social selection*, saying that

in a relatively stable society (or class) with its typical social character, there will always be deviant characters who are unsuccessful or even misfits under the traditional conditions. However, in the process of socioeconomic change, new economic trends develop for which the traditional character is not well adapted, while a certain heretofore deviant character type can make optimal use of the new conditions. As a result the "ex-deviants" become the most successful individuals and the leaders of their society or class. They acquire the power to change laws, education systems, and institutions in a way that facilitates the development of new trends and influences the character formation of succeeding generations. Thus the character structure is the selective factor which leads to the successful adaptation of one part of the population and the social failure and weakening of another. The "superior" sector will have the advantage of greater wealth, better health, and better education. While for the "defeated" sector the opposite will be true. The stability of such characterological classes will, of course, be all the greater the longer the period of social stability. But however long it is, historical evidence shows that deviant and secondary trait personalities never fully disappear and hence social changes always find the individuals and groups which can serve as the core for a new social character. (Fromm and Maccoby, 1996 [1970]: 232)

In the case of the village study itself, it was the productive-exploitative new entrepreneurs, who were the ex-deviants, now taking advantage of the opportunities for capitalist enterprise that had previously been socially limited.

So poorly is the Mexican study known that there have been very few appraisals of it. What is apparent is that, as is the case with Fromm's previous studies, there can be questions raised around his use of correlation, inference, and the level of "proof" that the study provides. While this may be so, the study is undoubtedly yet another groundbreaking piece of work that merits greater attention (unfortunately, a detailed discussion is beyond the scope of the present work; I will, however, go into greater detail in a chapter in *Sociological Amnesia: Cross-currents in Disciplinary History*, a forthcoming collection to be published by Ashgate). The correlations between social character and social activity, which have been, if not proven, then at least strongly suggested here, are potentially significant ones for social and political thought. In particular connection to revolutionary change, the study suggests that the process of social selection can be mediated by political revolutions but that these revolutions will not lead to lasting changes unless new socioeconomic conditions have developed sufficiently to attract the latent "characterological minorities" (or, in terms reminiscent of his criticism of Marx: until we have also lost our "psychological chains"). Importantly, Fromm was to use this idea as the basis for his own strategy of social change, a strategy that will be discussed in chapter 6.

Psychoanalytic Social Psychology Appraised

With his social psychology as outlined above, Fromm finds himself on similar terrain to the "culture and personality" tradition as exemplified by Ruth Benedict, Margaret Mead, Abram Kardiner, Ralph Linton, Clyde

Kluckhohn, and Erik Erikson (although his Marxism and his radical humanist account of Freud separates him quite clearly from these thinkers). There are also clear parallels to sociologists writing at the same time, such as Hans Gerth, C. Wright Mills, and Talcott Parsons, as well as to symbolic interactionists such as Sheldon Stryker, whose social structural symbolic interactionism evinces an uncanny similarity to aspects of Fromm's thought. An interesting contemporary connection can also be said to exist with the thought of Pierre Bourdieu. Bourdieu's concept of *habitus* and his general structural-phenomenological account of being covers much of the same ground as Fromm, although from different premises and to a different effect.

As an account of the social process, Fromm's social psychology ultimately falls a little short in terms of the levels of sufficiency required, failing, on the score of detail at least, to match up to most of the aforementioned authors. His historical social psychology is somewhat general, missing levels of social reality that it needs to engage with, and his empirical social psychology suffers from a lack of sophistication resultant of its pioneering status. A surprising failing, given his Marxian stress, is the lack of a detailed account of social structure, of institutions, class, roles, etc. Although Fromm was clearly aware of the importance of these factors, his work only really deals with minimal kinds of structures or processes in structural reproduction. As Fromm states time and time again in his early writings, extensive knowledge of the socioeconomic situation of the group under study is essential. This was a principle of Fromm's as far back as 1931, when he stated that what was required for social psychology was "the exact knowledge of the economic, social and political situation of the group to be analyzed" (1989 [1931]: 216). Although Fromm does make efforts to chart these conditions, he does not quite live up to the promise his methodological stipulations suggest.

Questions also remain over Fromm's characterology. The persisting doubt that will shadow his work in this regard is the issue of "proof" and whether or not psychoanalytic inferences will be seen as admissible. Fromm's contentions on psychoanalytic social psychology depend for their success on the degree to which it can be argued that psychoanalysis has shown that human conscious psychic activity is only a relatively small sector of psychic life and that many impulses behind psychic behavior are unconscious. Fromm was well aware of this, but was unstinting in his conviction:

> Although psychoanalysis does not live up to the ideal which for many years was the ideal of academic psychology, that is, the approximation of the experimental methods of the natural sciences, it is nevertheless a thoroughly empirical method, based on the painstaking observation

of an individual's uncensored thoughts, dreams and phantasies. Only a psychology which utilizes the concept of unconscious forces can penetrate the confusing rationalizations we are confronted with in analyzing either an individual or a culture. A great number of apparently insoluble problems disappear at once if we decide to give up the notion that the motives by which people *believe* themselves to be motivated are necessarily the ones which actually drive them to act, feel, and think as they do. (1969 [1941]: 136)

Fromm's understanding of science clearly does not emanate from the Newtonian-Galilean tradition but, rather, from the Aristotelian one, in which the degree of formalism appropriate to each science is seen as dependent on the nature of the phenomena under study. Fromm in fact likens psychoanalysis to medicine (an "art" in which certain theoretical principles are applied to empirical data), giving as a fruitful analogy the example of an X-ray picture:

In the case of a typical picture, even most beginners will give the same interpretation; on the other hand in an atypical picture even the most experienced specialists may disagree among themselves. Only the further course of the illness or surgery can decide which interpretation was correct. But when the interpretation has been made and serves as the basis for further treatment, one trusts the patient's life on the assumption that the interpretation of a skilled physician is likely to be correct. There is, in fact, nothing subjective, in the usual sense, in his diagnosis. He is a highly trained observer whose judgment results from a mixture of experience, skill, intelligence, and concentration. However, he cannot *prove* the correctness of his interpretation in a way which would convince everybody (which is, incidentally, also sometimes the case in highly sophisticated scientific experiments) and least of all those physicians with less skill and talent than his own; and eventually there is, of course, the possibility that he may be wrong. (Fromm and Maccoby, 1996 [1970]: 27)

Like Freud, Fromm was trying to go where others would not. He was open about the fact that "a certain amount of uncertainty is the price the psychoanalytic researcher pays for the attempt to arrive at a deeper understanding of the most relevant data" (Fromm and Maccoby, 1996 [1970]: 27).

Beyond this, there is a doubt over the accuracy and efficacy of his account of the character orientations. At perhaps the most basic level it must be asked whether the character orientations do not in fact inflate and reify transient, conflicting personality aspects. This has been argued by Adorno, among others, despite that fact that Adorno comes to utilize Fromm's idea of social character fairly centrally in *The Authoritarian Personality*. Fromm's response to Laing's work—which he praised as a form of radical humanism—is worth recounting here. In his appraisal of Laing, Fromm disagrees in only one respect with what he says—that is, over Laing's claim that there is no "basic personality," or no "one internal system":

> I only want to say that the assumption of a basic character system in person A does not exclude the possibility that this system is constantly being affected by systems B, C, D…with which it communicates, and that in this interpersonal process various aspects of the character system in person A are energized and others lose in intensity. The simplest example is the person characterized by a sadomasochistic system. In his encounter with one system (B) his sadism will be activated; in his encounter with another (C) his masochism will be activated. However, the person in whose system sadomasochism is not pronounced will react neither masochistically nor sadistically when he encounters systems B or C, respectively. (1992: 62–63)

This said—and as Fromm himself notes—an almost endless number of combinatory possibilities exist. In light of this, it may be legitimately asked how useful for social analysis such designations can be? Is it a system that is too complicated to sustain any useful or sufficiently rigorous study? Michael Maccoby's own work on social character offers a profitable comparison here, focusing as it does not on the application of hypostatized categories but flexible ones tailored to the situation which nevertheless refer back to a generalized typology (Maccoby, 1976). In *The Gamesman*, a study of the values and motivations of corporate managers and engineers creating new technology, Maccoby redescribes Fromm's character types in a language he thought would be accepted by the managers and engineers themselves and become part of their conversation. For instance, Maccoby identified the following character types as translations of the Frommian schema: the *craftsman/woman* as a productive hoarding type; the *jungle fighter* as an exploitative type who might be either a more productive protector of his followers or an nonproductive manipulator; the *company man/woman* as a more receptive type; and *the gamesman/woman* representing a new social character type who was then rising to top of companies and who treats work and life as a game to be played and won. This approach offers the possibility of avoiding what can be seen as the rather stark categorizations that Fromm makes, categorizations which "run the risk of over simplistic and perhaps even prejudiced pigeonholing" (Thompson, 2009: 47–48). It is interesting to note, however, that this was the policy that Fromm followed in his psychoanalytic practice, and that, therefore, what Maccoby does here is the logical continuation of Fromm's own thought as applied to social analysis. Either way, it should be stressed that Fromm's instinct remained an important one: to clarify character types as a means of promoting sociological understanding.

On top of all of this, the issue of functionalism remains to be decided. While Wiggershaus's accusation of a seamless functionalism (Wiggershaus, 1994: 125) in Fromm is clearly an exaggeration, there is a tension in Fromm between his insistence on the existential freedom of an individual in society and the greater or lesser determination of that individual by the objective needs of society. What is obvious is that while Fromm was insufficiently precise here, he was not a crude functionalist. The individual, in his account, does not simply mirror the structural properties of the society in which he or she lives. As a social psychoanalyst, Fromm was always aware of the determining role of structure alongside the always-existent possibility of "waking up" to this determination. He saw the social and the individual as fundamentally related and in constant interaction. What mattered for Fromm, in humanist terms, was "not so much the content of what is repressed, but the state of mind and, to be more precise, the degree of awakedness and realism in the individual" (2006 [1962]: 97). While this is so, Fromm might have achieved more by way of explicitly explaining and linking social structures and networks with his account of individual action.

Despite these issues, the strengths of Fromm's social psychology are insufficiently recognized. His social psychology was a radical humanist, Marxian attempt to improve upon the sexual reductionism of the early psychoanalytic researchers and to extend Weber's analyses into regions where he had not ventured.[12] Social action theory is in strict need of a well-developed system of social psychology, a schema for analyzing the significance for social action of an actor's expressions, feelings, wishes, and thoughts. As Craib has said: "if people believe or act in a way that can be attributed to the effects of social forces, then it is only because the internal psychodynamics of the character structure allow them, or force them, to do so... To be *only* sociological is to turn partial, and often dangerous, aspects of the self into the whole self" (Craib, 1989: 194). It is also important to note that Fromm's work here offers the opportunity to retain the analytical correlates of humanism—that is, the subject, the self, etc.—elevating to a considered analytical status the idea of a basic psychological dynamism that underlies human experience and that figures as a fundamental variable in the social process. Retaining these correlates and raising the phenomenon of a basic psychological dynamism to such a status is not only crucial for a proper explanation of the social process; it also enables the reintegration of normative categories that relate to these correlates and, therefore, enables the transcendence of the facile fact-value separation that polices social scientific and social theoretical thought. In this regard, Fromm's work does point out the right path for a radical humanist Marxian social psychology, despite the fact that his analyses may have sometimes fallen short of fulfilling the demands that he set for them. What was important in his account was the attempt to explain how psychological factors interact with the other factors in the social process. This gets directly to the heart of the issue for much social theory in that it is a methodological bulwark against the sociological reductionism that can be found there. It also avoids the libido-obsession of Reich, the effective mechanicism of Adorno, and the hyper-individualism of Marcuse. As Neil McLaughlin has remarked,

> the strength of Fromm's approach to psychoanalysis was that he viewed the tradition as an empirically based social theory, an important counterweight to a sometimes excessively abstract and speculative Freud preferred by post-modern theorists in the humanities. Psychoanalysis can contribute to social science only if the insights of the tradition are articulated clearly and concisely in ways that engage debates outside Freudian institutes and conferences of psychoanalytic influenced academics. Fromm's work, more so than either Adorno or Lacan, can help in encouraging a dialogue between psychoanalytic perspectives and mainstream social scientists unwilling to enter the hermetically sealed world of critical theory. In addition, Fromm's focus on emotions and the irrational can provide a useful corrective to what some argue is the overly rationalist version of critical theory developed and promoted by Habermas. (McLaughlin, 1999: 18–19)

That he fell short can be seen to be partly a consequence of the pioneering nature of his work and partly a result of his public intellectual commitment to advancing humanism in the world. This advancement of humanism will be the central point of discussion in chapters 5 and 6.

CHAPTER 5

Anti-Humanism: A Radical Humanist Defense

Taken as a whole, Fromm's writings amount to the development of an extended manifesto for human unfolding; in particular, for the unfolding of our capacities for love over hate, rationality over irrationality, productiveness over destructiveness, and authenticity over conformity. It is a vision that is built on the basis of a restated and radicalized humanism that sees itself as the completion (in inverted form) of classical Judaeo-Christian humanism and, as this, the realization of messianic socialism. Transposed, as it is, into revised psychoanalytic terrain, it is a philosophy that posits the self as at once its radical goal and means and that is grounded on a qualified essentialist account of the human being based on an evolutionary account of human genesis. But this is a vision that is under threat today from an anti-humanism that directly challenges its very tenability. A product of various disparate thinkers lodged in certain sectors of the social sciences and humanities, this anti-humanism centrally reduces to an attack on the axiomatic precepts of humanism namely, the idea of "man," of "the subject," of "the self," and of history as the realm in which human perfectibility (or flourishing) can manifest itself. The popularity of structuralist and poststructuralist thinkers (and those grouped as such, despite the various disavowals), and the loose body of thought generally described as "postmodernism," is instrumental in this attack, which is as potent as it is restrictive. In the last 50 years or so, the idea of the "death of man," of "the subject," of "the author," etc., has been proclaimed alongside the intricate elaboration of a variety of non-foundational, semiological, linguistic, or simply extra- and sub-personal explanatory models, which, in one way or another, proffer a cultural (and at times epistemological or even ontological) relativism that is allergic to meta- or grand-narratives.

Although Fromm never commented publicly on the strands of anti-humanist thought that were coming to prominence during the later years of his life, he was strongly opposed to relativism (particularly ethical relativism, but even, to a certain extent, cultural relativism), anti-humanism and "postmodernism" being merely its current embodiments (Gellner, 1982). Fromm did, however, comment on what can be said to be the most prominent forms of relativism of his time—namely, behaviorism and existentialism—and was scathing in his commentary. Anti-humanism, however, is slightly different in that it is not primarily the result of positivism (as in the case of behaviorism) or idealism (as in the case of existentialism), but a reaction to these modes of thought which, at the same time, plays on their theme of antiessentialism, extending it further into stronger or weaker forms of constructionism. Though the various anti-humanist arguments clearly involve the needed problematization of the naïve ethnocentricity of the classical humanist constructs, these arguments have a tendency to get caught up in this very problematization, in excessive attributions of linguistic and cultural determination or one-sided stresses on fragmentation and discontinuity.

Crucially, although he was opposed to a strong form of relativism, Fromm is not wholly without connection to the themes that underlie this anti-humanist frame of thought. As should be clear by now, Fromm was not a naïve humanist. As I tried to show in the account of his theories of social character and the social unconscious, Fromm was aware of the importance of cultural difference and the constitutive power of language. He was also, as someone following in the footsteps of Marx and Freud, fundamentally aware of the challenges posed to rationalism over the last few centuries. What is characteristic of Fromm, however, is that although centrally influenced by Marx and Freud, and thereby positioning himself at variance with the claims of the Cartesian cogito, he did not seek to abandon the grounding assumptions of his humanist predecessors—that is to say, the ethical belief in "the human" as a possibility and the underlying assumption that there is a generally shared human situation. His thought is characterized, rather, by the retention of these humanist assumptions alongside the recognition of humanism's myopic tendency, pursuing a policy of refined continuation, which is greatly instructive and, in fact, finding greater recognition today.

The Anti-humanist Paradigm—Part I

The term "anti-humanism" was first used by Louis Althusser in relation to the proliferation of socialist humanist thought in the wake of the publication of Marx's *Economic and Philosophic Manuscripts*. A member of the French Communist Party, Althusser saw socialist humanism as a blatant contradiction in terms, trying to, as he saw it, combine bourgeois idealism with class and, therefore, "true" humanism. Drawing on Bachelard, Althusser stresses the distinction between science and ideology, famously positing the existence of the "epistemological break" that separates the early, "idealist" from the later, "scientific" Marx. On this reading, Marx's contribution to thought is seen as consisting of the works of his later, scientific period, which Althusser argues are premised on a theoretical or philosophical anti-humanism that breaks with "every theory that based history and politics on an essence of man" (Althusser, 1969: 227). Despite his protestations to the contrary (Althusser claims he was a Spinozist rather than a structuralist), Althusser's Marxism advances what seems to be a deep structuralist account of the social process that operates without recourse—and in strict opposition—to the category of the subject. Expressly opposed to the idea of "the Essence of Man [as] the Origin, Cause and Goal of History," for Althusser there can be no "Subject as Absolute Centre, as Radical Origin, as a Unique Cause" (Althusser, 1976: 96). History, for Althusser, "really is a 'process without a Subject or Goal(s),' where the given *circumstances* in which 'men' act as subjects under the determination of social *relations* are the product of the *class struggle*" (Althusser, 1976: 99). On Althusser's understanding, capital defines for the capitalist mode of production the different types of individual required and produced for that mode, according to the functions, of which the individuals are "supports" (*Träger*), in the division of labor, in the different "levels" of the structure (Althusser and Balibar, 1970: 112).

Although perhaps superficially similar to Fromm's account of social character, there are clear and fundamental differences. First of all, Althusser's account, unlike Fromm's, has effectively obliterated the subject. It also, contrary to Fromm, wants to "abandon the issue of anthropology," "this anthropological 'given'" (Althusser and Balibar, 1970: 180). As he states in *For Marx*: "If the essence of man is to be a universal attribute, it is essential that *concrete subjects* exist as absolute givens; this implies an *empiricism of the subject*. If these empirical individuals are to be men, it is essential that each carries in himself the whole human essence, if not in fact, at least in principle; this implies an *idealism of the essence*. So empiricism of the subject implies idealism of the essence and vice versa" (Althusser, 1969: 228). Such a view wholly opposes as an ideological myth the abstraction of a common essence from the multitude of concrete individual human beings, which, as was shown in chapter 2, is wholly contrary to Fromm's approach.[1]

As a term, anti-humanism has come to be extended beyond its original sphere of usage in Althusser, being applied to aspects of thought sharing similar themes to Althusser's, which have, over the last half-century or so, formed into an influential paradigm in the social sciences and humanities. Constructed in self-conscious opposition to the dominant form of European thought since the Renaissance and the Enlightenment, this paradigm—which is often given the blanket description "postmodernism"—is concerned with the problematization of the central concepts of said dominant form of thought. The concepts of "man," "the self," "the subject," etc., are repudiated as ethnocentric relics, their essentialist ahistoricality wrought up with theological absolutism and associated with the forms of ethnocentrism that accompanied colonial conquest. As with any paradigm, there are antecedents along the way whose influence has been contributory to its formation. A line can be traced from current anti-humanist thought as far back as the atomists in classical Greece, to Hume and the Empiricists during the time of Enlightenment, although none have been more important to the direct constitution of this paradigm than the thought of what can be called the counter-Enlightenment, best exemplified in Nietzsche and Heidegger (and, depending on the reading, Marx and Freud).[2] Fromm's closest connection to this paradigm, however, is through his Institut ex-colleagues, and particularly Adorno, who was indebted to Nietzsche although highly critical of Heidegger.

Preceding Althusser, the Frankfurt School's development of critical theory, with its grounding in a nonidentity philosophy, has many conceptual and thematic similarities to the anti-humanist paradigm. (This is particularly the case with for Adorno, it is less so with Horkheimer and Marcuse. Even in the case of Adorno it must be stressed that there are crucial differences, Adorno's critique of idealism (as with that of Horkeimer and Marcuse) containing a strong materialist pretension that places him in a more proximate position to Fromm in certain crucial respects than the others considered in this chapter). This philosophy—which was touched on in chapter 3—is a form of Left Hegelian process philosophy, which holds that reification is such in capitalist society that philosophical thinking itself has become reified, giving over to the false identity of subject and object. As with any form of process philosophy, the central place customarily accorded to what is seen as objectively existing reality is subsumed in nonidentity philosophy by that of the *process of becoming*. The staticness of the object, of the existing world, must be transcended in thought by a focus not on what is at hand, so to speak, and part of the existing conceptual framework, but on the internal combustion of this framework itself. Adorno seeks to achieve this through the proffering of a methodological *negative dialectics* in which the Left Hegelian trope of "negativity" is mixed with Nietzschean aspects with the aim of freeing dialectics from affirmative traits that are entailed in Hegel's notion of the negation of the negation. Adorno shares with Althusser a common opposition to the humanist Marxist faith in the assertion of the universal man as the creator of history and its absolutizing of the solitary individual (Jay, 1972: 304). For Adorno, "man is the ideology of dehumanization" (Adorno, 2003: 48), and humanism a secret form of Fascism, saying in *Minima Moralia* that "in the innermost recesses of humanism, as its very soul, there rages a frantic prisoner who, as a Fascist, turns the world into a prison" (Adorno, 2005: 89). In addition to this, in his magnum opus *Negative Dialectics*, Adorno levels criticism at this philosophy and a thinly veiled swipe at the "poor romanticism" of Fromm. "The thinker," he states, "may easily comfort himself by imagining that in the dissolution of reification, of the merchandise character, he possess the philosophers' stone. But reification itself is the reflexive form of false objectivity; centering theory around reification, a form of consciousness, makes the critical theory idealistically acceptable to the reigning consciousness and to the collective unconscious. This is what raised Marx's early writings—in contradistinction to *Das Kapital*—to their present popularity, notably with theologians" (1973: 189–190).

Like Althusser, Adorno was opposed to what he saw as the abstract and reactionary philosophical anthropological search for essences, arguing that the fact that we cannot tell what man is rules out the possibility of any anthropology. His negative dialectical position, in fact, necessitates that "every 'image of man' is ideology except the negative one" (Adorno, 1968: 84). The stress on negativity here is important in that, to speak positively is to imply that humanity is realized in present society, which in turn is to "reinforce and affirm all those features of society that prevent the realisation of man" (Rose, 1978: 75). To concretize existing reality with talk of "the self," therefore, is in fact what is inhuman. As such, Adorno accuses psychoanalysis of collaborating in human domination: "In appealing to the fact that in an exchange society the subject was not one, but in fact a social object, psychology provided society with weapons for ensuring that this was and remained the case" (Adorno, 2005: 63). Furthermore, in *Dialectic of Enlightenment*, Adorno—with Horkheimer—equates the denigration of nature into an external other with the humanistic maxim of man as the measure of all things—an anthropomorphism that reduces nature into an object for domination (Adorno and Horkheimer, 1997: 224, 232–233). This process is fundamentally connected with the rational domination of nature, which, though older than the Enlightenment itself, is formalized there in paradigmatic form. This rational domination of nature is also a domination of interior nature, that is to say, of men themselves, by their self—"subjection to the nature of the Self" (Adorno and Horkheimer, 1997: 32). Enlightenment is seen, in fact, as a reversion to mythological thinking under the banner of rational progress: "Myth turns to enlightenment, and nature into mere objectivity. Men pay for the increase of their power with alienation from that over which they exercise power. Enlightenment behaves towards things as a dictator towards men. He knows them only insofar as he can manipulate them" (Adorno and Horkheimer, 1997: 9). *Dialectic of Enlightenment* ends (if not literally then effectively) with one final grim claim: namely, that "the conclusion that terror and civilization are inseparable, as drawn by the conservatives, is well-founded" (Adorno and Horkheimer, 1997: 217).

The kind of overt Marxism that plays a more or less central role in the thought of Althusser and Adorno, while offering a clear point of connection with Fromm, has largely slipped out of intellectual fashion today. What it has tended to be replaced with is a by and large non-Marxian cultural theory best represented in its earliest stages by the figures of Claude Lévi-Strauss and Michel Foucault, the former preceding, and the latter a student of, Althusser. To call this thought non-Marxian is not to disclaim any affinity to Marx—in both Lévi-Strauss and Foucault an affinity has been remarked on, although it is an affinity to the supposedly "anti-humanist" Marx, and one that is relatively unspoken. What is characteristic of both Lévi-Strauss and Foucault is the desire to, in Lévi-Strauss's words, "dissolve" man—"I accept the characterization of the aesthete insofar as I believe the ultimate goal of the human sciences not to constitute, but to dissolve man" (Lévi-Strauss, 1966: 247)—and to explore the other side of Enlightenment dream as represented in the forms of the devalued knowledge and rationalities of the marginal and far away.

As with many of his generation, Lévi-Strauss's thought can be said to be a reaction to the methodological individualism of Sartre. His social (or structural) anthropology, influenced as it was by Ferdinand de Saussure's projection of a science of *semiology*, as well as structural-functional aspects found in Radcliffe-Brown, Durkheim, and Mauss, was premised on the rejection of the idea of the subject as the location or source of meaning, its central role being replaced by that of language or of significatory systems. Lévi-Strauss's view of anthropology is as "the *bona fide* occupant of that domain of semiology which linguistics has not already claimed for its own" (Lévi-Strauss, 1977: 9–10). Although it is true that in the final volume of *Mythologies*, Lévi-Strauss does state that only subjects speak and that every myth has its origin in individual creation, he also stresses that the individual activity of the human subject is "contingent" (Giddens, 1979: 24). As such, its central occupation is the mapping out the synchronic (invariant) structures, particularly myths, relatively unaffected by the transformations of history, or, in Lévi-Strauss's famous line, to show "not how men think in myths, but how myths operate in men's minds without their being aware of the fact" (Lévi-Strauss,

1969: 12). In a similar sense to Althusser after him, although in different terrain, Lévi-Strauss sought to arrive at the "scientific" analyses of kinship systems, etc., seeking that (unconscious) structure lying beyond empirical observation that is nevertheless the backdrop to human social institutions. Without meaning or subject, history has no need for a transcendental humanism. It also has no need for talk of a general humanity to which ethnographic reduction leads. For Lévi-Strauss, the concept of "man" was a creation of post-Renaissance European culture, which, as exemplified in the myth of the exclusive dignity of human nature, inevitably led to the subjectification of nature—a "first mutilation, one from which other mutilations were inevitably to ensue" (Lévi-Strauss, 1977: 41). Like Althusser and Adorno, Lévi-Strauss wanted his own true humanism, a "new" humanism, which was to be founded on the ethnological impulse of anthropology. This new humanism was to be built in the image of Rousseau (whom Lévi-Strauss credits as the spiritual founder of ethnology), looking, as Rousseau did, beyond the first-person viewpoint of the Cartesian Cogito toward the spontaneous identification of the self with the Other found in the traditional ethnological encounter. Compassion and pity are raised as the central values, to be realized in the act of identification with the Other, and in fact with "any living being, seeing that it is living" (Lévi-Strauss, 1977: 38).

The thought of Foucault, particularly of his early works, represents in certain respects (and in spite of his disavowals) an extension of the structuralism of Lévi-Strauss. As with Lévi-Strauss (and Althusser), Foucault held that that there was no such thing as history as it is generally conceived, that is to say, history as the realm of the self-wrought progress of the meaning-giving subject. The point of his early work was, on the contrary, to show how discursive structures, as opposed to individuals, constitute history, and thereby to "free the history of thought from its subjection to transcendence" (Foucault, 2002a: 223). What this amounted to for Foucault was the stripping away of the subject by an "archaeological" focus on the discourses of various social scientific disciplines (archaeology understood here as the attempt to disclose the constraints on speaking and thinking that such discourses entailed). Foucault's analyses in *Madness and Civilization, Birth of the Clinic*, and *The Order of Things* purported to show how discourse speaks through humans, rather than humans through discourse. While Lévi-Strauss spoke of "dissolving man," Foucault foresaw the "death" of man, "erased, like a face drawn in the sand at the edge of the sea" (Foucault, 2002b: 422).

Foucault, however, also represents a break of sorts from the classical structuralist pattern. As opposed to what seemed to be the relatively ahistorical nature of structuralist thought, Foucault realized the need to account for *how* it was that structure functioned on the micro-level, facilitating change and discontinuity. In as much as this is the case, his thought also represents the move toward a poststructuralist stance, particularly so in the development of his "genealogical" approach. Foucault gives an account of this approach in his "Nietzsche, Genealogy, History" essay:

> Where the soul pretends unification or the self fabricates a coherent identity, the genealogist sets out to study the beginning—numberless beginnings, whose faint traces and hints of color are readily seen by a historical eye. The analysis of descent permits the dissociation of the self, its recognition and displacement as an empty synthesis, in liberating a profusion of lost events. (Foucault, 1984b: 81)

Although Althusser, Adorno, and Lévi-Strauss can claim that they sought to problematize the idea of the subject, Foucault was the only one who can claim to have really focused on the constitution of what we take "the subject" to be. Particularly in his later writing, Foucault seeks to understand the effect of social practices subjectively—this can be seen most clearly in *The Use of Pleasure* and *The Care of the Self,* the final installations of his *The History of Sexuality* trilogy. In these works, Foucault focuses on what he terms "technologies of self"—the practices by which the self is cultivated. Although this is an attempt at a deeper subjective understanding than that found in structuralist analysis, it is an understanding that has neither relinquished the structuralist concern with determination, nor Foucault's own concern with power. That is so is evident from *The Will to Knowledge,* the first volume of the trilogy, in which Foucault introduces the ideas of "bio-history" and "bio-power" (Foucault, 1978: 143). The human body, as conceived here by Foucault, was a body penetrated by techniques of knowledge and power, subjugated by them, despite all appearances. What was particularly stressed in this account was the issue of *normativization* and its deep interconnection with subjectivity.

Despite this greater focus on subjectivity, what is evident in the latter Foucault is the fact that his anti-foundationalism remains strong: "Nothing in man—not even his body—is sufficiently stable to serve as the basis for self-recognition or understanding of other men" (Foucault, 1984b: 87–88). His focus is now fully poststructuralist: searching for a descent, not for foundations, and with the aim of disturbing what was previously considered immobile so as to bring out its inherent fragmentation and heterogeneity. This was the continuation of Nietzsche's challenge of the pursuit of the origin (*Ursprung*): "The purpose of history, guided by genealogy, is not to discover the roots of our identity, but to commit itself to its dissipation. It does not seek to define our unique threshold of emergence, the homeland to which metaphysicians promise a return; it seeks to make visible all those discontinuities that cross us" (Foucault, 1984b: 95). Despite this anti-foundationalism and problematization of the self, Foucault is adamant that he wanted to reclaim possibilities for the constitution and development of the self, to "promote new forms of subjectivity" through the refusal of the "type of individualization which is linked to the state" (Foucault, 1982: 216).

His strategy for achieving this was based on a rejection of the traditional approach of striving for an essential freedom and its replacement with what he termed "agonism," a form of combat relationship, of permanent provocation, "which is at the same time reciprocal incitation and struggle" (Foucault, 1982: 222). This approach was justified on the insight that "power relations are rooted deep in the social nexus, not reconstituted 'above' society as a supplementary structure whose radical effacement one could perhaps dream of" (Foucault, 1982: 222).

The Anti-Humanist Paradigm—Part II

What was discussed in the preceding section was, in the main, the opposition to the traditional humanist notion of the subject as the agent of history and the predominantly structuralist analytical strategies of bypassing the subject in order to get to the truly determining categories of history (this and the rejection of traditional philosophical anthropology, more generally). In this section, I want to continue the discussion of the anti-humanist paradigm with reference to the thought of a number of thinkers—Jacques Lacan, Jacques Derrida, Jean-François Lyotard, and Richard Rorty—who, while having much in common with the those previously discussed, have a less overt connection to (or even an outright *dis*-connection from) Marxian thought, as well as a greater focus on the linguistic problematizing of the subject and the decentering of the self. Broadly poststructuralist (other than Lacan—who might have been swapped for Foucault but for the purpose of discussion), these thinkers can be seen to develop their thought to an extremity, the substance of which is useful to outline before engaging in deeper discussion of Fromm's radical humanism.

Lacan is a good place to start the second part of this discussion. A colleague of both Lévi-Strauss and Althusser, and a practicing psychoanalyst, Lacan famously proposed the "return to Freud" in which the unconscious was seen as "the whole structure of a language" (Lacan, 2001: 163). He sought to employ structural linguistics to explain the workings of the unconscious and, thereby, to illustrate the agency of language in the subjective constitution. This amounted to the fundamental decentering of the unconscious and thus the displacing of the constitutive power of the "I," involved as it is in a system of signification that precedes and constitutes it—"the subject, too, if he can appear to be the slave of language is all the more so of a discourse in the universal moment on which his place is already ascribed at birth, if only by virtue of his proper name" (Lacan, 2001: 163). Lacan, therefore, spoke of the unconscious as the "discourse of the Other," by which he means to signify that speech originates not with the Ego or the subject, but in the Other, and therefore beyond the subject's conscious control. Lacan also, in his account of the "mirror stage," sought to show that the positioned subject only emerges in the course of psychological development as the result of affective identification with its own specular image, or imago, which is in fact the creation of what he terms the "Ideal-I' (Lacan, 2001: 2). It is worth quoting Lacan in full here:

> This moment in which the mirror-stage comes to an end inaugurates, by the identification with the *imago* of the counterpart and the drama of primordial jealousy (so well brought out by the school of Charlotte Bühler in the phenomenon of infantile *transitivism*), the dialectic that will henceforth link the *I* to socially elaborated situations...It is this moment that decisively tips the whole of human knowledge into mediatization through the desire of the other, constitutes its objects in an abstract equivalence by the co-operation of others, and turns the I into that apparatus for which every instinctual thrust constitutes a danger, even though it should correspond to a natural maturation—the very normalization of this maturation being henceforth dependent, in man, on a cultural mediation as exemplified, in the case of the sexual object, by the Oedipus complex. (2001: 6)

But this is a misunderstanding (*méconnaissance*). What happens here is that the subject becomes alienated from itself and is integrated into the Imaginary order. Unlike existential philosophy, which posits a picture of the self-sufficiency of consciousness, Lacan wants to stress that it is fundamentally *méconnaissances* that constitute the ego, the sense of "I" being "the illusion of autonomy to which it entrusts itself" (Lacan, 2001: 7).

Lacan's concept of the person, then, is as radically *split* or *divided against* itself, the self denied any point of reference from which to be restored. Lacan, therefore, speaks of "the self's radical ex-centricity to itself" and criticizes "the moral tartufferies of our time [for] forever spouting something about the 'total personality' in order to have said anything articulate about the possibility of mediation" (Lacan, 2001: 189).

Who, if not us, will question once more the objective status of this "I," which a historical evolution peculiar to our culture tends to confuse with the subject? This anomaly should be manifested in its particular effects on every level of language, and first and foremost in the grammatical subject of the first person in our languages, in the "I love" that hypostatizes the tendency of a subject who denies it. An impossible mirage in linguistic forms among which the most ancient are to be found, and in which the subject appears fundamentally in the position of being determinant or instrumental of action. (Lacan, 2001: 26)

As such, Lacanian analysis is so arranged as to deconstruct the *méconnaissances* of the self and to enable the reclamation of the true fragmentary nature of being.

In the case of Derrida, we have a critique of structuralism that is in fact a continuation of certain of its anti-humanist themes. Generally described as a poststructuralist, what Derrida sought to offer was a qualified diversification of the semiotic principle as formulated by Saussure, which would reclaim writing for the field of linguistics as the paradigm form. In particular, Derrida was concerned to produce "a new concept of writing," which can be called *gram* or *différance* (Derrida, 1981: 26). *Différance* is understood by Derrida as "the systematic play of differences, of the traces of differences, of the *spacing* by means of which elements are related to each other" (Derrida, 1981: 27). Similarly to Foucault, Derrida was seeking to add dynamism to the structuralist account: "Neither fallen from the sky nor inscribed once and for all in a closed system, a static structure that a synchronic and taxonomic operation could exhaust... [d]ifferences are the effects of transformations, and from this vantage the theme of *différance* is incompatible with the static, synchronic, ahistoric motifs in the concept of *structure*" (Derrida, 1981: 27). But crucially, Derrida stresses that *différance* is not astructural: "It produces systematic and regulated transformations which are able, at a certain point, to leave room for a structural science. The concept of *différance* even develops the most legitimate principled exigencies of 'structuralism'" (Derrida, 1981: 28). Thus, despite the added dynamism brought in by the concept of *différance*, the subject is conceived as outside of the movement of *différance*. "There is," Derrida tell us, "no subject who is agent, author, and master of *différance*, who eventually and empirically would be overtaken by *différance*. Subjectivity—like objectivity—is an effect of *différance*, an effect inscribed in a system of *différance*" (Derrida, 1981: 28). The intention of this is to confirm what Saussure said about language—namely, that it "is not a function of the speaking subject" (Saussure, quoted in Derrida, 1981: 29). The subject for Derrida, then, "depends upon the system of differences and the movement of *différance*" and "is constituted only in being divided from itself, in becoming space, in temporizing, in deferral" (Derrida, 1981: 29).

In addition to, and as part of this decentering of the subject, Derrida's thought constitutes a challenge to the traditional "metaphysics of presence." Like Heidegger, Derrida tries to step outside of the Western metaphysical tradition, rejecting, as Heidegger did, the "correspondence theory of truth." For Derrida, all the conceptual oppositions of metaphysics "amount, at one moment or another, to a subordination of the movement of *différance* in favour of the presence of a value or a *meaning* supposedly antecedent to *différance*" (Derrida, 1981: 29). "The play of differences supposes, in effect, syntheses and referrals which forbid at any moment, or in any sense, that a simple element be *present* in and of itself, referring only to itself" (Derrida, 1981: 26). "*There is no thing outside of the text* [there is no outside text]" (Derrida, 1976: 158). Derrida here does not mean that there is nothing outside of the text in a literal sense, but that, following Saussure as much as Heidegger, a sign is always a substitution for another sign, with no anchoring point; there is nothing that is ever conceived of outside of differential opposition, and that therefore no singular beginning or origin is available to us.

> Whether in the order of spoken or written discourse, no element can function as a sign without referring to another element which itself is not simply present. This interweaving results in each "element"—phoneme or grapheme—being constituted on the basis of the trace within it of the other elements of the chain or system. This interweaving, this textile, is the *text* produced only in the transformation of another text. Nothing, neither among the elements nor within the system, is anywhere ever simply present or absent. There are only everywhere, differences and traces of traces. (Derrida, 1981: 26)

Nothing exists as pure difference (by which is meant nothing exists purely in and of itself), and thus there is nothing outside of context.

Jean-François Lyotard, friend and contemporary of Derrida, and one of the only thinkers to self-consciously appropriate the label "postmodern" (although even Lyotard's appropriation comes with caveats), represents a further deepening of the anti-humanist position—although in a particular way. In defining the postmodern as "incredulity toward metanarratives" (Lyotard, 1984: xxiv) and the reduction of everything to language games, there is even less room for the old humanist worldview. Lyotard can be seen as the most militant of those discussed, or at least the most expressive in his opposition to the traditional humanist and Enlightenment concerns. He explicitly and flamboyantly speaks out against the "white terror of truth," the "grip of the unity-totality," and "the chill of the clear and distinct" (Lyotard, 1993: 242), calling for us to "wage war on totality; let us be witness to the unpresentable; let us activate the differences and save the honor of the name" (Lyotard, 1984: 81–82). As with all post-structuralisms, however, Lyotard's is still tied to that which he seeks to supersede: "the possibility of reality, including the reality of the subject, is fixed in networks of names 'before' reality shows itself and signifies itself in an experience" (Lyotard, 1988: 46). The self does not exist in the reliable terms in which it is generally conceived: "a *self* does not amount to much, but no self is an island; each exists in a fabric of relations that is now more complex and mobile than ever before. Young or old, man or woman, rich or poor, a person is always located at 'nodal points' of specific communication circuits, however tiny these may be" (Lyotard, 1984: 15). In a similar manner to Foucault and Derrida, although more pronouncedly, Lyotard gives more stress to the celebration of difference and diversity. His stress on the heterogeneity of language games, or "phrase regimens," is used to denote the multiplicity of communities of meanings and the fact that we live in a world of such intensive and extensive difference that there can be no single story or account that synthesizes or adequately reconciles these differences.

What was central to Lyotard's account was the necessity of acting on the fact of the "impermissibility of universals." For Lyotard, justice and injustice can only exist in terms of language games, and so the universality of ethics is impossible. He stresses the "multiplicity of justices," and therefore that the justice of an idea can only be judged without determinate criteria. For Lyotard, the forwarding of prescriptive politics by appealing to a literal, describable state of things necessarily totalizes one narrative as literal and victimizes those excluded. Similarities to Foucault, with his allergy to any kind of authority, are evident here. In fact, Lyotard's idea of "paganism" has some crucial similarities to Foucault—particularly its aim of upsetting the given balance of power within a given area or field and his stress on the little narrative (*petit récit*). Where it can be said to go beyond Foucault is in its stress on the "divine affirmation of the singularity of events"; events conceived as energetic intensities that resist recuperation into utilities. Like Deleuze and Guattari's "schizophrenic" ethics, Lyotard focuses on *surviving* capitalism, rather than changing it, through the proliferation of desire.

Richard Rorty is an apt choice to bring the discussion of the anti-humanist paradigm to a close. He is in many ways the culmination of all the thinkers discussed in this section, but, as an American, perhaps, he translates the ideas held in common in revealing clarity. Like Derrida (and Heidegger before him), Rorty rejects the correspondence theory of truth (Rorty, 1980). All there are for Rorty are contingent "vocabularies"; only descriptions can be true or not, the world cannot, and the suggestion that the truth (and the world) is out there is "a legacy of an age in which the world was seen as the creation of a being who had a language of his own" (Rorty, 1989: 5). He also saw that the idea of the intrinsic self was a remnant of the idea that the world is a divine creation, and interpreted Freud as helping us see that there is no central faculty, no self, called "reason" (Rorty, 1989: 21, 33).[3] What is perhaps most characteristic of Rorty is the fact that he spoke of "solidarity" and "love"[4]—and therefore has a more outward connection to the traditional humanist paradigm than found in the other thinkers discussed—but that he does so directly alongside a stringent, anti-foundationalist pragmatism which de facto rules out any recourse to the idea of a common humanity. Rorty fully accepts the growing willingness to neglect the issue of human nature and the reference to ontology and history as a guide to living: "We have come to see that the main lesson of both history and anthropology is our extraordinary malleability. We are coming to think of ourselves as the flexible, protean, self-shaping animal rather than as the rational animal or the cruel animal" (Rorty, 1998: 169–170).

So Rorty was avowedly committed to the advancement of solidarity in the world, seeing moral progress as both real and attainable—but this does not consist for Rorty in the recognition of a human essence or a core self in all beings. In *Contingency, Irony, and Solidarity*, Rorty advances the argument that the reason some Jews were saved from the gas chambers was not because of an identification on the part of those doing the saving with the idea that the Jews shared in a common human nature but, rather, because of more parochial identifications such as "this particular Jew was a fellow Milanese, or a fellow Jutlander, or a fellow member of the same union or profession, or a fellow bocce player, or a fellow parent of small children" (Rorty, 1989: 190–191). For Rorty, local identifications such as these carry more force than the universalistic "one of us human beings" (Rorty, 1989: 190). In his Amnesty lecture "Human Rights, Rationality, and Sentimentality," which is published in his *Truth and Progress* collection, Rorty argues that "most people—especially people relatively untouched by the European Enlightenment—simply do not think of themselves as, first and foremost, a human being. Instead, they think of themselves as being a certain *good* sort of human being—a sort defined by explicit opposition to a particularly bad sort" (Rorty, 1998: 178). Moral progress toward solidarity, then, consists in the ability to see more and more traditional differences as unimportant when compared with similarities with respect to pain and humiliation (Rorty, 1989: 192).

For Rorty, this consists in the appeal to human rights as grounded in sentimentality (Rorty, 1998). Although Rorty claims that his concerns here have nothing to do with questions of realism and antirealism (which is strange, in that surely this is what his earlier position as regards the correspondence theory of truth seems to entail), he advocates dropping foundationalism and concentrating our energies on manipulating sentiments and on sentimental education. This ties up with his picture of a *liberal ironist utopia* in which citizens are fully aware of their placement in history and of their philosophical vocabulary but who have extended (and continue extending) their sense of "we" to others who we previously thought of as "they" (Rorty, 1989: 192). As Rorty explains, his ironist is someone who fulfills the following three conditions: "(1) She has radical and continuing doubts about the final vocabulary she currently uses, because she has been impressed by other vocabularies, vocabularies taken as final by people or books she has encountered; (2) she realizes that argument phrased in her present vocabulary can neither underwrite nor dissolve these doubts; (3) insofar as she philosophizes about her situation, she does not think that her vocabulary is closer to reality than others, that it is in touch with a power not herself" (Rorty, 1989: 73). Rorty is clear on the purpose of this ideal liberal society, which is nothing other than to "make life easier for poets and revolutionaries" (Rorty, 1989: 60–61).

The issues stemming from this discussion of the anti-humanist paradigm are many and varied and not suited for containment in a single chapter. I will discuss the most immediately pertinent ones presently, but the discussion will not be completed—to the extent it can be completed at all—until chapter 6.

Humanism and Human Nature

Contrary to the thinkers discussed above, Fromm's thought is conceived and conveyed in relative continuity with the themes of the Renaissance and Enlightenment humanists. Despite the fact that he saw them as lacking a proper understanding of the connections between theory and practice—and therefore as inferior to Marx, who was in other respects their heir—Fromm praised the Renaissance and Enlightenment humanists as the guardians of the Judaeo-Christian messianic ideal. This ideal—the "messianic time" of the prophets, to be realized in the here and now through development of our capacities for love and reason—was the guiding principle of Fromm's thought. As was shown in chapter 2, the idea of messianism is premised on the idea of universalism implied in the ideal. Fromm's rather archaic language—in particular, his use of the generic, sexless "man"—is a manifestation of this connection, and this, together with his other humanist "baggage," clearly puts him at variance with the axioms of the anti-humanist paradigm. A Marxian who criticized Freud for his ethnocentrism and who had an appreciation of the importance of cultural diversity and the constitutive power of language, Fromm was, nevertheless, outspoken in his criticism of the relativistic denial of a universal humanity. Particularly critical of the idea, increasingly popular as the twentieth century wore on, of the human being as "a blank sheet of paper on which culture writes its text" (2006 [1962]: 21), Fromm argued that there *is* a human nature characteristic of the human species—not fixed and unchangeable, but not infinitely malleable or conditionable either:

> It is true that man can adapt himself even to unsatisfactory conditions, but in this process of adaptation he develops definite mental and emotional reactions which follow from the specific properties of his own nature... He can adapt himself to almost any cultural pattern, but in so far as these are contradictory to his nature he develops mental and emotional disturbances which force him eventually to change these conditions since he cannot change his nature. (2003 [1947]: 15–16)

The human being, for Fromm, is "an entity charged with energy and structured in specific ways" (2003 [1947]: 16); and while this entity is always embedded in a culture and society, the conditions of this embedding are predicated on the priority of the ontological structure of the kind of entity that the human being is.

Talk of "human nature," or of the human "essence," is generally viewed as embarrassing today, associated with restrictive, reactionary thinking that is seen to stem from (or even be a direct part of) outmoded theological discourse. What must be openly stressed here is that Fromm's discussion of "the human situation," as he often liked to call it, *does* have some connection to this discourse. His idea of the existential dichotomy, as discussed in chapter 3, clearly has certain parallels to the Judaeo-Christian idea of the fundamental split in man's nature. But although sometimes expressed with the aid of biblical analogy, Fromm was concerned that his account of the fundamental human dichotomy be put forward as consistent with evolutionary biology. In *The Anatomy of Human Destructiveness*, Fromm is unequivocal: "We have to arrive at an understanding of man's nature on the basis of the blend of the two fundamental biological conditions that mark the emergence of man" (1997 [1973]: 300). The first of these conditions is "the ever decreasing determination of behaviour by instincts"; the other is "the growth of the brain, and particularly the neocortex" (1997 [1973]: 300–301). As such, Fromm concludes that "man can be defined as the primate that emerged at the point of evolution where instinctive determination had reached a minimum and the development of brain a maximum" (1997 [1973]: 302). The idea of the existential dichotomy (or contradiction in existence) can, then, on this view, be seen as the result of a unique break in the evolutionary process (the "freak of nature"), and, therefore, as consistent with an evolutionary biological understanding. Emerging at a certain and definable point in evolutionary history, the species Homo sapiens is constituted by the inheritance of certain distinguishing features—morphological, anatomical, physiological, and neurological data—which mark it out as a distinct species (1997 [1973]: 27).

In a posthumously published essay, Fromm describes his account, in fact, as "sociobiological" (1992: 6). With a welcoming willingness to attempt to bridge the generally upheld sectarian divide between sociology and biology, Fromm criticizes as a false dichotomy the view that the two are fundamentally removed. The account Fromm offers, it must be stressed, is clearly far from a stereotypical representative of accounts that generally go under the name "sociobiological." It does, however, share in one crucial aspect: namely, the understanding of the human condition as the result of Homo sapiens having emerged at a particular point in evolutionary history and as primarily motivated with the pan-evolutionary concern for survival. It is obvious that, in his account, Fromm does not ignore sociology and is not guilty of biological reductionism, as is found in the more stereotypical sociobiological accounts. His idea of the "evolutionary break" is a clear recognition of the relative indeterminacy of human nature as made possible through the reduction in instinctive fixation that characterizes human existence (and thus of the role of social and cultural determinants), and his account of character is explicit in its acknowledgment of the variety of responses to this relative indeterminacy.

As was noted in chapter 2, Fromm saw his account here as fundamentally in keeping with the distinction Marx makes in *Capital* between human nature *in general*, and human nature as *historically modified* (Marx, 1990: 758–759). This distinction, which Fromm makes explicit reference to, allows that in the human being a nature exists that is relatively constant but that there are also many variable factors that lead to the constitution of different types of human beings, that is to say, different cultural manifestations in different times and different places (and within the same time and place, as his characterology suggests). The human being, in acting upon external nature, changes it, and thereby simultaneously changes its own nature (although to say it changes its own nature is to say it changes its nature as manifest, not the underlying biological or ontological constitution, which remains relatively permanent—at least on the historical timescale in which Homo sapiens have existed). Crucially, Fromm's "sociobiological" account is also psychologically informed. This can be seen as a further extrapolation of the evolutionary biological principle: since Homo sapiens can be defined in anatomical, neurological, and physiological terms, then surely they can also be defined in psychical terms. As was seen, Fromm's idea of character is conceived as a dynamic adaptation to reality (and his idea of the social character as a dynamic adaptation to the structure of society): "The sociobiological orientation is centered around the problem of survival. Its fundamental question is: How can man, given his physiological and neurophysiological apparatus, as well as his existential dichotomies, survive physically and mentally?" (1992: 6). His account then can be seen as *biopsychosocial*, and thus avoids reduction to any of the three levels accommodated in it.

Although Fromm's account, as outlined above, is useful in its willingness to try to combine biology, sociology, and psychology, it has been charged with anthropocentrism. What must be said is that Fromm does, in fact, appear guilty of anthropocentrism on a number of occasions. His idea of the "evolutionary break" itself, with the distinction made between the "active" nature of man and the "passive" nature of other animals, and his suggestion that animals live in "harmony" with nature, would seem to be a prime example of this. David Ingleby, in his introduction to the Routledge edition of *The Sane Society*, jumps on this as evidence of Fromm's impoverished view of animal sentience. But while Fromm's language here is poorly chosen, and his distinction overwrought, it is clear that he cannot mean "passive" in the sense that Ingleby takes him to mean. Fromm explicitly states that animals *do* possess intelligence (2002 [1955]: 23); similarly, Fromm qualifies what he means by "harmony": that is, that the animal has a specific ecological niche (as compared to our pan-ecological niche). It is also clear that Fromm's distinction between humans and animals, while overstated, does not spill over into an exploitative attitude toward animals and the natural world. Yes, the working on—and development of—nature is part of his account of a productive human life (belying the Marxian influence as much as any religious influence); but, as his account of technological domination and of the destructiveness of humanity more generally (discussed more fully in chapter 6) shows, Fromm is not anthropocentric in an unreflective sense. For, while Fromm offers a generally overwrought distinction between humans and other animals (done in characteristic binary fashion so as to draw out the essence of what it means to be human), he explicitly calls for a "new ethic" toward and attitude of "cooperation" with nature (2009 [1976]: 7, 131), criticizing the preoccupation with conquering nature that has dominated the more recent part of human history. An adherent of the messianic vision of harmony between mankind and nature, the relationship between humanity and nature in Fromm, then, most logically centers on "the progressive realisation of human potential and the transformation of relations between human nature and non-human nature, in which respect for the latter is a sign of the maturity of the former" (Wilde, 2004b: 168).

While this is so, his idea of an "evolutionary break" simply does not equate to the current biological accounts of human evolution. As Cortina (1996) has pointed out, there is an overemphasis in Fromm on evolutionary discontinuities. Citing John Bowlby's attachment theory and Stephen Jay Gould's concept of *neotony*,[5] Cortina contends that "humans did not evolve by 'losing' their instinctual equipment but by its transformation" (Cortina, 1996: 123), and that where humans diverge from other primates is in the meaning that pro-social ties come to have for them. The increase in behavioral flexibility evidenced in primate evolution, as Cortina argues, is not due to our "break" with nature, and thus the dualistic aspect of Fromm's thought here is unfortunate. Cortina (1996), Cortina and Lotti (2010 and Forthcoming) and Ted Benton (2009; 1999; 1991) have written extensively on this matter, stressing the naturalistic basis and, in Benton's words, the human/animal continuism, that ought to inform any account of human nature. Fromm's account is laudable, however, even if ultimately overstated, in his stress that "man has to be looked upon in all his concreteness as a physical being placed in a specific psychical and social world with all the limitations and weaknesses that follow from this aspect of his existence" (Fromm and Xirau, 1979 [1968]: 9). On such a reading, it is possible to redeem the worst excesses of this common dualism, even if it might be more accurate to see our ways of living as extensions (sometimes extensions where it is hard to see this origin) of more common animal needs.[6]

In both instances discussed above—the hyperbolic (and incorrect) choice of a "break" with nature as explaining the characteristic evolutionary status of Homo sapiens, and the implications this can be seen to have for other animal species—the legacy of Fromm's religious past can be seen as partly to blame. That said, relative freedom from instinct, though wrongly conceived by Fromm as fully unique to humans, is certainly *particularly* evidenced in humans. The "break" that Fromm posits, then, is less a renunciation of the evolutionary principle than a *diversification within it*. And though Fromm's account is based on an outmoded biological conception (including his occasional remarks on the distinction between humans and animals), the fact of differentiated continuity does not alter the basic constitution: reduced rigidity of instinct-patterns, more freedom, development of conscience, compassion, guilt, awareness, etc., *do* amount to, if not a contradiction or dichotomy, then certainly a *predicament* or *condition*, which can be said to be more pronounced in humans than in other species. What is important is that, despite his misconception of the evolutionary process as manifested in human beings taken in themselves and as considered vis-à-vis other species', Fromm's account is much fuller in this regard than the various anti-humanist thinkers so lauded today. What is characteristic of their various accounts is the lack of any significant reference to the human being in whatever sense.

In these accounts, a positive picture of "man" (Homo sapiens, the human being) is more or less absent. What I want to argue here is that Fromm's reliance on an outmoded biological model is less serious a problem than the apparent ignorance (or at least willful neglect) of biological theories in toto. Even if it is the case that the accounts of the various anti-humanist thinkers discussed were formed partly with the intention of countering crude naturalistic descriptions, the lacuna remains and is something that is far from inconsequential in terms of the overall sufficiency of the accounts in question. As it turns out, Fromm's idea of man as the "freak of nature," although not intended in this sense and not really legitimate (in that they do not tend to speak of "nature" at all), is rather fitting as a description of the undefined referent in most anti-humanist accounts—a being without any apparent connection to the natural world from which it arises and in which it inescapably resides. This effective *naturephobia* (Benton, 2001) stems, in fact, from a deeper antiessentialist, anti-ontological, and even antirealist worldview. Though this issue affects all those discussed above to various degrees, and is the main flaw in their accounts, perhaps the most illustrative example is that of Rorty, whose clear and straightforward attempt to formulate a theory of human rights on a nonessentialist basis is revealing in its failure. That Rorty's account fails, taken on its own terms, has been convincingly argued by Norman Geras in *Solidarity in the Conversation of Humankind*.

As was shown above, Rorty's liberal ironist approach to solidarity is based on an anti-foundationalist pragmatism which rejects the existence, and, therefore, argumentative recourse to, the idea of a human nature. What Geras shows is that, despite his proclamations to the contrary, Rorty's account actually *relies* on a conception of human nature.[7] Rorty's denial is, therefore, rhetorical, and cannot be sustained. Geras notes that this comes about through a "continual shifting of ground, so that now in one, now another meaning, a human nature is denied by Rorty, even while in one or other of the meanings not currently being denied a human nature is also implicitly affirmed by him" (Geras, 1995: 48–49).

In fact, Geras notes that Rorty, seemingly oblivious to what he is doing, actually advances a universalist basis for extensive solidarity in his focus on pain and humiliation. In his stress on these potentialities, Rorty is clearly falling back on something intrinsic in the human (and, as it happens, animal) condition. As Geras notes, if we truly do just invent our own nature, then why not make one up that is immune to suffering, humiliation, etc.? "Why not just tinker with ourselves so that we are never hungry etc?" (Geras, 1995: 67) Crucially, Geras points out that the basis to Rorty's juggling here is the framing of his argument such that "in order to subscribe to a notion of human nature you must be committed to something so excessively narrow and specific as to have to overlook differences, historical, cultural, or simply inter-individual, that are manifest and impossible to deny" (Geras, 1995: 49). This applies in many instances of the denial of human nature—and was something of which Fromm was acutely aware (Fromm and Xirau, 1979 [1968]: 5). This outright (or effective) denial of the human body is a continuation of anti-ontology, which can even be found in Foucault. Despite the fact that Foucault talks of "the body" and the practices that work on it, his discussion is relatively contentless with respect to what the body actually *is*. There is no talk of *what* it is about the body that allows society to do the things it does to it. As Margaret Archer has noted, the fascination with "the body" has actually been the final chapter in the project of demolishing humanity: "Bodies are no longer respected as something non-reductively material, which mediate our traffic with the world, but only as a permeable medium which takes the ideational impress" (Archer, 2000: 316). Ultimately, Foucault lacks any "embedding structures" at all, even though they provide some of the criteria upon which the "creative activity" that is implied in his later accounts of the "care of the self" and the "art of living" makes sense. His criticism of grandiose humanisms that conceal technologies of power behind their mask of benign progressivism is good and important, but it misses these more basic fundamental connections.

Although he does not speak as clearly as Rorty, or even Foucault, Adorno too can be said to be seeking his own ideal society—a "true" or "real" humanism (Thornhill, 2005). The problem for Adorno is that his nonidentity process philosophy suffers from a similar, but distinct, problem to that of Rorty's liberal ironist anti-foundationalism. Whereas Rorty rejects the idea of essential human qualities but then brings them in through the back door, any significant reference to the human being as a particular entity is conspicuous by its absence in Adorno's account. That this is so is necessitated by Adorno's extreme concept of reification in which all individual qualities are inexorably reduced to the exchange nexus that totally dominates society.[8] His negative dialectical nonidentity philosophy that goes with it is supposed to offer a privileged point of access to this domination; despite this, it really must be asked: what is "nonidentity" other than the realization that concepts are not fulfilled? What is certain is that a lot of effort and verbiage is involved in Adorno's thinking here; how far it gets it is, however, debatable, despite its undeniable conceptual accuracy. A strong case could be made that it does not get very far at all—and certainly not far enough to rule out the older, more traditional forms of thought against which it was composed. Essentially, the defining feature of Adorno's negative dialectics, in this connection, seems to boil down to the idea that to think dialectically means to think in contradictions: the idea is that thinking in contradictions would obviate the need to dominate through conceptual identification. But while this is so, Adorno himself states that "we can see through the identity principle, but we cannot think without identifying. And definition is identification" (Adorno, 1973: 149). Either this is ironic or it is contradictory (and not in a "dialectical" sense). The fact that he states that definition also approaches that which the object itself is in its nonidenticality—that "nonidentity is the secret *telos* of identification. It is the part that can be salvaged; the mistake in traditional thinking is that identity is taken for the goal" (Adorno, 1973: 149)—suggests the latter option.[9] The argument really does not seem to be particularly remarkable at all. That "'A' is to be what is not yet" (Adorno, 1973: 150), while agreeable, is clearly already implied in traditional Marxian thought, and, in turn, is clearly appreciated by Fromm.

Incidentally, this can also be said to apply to Derrida. If, as is the case, Derrida does not mean that there literally is nothing outside of the text, and therefore corporeality and sensuousness (and an external world) are not ruled out, then he does not seem to be so disagreeable (incidentally, it is notable that Lyotard criticizes Derrida in the former instance for effectively ruling corporeality and sensuousness out)[10]. But even if it is accepted that there is no such thing as pure difference, no singular position from which to begin, in what sense does this amount to the denial of traditional metaphysics? If he is suggesting that the constituents of the world are inextricably bound together—even if more than is ordinarily thought to be the case—then "the world" (as inclusive of these constituents) still remains as the basis upon which these things are bound. If he is suggesting that we cannot know the world other than through interpretation, then it is a suggestion that is neither particularly unique nor powerful; moreover, it is guilty of what Roy Bhaskar has termed the "epistemic fallacy" namely, the definition of being in terms of knowledge (Bhaskar, 2008: 16). Even though Derrida's thought has its own strategy and own important sphere of relevance, its focus ensures the denigration of human sensuous qualities and their biological (although, of course, not only biological) structurings.

The issue here is an excessive constructionism, and it is found in all anti-humanist thinkers. It points at the necessity for ontology (in the realist sense), biology, and a form of essentialism *alongside* the appreciation of the insights of constructionism—otherwise, thought tends to give way to an excessive culturalism and/or linguistic relativism. Although the opposition to realism, biology, and essentialism is generally conflated, it is particularly essentialism that is objected to. The fact that it is so routinely objected to is partly understandable. Essentialism—the view of the world as consisting of entities that can be meaningfully and knowledgably distinguished from one another based on what we know about them—has, for a long time, been associated with ahistorical, reactionary, and regressive thinking, positing human beings as unchanging and reified, and thus belying a naïve unrelational understanding. Such simplistic, pre-sociological thought is rightly opposed. However, when it is said that "there is no such thing as a human nature," the person making the statement is either speaking incoherently or is trying to deny an inadequate conception of human nature—and you do not prove the nonexistence of something by arguing against an inadequate conception of it. They may be seeking to denounce some unduly reactionary conceptions of human nature that focus either fatalistically upon a set of characteristics often exhibited by members of the human species (such as the idea of humans as naturally lazy or selfish) or discriminatorily on the defilement of certain societal taboos (such as in the case of homosexuality or women working in "masculine" professions). But after these denunciations, the problems that Geras identified in Rorty's account will remain.

An ontological view of the world that does not deny the very existence of that world necessitates an at least *basic* essentialism, that is to say, the idea that the world is made up of irreducible entities that belong to particular kinds of things by virtue of their essence (essence here simply denoting that by virtue of which a thing is what it is—this idea making at least some reference to underlying ontological structures). As Fromm himself noted, we "must start out with the premise that something, say X, is reacting to environmental influences in ascertainable ways that follow from its properties" (2003 [1947]: 15). This, in its original and literal sense, is all that "metaphysics" need entail (ontology and essentialism merely being further descriptive realms of metaphysical inquiry). This is what every structuralist, linguistic, and poststructuralist account is predicated on, whether it accepts this is the case or not. We are only affected by structures, language, etc., *because* of the kind of being we are. Yes, we are inescapably relational beings; but relations cannot exist without referring, in some sense, to some kinds of wholes that relate.[11] It is an elementary logical point that to acknowledge that something is never in existence on its own, strictly speaking, is not to deny its existence per se: there are many things that are not ontologically distinct but are, nonetheless, identifiable features of life (for instance, we do not deny the existence of language and relations of production even though they cannot be said to be ontologically separate realities). Just because the general, natural characteristics of human beings are not fully separate, ontologically independent from qualities that are culturally induced, that is not to say that there is no such thing as "human nature." A failure to see this is a failure to appreciate categorical thought and the validity of abstraction.

Importantly, the recognition of a human "essence" or "nature" in no way precludes the mutual recognition of the facticity of culture, language, or whatever else one wants to point to. To recognize the existence of a human essence or nature is simply to recognize the logical counterpart to our manifest variability and conditioning (manifest variability and conditioning being part of such a nature). Fromm himself remarks: "If [man] lives under conditions which are contrary to his nature and to the basic requirements for human growth and sanity he cannot help but *reacting*: he must either deteriorate and perish, or bring about conditions which are more in accordance with his needs" (2002 [1955]: 19). Again, it is quite an elementary logical point that a reaction presupposes the existence of some *thing* that reacts; some *thing*, which, by virtue of the properties it possesses, is affected by the determining influence; some *thing* that is therefore distinct from this influence, although it may also be largely determined by it. So while we are not immutably set, we are not *tabulae rasae* either; we are not free-floating and centerless—if we were, there would be no reaction, no development or underdevelopment, and, ultimately, no human.

Having said this, there is clearly much more work that needs to be done in the specification of what this essence is—a difficult, if ever completely realizable task. Although Fromm's contribution to psychology is crucial in pointing to what is surely a generally universal facet of human life, his account of the evolutionary biology that underlies it was overstated, if not dualist, and his account of the "existential needs" was imprecise and inconclusive, as helpful as it was that he offered it in the first place. What is clear is that essentialism needs to mix productively with constructionism, enabling it to properly accommodate the relational and processural reality of life alongside its own truth—in fact, a proper essentialist account would include as part of its description these relational and processural facts. As much as this is so, the essentialism/antiessentialism binary dichotomy is far too blunt. The resolution is to be found through refinement in a qualified essentialism[12] similar to that which Fromm offers. Some critical realist thinkers— particularly Ted Benton, Margaret Archer, and Christian Smith—have been working on similar ground here. Benton calls for a social theory to make the case for naturalism (which is more or less what I mean by essentialism here) that avoids the pitfalls of unwarranted reductionism (Benton, 2009). Although Archer's work focuses predominantly on the resolution of the structure/agency problem and the mapping out of a sociology consonant with such a resolution, she is explicit in her recognition of homo sapiens as "a natural kind" and that "our particular species-being, endows us with various potentials, whose full development is socially congruent, whose pre-existence allows us to judge whether social conditions are dehumanising or not" (Archer, 2007: 144). Christian Smith, who has gone further than Archer in essentialist terrain, has sought in recent years to develop "a theoretical model of the ontology of the nature of human being" linked to a "descriptive anthropology of human personhood" (Smith, 2003: 10, 5). Smith's account here shows many thematic connections to Fromm's attempt to explain the human situation, although he notably fails to make any mention of Fromm, whose work fulfills many of the criteria he lays down, including having a well-developed theory of the human unconscious (Smith, 2010: 44).

The connections between critical realism and essentialism, in fact, are potentially extremely fruitful—the idea of something essential in what it is to be human corresponding with the idea of underlying ontological structures centrally advanced by critical realist thought. The critical realist stress on the phenomenon of "emergence" (the creation of new, higher-level properties through the combination of lower-level properties to which the higher-level properties are irreducible) allows the world to be seen as composed of a variety of stratified levels—the following list of levels provided by Smith giving an idea of the kind of complexity involved: subatomic, atomic, molecular, chemical, biological, zoological, ecological, meteorological, mental, social, global, galactic, and cosmological (Smith, 2010: 35). Though these levels are distinct and are dealt with at the highest level by the specialized sciences devoted to studying them, they are all fundamentally connected, and it is only through the recognition of these connections *at the same time as* studying the irreducible realities found at each level that we get an accurate picture of the world. Although Fromm does not formulate the idea of emergence explicitly, it is clearly implied in his work. His account of man's essence as "contradiction in existence," while not reducible to one strata, explicitly makes reference to underlying evolutionary reality, and thus with reference to biology and psychology. Similarly, his social-psychological account of character is not reducible to biology or psychology, but does make significant reference to them. Connected to this discussion is the need to tease out Marx's distinction between human nature in general and as modified, finding empirical evidence that it exists, and being able to specify with greater certainty what can said to be the existential needs of man. Suffice it to say that the issues involved here are immensely complex and not conducive to a short and straightforward definitive answer. I hope to pursue the connections involved in a further study.

The Subject and the Self

The same antiessentialism that leads the anti-humanist thinkers to reject any positive substantial account of the human being as an entity is also effective (and necessarily so) in the inability of these very thinkers to provide a positive and meaningful account of the human being as a subject possessed

of causative agentic powers. Without an idea of the human being as a particular natural kind possessing particular natural, but also culturally mediated,
qualities, it becomes close to impossible to offer such an account on any consistent kind of basis. The failure of the anti-humanist schemes to sufficiently
stress that (and/or explain why) agents possess properties distinct from the
determining forces of structural forms, therefore, is ultimately detrimental
to the sufficiency of the account offered. In the case of Fromm, however, the
idea of a subject possessed of causative agentic powers is central, working
alongside his idea of the determination of the individual by cultural and
unconscious factors. As early as 1929, Fromm makes his position clear, quoting the following passage from Marx: "History does nothing, it possesses no
immense wealth, it fights no battles. It is instead the human being, the real
living person, who does everything, who owns everything, and who fights all
battles" (1989 [1929]: 39). For Fromm, "the basic entity of the social process
is the individual his desires and fears, his passions and reason, his propensity
for good and evil. To understand the dynamics of the social process we must
understand the dynamics of the psychological processes operating within
the individual, just as to understand the individual we must see him in the
context of the culture which molds him" (1969 [1941]: x). Fromm, who is
in direct opposition to structuralist thought here, takes the opposite lesson
from history that Rorty took: namely, that history has shown man to be an
agent whose intrinsic properties react strenuously against powerful pressures
and unfavorable social and cultural circumstances (2003 [1947]: 15).

As was argued in chapter 4, although Fromm's account of the social
process is less developed than it might have been in terms of its depiction
of social structure and social institutions, it is an account that manages to
retain a central place for the social actor. Fromm saw the structure of a society as largely, but not wholly, defining the individuals within it, with these
individuals always retaining the potential for agentic, subjective creation. In
as much as this is the case, Fromm's thought begins from a superior position to that of the anti-humanist thinkers, who tend to effectively write out
agency in any significant sense. This is important, for without the idea of a
subject we can have no recourse to capacities for self-reflection and self-ac-
tualization, and thus cannot account for the lived nature of much of human
life represented in the idea of personal agency. In the same manner that
the almost total lack of explicit statement as to what it means to be human
detracts from the explanatory power of the anti-humanist accounts, their
failure to adequately account for the social actor makes individual change,
innovation, and creativity almost unimaginable in their systems.

This denigration of the subject is, of course, the result of decades of
unsustainable sociological reductionism that is kept in place in large

measure by virtue of the rigid separation of the disciplines. That this is so has been stressed by certain recent prominent sociological thinkers, most impressive of whom perhaps being Margaret Archer. Archer, in a particularly promising development (even if, in fact, a redevelopment), has focused on the empirical study of the "internal conversation" (Archer, 2000; 2007), showing that "reflexivity"—the regular exercise of mental ability—is necessary for day-to-day activity and thus central to the mediation of structure. Playing the role of mediator between the objective structural or cultural power and social action, it is indispensable to the societal process, and thus to the reality of the phenomena to which structuralist thought outlines. But what enables this reflexivity? Surely, as Archer herself notes: a "continuous sense of self" (Archer, 2000: 2), or, in psychological language, what is more plainly known as *the self*. It is important to be clear about what is being spoken of here. The self, or rather, the *psychological* self, describes the *reflective function* of the subject, that is to say, the cognitive and affective representation of one's identity (or, in plainer terms still, the *subject of experience*). So as to avoid accusations of unempirical etherealness, this idea of the self can be conceived in essentialist terms—that is to say, with connection to the functioning of the human organism to which it is inescapably connected. Archer herself is clear on this, stressing that our continuous sense of self emerges from our practical activity in the world and relates to this activity as the necessary facilitator (Archer, 2000: 3).

Over and above Archer and her important sociological recognition of the naturalistic basis of the self, Antonio Damasio, writing from a neurobiological perspective, has theorized the biological rootedness of the self. Using the grounding reference of the body—in which the brain is inescapably and integrally implicated—Damasio contends that the experience of self is rooted in successive neural states, in ongoing mental processes that form part of the functioning of the human organism. By reference to a distinction between the core consciousness of what he calls the "core self," "a transient entity, ceaselessly re-created for each and every object with which the brain interacts" and the self of extended consciousness of what he calls the "autobiographical self," constitutive of systematized memories of core consciousness (Damasio, 2000: 17), Damasio seeks to resolve William James's apparent paradox of the continuing but always present (and therefore ever-new) sense of self. The solution that he offers is found in the simple fact that the seemingly changing self and the seemingly permanent self, although closely related, are not one entity, so to speak, but in fact two (Damasio, 2000: 217). As Damasio says:

> At any given moment of our sentient lives...we generate pulses of core consciousness for one or a few target objects and for a set of accompanying,

reactivated autobiographical memories. Without such autobiographical memories we would have no sense of past or future, there would be no historical continuity to our persons. But without the narrative of core consciousness and without the transient core self that is born within it, we would have no knowledge whatsoever of the moment, of the memorized past, or of the anticipated future that we also have committed to memory. Core consciousness is a foundational must. It takes precedence, evolutionarily and individually, over the extended consciousness we now have. And yet, without extended consciousness, core consciousness would not have the resonance of past and future. The interlocking of core and extended consciousness, of core and autobiographical selves, is complete. (Damasio, 2000: 218–219)

This discussion of Damasio is important. The idea of the differentiated self as rooted in (neuro)biology acts as an important challenge to anti-humanist thought, particularity its excessively relativist or culturalist aspects.[13] First of all, it must be stressed that the claim that the self is wholly a product of socialization, as is often contended by anti-humanist thinkers, is clearly erroneous. As Archer has pointed out (and as is evident from Damasio's neurobiological writings), we clearly have a pre-linguistic developmental sense of self. From birth we are possessed of a developing, *practical*, sense of self which pre- and antedates language acquisition—a sense of self that is ontologically inviolable (Archer, 2000: 2). As Archer notes, socialization is dependent on this sense of self and the crucial ability it offers to make the primary distinction between self and others. The sense of self, therefore, is primarily *monological* not dialogical, as it is commonly held to be in anti-humanist thought. In saying this, it must be stressed that to argue the foregoing is not to say that dialogue plays no part—dialogue clearly plays a crucial role in the development of selfhood, supplanting in many ways, but never wholly, the monological self in the construction of the adult individual. Neither is it to deny the constitutive power of language—Freud has shown that even the unconscious speech of the body (in hysterical paralyses, for instance) is conditioned by language (Freud, 1953). The point being stressed here is that ignoring the naturalist presuppositions which make language and socialization possible, is an elementary and surprisingly common mistake among linguistically based social theorists and one that is significantly detrimental to the sufficiency of their accounts. That this is so, applies to none more than Lacan.

Lacan, as with others, seems to ignore that the ability to learn a language presupposes certain physical attributes: vocal chords, and certain innate abilities to think and talk, to string words together in a certain order, etc. Even the ability to recognize oneself in the mirror presupposes certain abilities of a subject for recognition that precede language (Craib, 1989: 123).[14] In fact, Lacan's mirror argument "fails to specify the psychic processes interior to the individual which makes misrecognition possible—for the individual to even begin to recognize itself in the 'mirror' it must surely already possess a more rudimentary sense of self" (Craib, 1989: 110). As such, "the human subject is not constituted as 'self-divided' merely because of its insertion into language. Rather, the traumatic divisions and splits which people experience via the whole field of the socio-symbolic order are intimately linked to concrete relations of power and ideology" (Elliott, 2002: 110). This picture is very close to that which Fromm puts forward.

The idea of existence of more than one self is an idea widely taken as given today. Stephen Mitchell speaks of a "plural or manifold organization of self, patterned around different self and object images or representations, derived from different relational contexts," saying that "we are all composites of overlapping, multiple organizations and perspectives" and that "our experience is smoothed over by an illusory sense of continuity" (Mitchell, 1993: 104). He notes that studies of bilingual patients suggest, especially when one language is learnt at a developmentally later point, that the languages reflect very different "orientations of self," and that this suggests "discontinuous, variously organized, developmentally sequenced versions of self" (Mitchell, 1993: 105). He says further that "discontinuities in self-organization are part of what enriches life, enabling conflicted domains of experience to be developed without the pressure of continual moderation and integration" (Mitchell, 1993: 105). But in a literal sense, of course, the idea of more than one self is incoherent. A self relates in a one-to-one relationship to the individual biological organism that is the human being. While this is so, it is surely the case that we can have multiple or conflicted orientations of self or, perhaps better, multiple or conflicted orientations of *identity* (to a greater or lesser degree, this is the very reality of mental functioning, corresponding to the different voices we generally use in our internal conversation); it also does not preclude a person *feeling* that they literally have multiple selves. The idea of conflicted orientations or self or identity is clearly not alien to Fromm's thinking. As has been shown, Fromm opposes existentialism and therefore rejects a view of the self as simply self-sufficient. At the same time, he does not see the self as necessarily decentered. It is a corollary of his essentialism that a self exists, and a corollary of his psychoanalytic position that the self is dynamic, overlapping, and potentially divided against itself (this latter point is the basis for much of his social criticism). But even if dynamic, overlapping, and divided, there is some *thing* or *capacity* that mediates, to a greater or lesser degree, the dynamism, overlapping, and division. We can acknowledge the existence of more than one *aspect* of self in the ongoing process of identity formation, but can still say that we respond, or are capable or responding, in terms of our "majority self" (Stevens, 1983: 10).

As Bentall has put it, the self is not a *thing*, as Cartesians assume, but a "set of ideas, pictures or beliefs (or, to use a generic term, *mental representations*) about who we are; some of these representations are explicit and available for contemplation, but others are implicit and take the form of vague assumptions or 'schemas'" (Bentall, 2003: 199). Like most mental representations, the self has fluid boundaries and overlaps with other kinds of thoughts and feelings, which is why it defies precise definition. Bentall suggests Daniel Dennett's metaphor of the self as the "centre of narrative gravity," which, like the center of gravity of a physical body, cannot be isolated and touched but around which our memories, stories that we tell about ourselves, and decisions we make, all revolve. We can, then, see the self as a stored reservoir of knowledge about the personality as the bedrock from which all other aspects of the self are derived. The point is that even in cases of multiple, conflicted orientations of self, agentic power is possible, and that a focus on this rather than on theoretically ruling it out is preferable.

A related issue that should be dealt with here is the common assertion that the experience of the self as discrete, bounded, and continuous, is a peculiarly "Western" phenomenon. Although the preceding discussion clearly indicates that this idea is erroneous, it is worth dealing with in some detail, seeing as it is surprisingly well-lodged in traditions of social theoretical thought with an affinity to the culturalist aspects of the anti-humanist paradigm. A classic influence in this regard is Clifford Geertz's "From the Native's Point of View." What Geertz argues here, after showing how peoples of different cultures have different concepts of self and personhood, is that "the Western conception of the person as a bounded, unique, more or less integrated motivational and cognitive universe, a dynamic center of awareness, emotion, judgment, and action organized into a distinctive whole and set contrastively both against other such wholes and against its social and natural background, is, however incorrigible it may seem to us, a rather peculiar idea within the context of the world's cultures" (Geertz, 1984: 126). Geertz cites examples from his fieldwork in Java, Morocco, and Bali, stressing how the identities he came across in these locations differed markedly from Western ones, generally in a variety of nondiscrete and unbounded forms.

While Fromm did not deal specifically with the contention that the experience of "the self" was a peculiarly "Western" notion, the idea clearly goes against the universalist basis of his thought. As it happens, Geertz's claim has been impressively countered by Melford Spiro (1993) and Nancy Chodorow (1999). What is clear from the analyses of Spiro and Chodorow is that Geertz commits a category mistake, confusing the cultural *conception* of self with *experience* of self—what Archer terms the "myth of cultural integration" (Archer, 2007: 26). Chodorow, in her account, notes, for instance, that Geertz fails to pay attention to any particular person's *experience* of cultural categories or to investigate how different people in a given culture might *experience* cultural meanings in different ways (Chodorow, 1999: 145–147). As she notes, such an approach "bypass[es] the idiosyncratic, divergent ways in which emotions develop and are experienced that lead to an energy, contestation, difference, and transformation that might themselves frame and provide impetus for political, economic, and social life" (Chodorow, 1999: 161). As with Chodorow, Spiro identifies Geertz's conflation of cultural concepts and experience, directly challenging his claim to be able to infer the manner in which people actually represent themselves to themselves based on a study of symbolic cultural forms alone. Writing from his own experience as a practicing ethnographer in Burma, Spiro stresses that the culturally normative idea of an "unbounded," non-Western self was incompatible with his own observations; he found that, in fact, the people he met experienced a subjective sense of self that ran contrary to the culturally dominant Buddhist norm of the egoless person. What Geertz seems oblivious to, then, is that in addition to a standardized public identity dictated largely by external cultural norms, the social actor possesses an individual and private identity that is not identical with cultural norms and that generally corresponds to the experience of the bounded, discrete, and continuous self of "Western" thought. The Geertzian distinction between two supposedly bipolar types of self—Western and non-Western self—is, as Spiro notes, "wildly overdrawn" (Spiro, 1993: 116).

The issues discussed so far in this chapter raise the question of the psychic unity of mankind, and whether there can be said to be a basic psychic structure stemming from the underlying existential and biological universalism. That there is such a structure was very much Fromm's view (this was touched on in the previous section in relation to the fact that he saw Homo sapiens as a species that can be defined in terms of its psychic and mental character). Effectively, Fromm saw the psychic laws as the same for all humans—at least insofar as they share "the essential features of bodily and mental equipment with the rest of mankind" (1970 [1951]: 18). Being of the same genus and facing a broadly similar existential situation, the basic psychic issues confronting human beings the world over generally reduce to an underlying basic similarity, which Fromm frames in terms of core existential needs—or *questions*—based on fundamental human existence.

As was noted in chapter 3, Fromm's account of the existential needs was not conclusive, and therefore cannot be taken as the basis for a positive account here. While this is so, the basic principle that underlies it seems theoretically sound and has, in fact, been argued for by Spiro (1984) and Gananath Obeyesekere (1990). Unsatisfied with the prevailing excessive relativism of his fellow anthropologists, Obeyesekere speaks of universal human nature, stating in terms reminiscent of Fromm that "the ground of this universal human nature is psychobiological: man as a kind of species possessed of a complex brain, relatively freed from the instincts, with a capacity for complex symbolization, especially in language and fantasy" (Obeyesekere, 1990: 101). Spiro, similarly unsatisfied, speaks of the principle of "the psychic unity of mankind," contending—in a manner almost identical to Fromm—that "the processes that characterize the working mind are the same everywhere—even though human cultures are different" (Spiro, 1984: 327). Illuminatingly, Spiro proffers a reinterpretation of Shelly Rosaldo's strongly relativistic account of the apparent differences which obtain between Ilongot and "Western" experiences of anger. Counter to Rosaldo's account—in which she suggests that the Ilongot do not repress or displace anger—Spiro's alternative interpretation suggests, in fact, that repression and displacement are *precisely* what occur (Spiro, 1984: 330–332). Rosaldo, in short, seems to be guilty of a modified version of what Geertz himself was guilty of: namely, confusing conscious cultural representation for unconscious individual reality.

In terms of his account of psychic universality, Spiro is less ambitious than Fromm, however, restricting it to his belief that "all humans have the capacity to distinguish fantasy from reality, to prefer pleasurable to painful feelings, to welcome nonconflictual over conflictual relations, and so forth" (Spiro, 1984: 327). While this is perhaps sensible, it does not seem theoretically impossible to extend this account to something approaching Fromm's, mapping out some fundamental needs on the basis of empirical cross-cultural investigation and philosophical anthropological analysis (this, as will be shown in chapter 6, was the task Fromm accorded the "science of man"). Obeyesekere, in fact, argues something similar to this in his discussion of "metatheories"—the theoretical bridges across cultures that "combine thick description with nomological adequacy and deductive order" (Obeyesekere, 1990: 258). A good metatheory, he argues, would be able to account for our common human nature through its "deductively interrelated set of nomological terms *as well as* dealing with the uniqueness of different life forms (Obeyesekere, 1990: 260). This, as Obeyesekere notes, is the kind of theory that we implicitly employ, but that because we do not recognize it for what it is we do so badly.

What is not being denied in the account being advanced here is that all thought is inescapably culturally patterned—this is clearly the case, and is a position basic to Fromm's social-psychological account. The fact that orthodox Freudian psychoanalysis universalizes developmental stages and assumes the existence of a universal family structure was a weakness that Fromm himself identified. As such, it is clear that Fromm is not guilty of a naïve universalism. Fromm was explicit that experience was organized and categorized in various ways according to culture—his analytic social psychology is given precisely the task of trying to understand the ways in which different social structures shape individual character. It is clear from this account that certain emotions and experiences are not permitted, either by virtue of the language or logic of the culture, or by direct prohibition in the form of taboos (this process is also facilitated by the domination of the news media by vested interests and the discouragement of critical thought that goes with it). While this is so, it is also clearly true that in his conception of the self, and of mental activity, Fromm was influenced by Freud's universalism. Fromm stressed that Freud built his system around the assumption of a universal human essence, "a universal man, not only man as he manifests himself in various cultures, but someone about whose structure generally valid statements can be made" (1970: 30).

The Freudian idea here, by which Fromm set so much store, was that once the unconscious is taken into consideration we are not so different from each other; that, as our unconscious is the repository for all social repressions (as well as all idiosyncratic individual repressions), when we get in touch with its contents we get in touch with our basic shared humanity. What must be said here is that, in his discussion of the unconscious as representing the whole of humanity, Fromm does seem to lapse into a form of quasi-Jungian speculation. He speaks of the "primary human experience," "the categories of thought buried in our unconscious and yet are an experiential core present in all men of all cultures," and of "the original man" (1997 [1973]: 306–307)—from all of which it must be assumed that Fromm had the view that the basic human experience was the same from the beginning of human evolution. But while what Fromm says here seems to contradict the sociological thrust in his thought, this is not necessarily so. His account allows for—and is built on—an underlying general universalism based on an idea of the common human predicament and the structural ordering of the psyche. Although realized in different cultures (and by different people within the same culture) in different ways, the underlying needs and strivings to avoid insanity, to be happy, to be related to others, etc., are seen as transcultural. On Fromm's account, these underlying issues are generally hidden from view, and we do not fully appreciate that the conflicts that stem from these constitutional problems work through the psychic structure in peculiar but structured (and comprehensible) patterns. In this sense, Fromm's talk about a "primary human experience" need not necessarily be clumsy. The fact that there is a basic psychic structure has been supported by Obeyesekere, who has argued that Freud's initial topography of the systems—*unconscious, preconscious, conscious*—seems to be universally represented in all cultures (something Damasio's research suggests must be the case). Obeyesekere argues, however, that Freud's second topographical account of the *ego-id-superego* is not universal, but, rather, based on the Judaeo-Protestant idea of conscience, which seems to be lacking in positive features, guilt and duty standing as the main motivators rather than compassion or kindness (Obeyesekere, 1990: xx, 251–253).

Fromm made precisely this point 40 years earlier, developing a distinction between what he termed the "authoritarian" and the "humanistic" conscience (2003 [1947]: 108–129). The idea of the humanistic conscience, the "voice of our true selves which summons us back to ourselves, to live productively, to develop fully and harmoniously—that is, to become what we potentially are" (2003 [1947]: 119)—contrasts with the authoritarian conscience, the voice of external authority represented in what Freud calls the superego. As Fromm conceives it, the humanistic conscience is "the reaction of our total personality to its proper functioning or dysfunctioning... a reaction of ourselves to ourselves" (2003 [1947]: 119)—an idea that has similarities to Damasio's idea of core and extended consciousness as arising from the general functioning of the human organism. Such a conscience exists primarily in an *affective* sense, that is to say, it is not necessarily something that we are intellectually aware of, other than through an inexplicable sense of anxiety. The fact that such an idea might seem so intangible is, for Fromm, partly due to the fact that in contemporary consumer culture we tend to listen less and less to this voice. Constantly bombarded by a multitude of different types of stimuli—television, radio, film (all of which, in their predominant forms, Fromm describes as "idle chatter"—and an apparent phobia of being along with ourselves, we are hardly aware of it (2003 [1947]: 120–121). Fromm contends, however, that we can see the existence of such a conscience in our dreams, during mediation, or in the analytic situation, where penetrating personal revelations that escape us during otherwise everyday life are frequent occurrences.

Despite this, other than in the passage above—and on one or two other occasions—Fromm rarely speaks of the idea of the "true" (or "real") self which aligns with his idea of the humanistic conscience. The idea of what we can call an *authentic self structure* is, however, centrally implied in his wider account of the need for the removal of false consciousness in social subjects. In *Escape from Freedom*, Fromm speaks of the "original self" and "pseudo self," the later acting as "subjective disguise for the objective social function of man in society" (1969 [1941]: 117), a way to escape the loneliness of freedom but at the cost of losing the original, and more authentic sense of self. In his account of "automaton conformity" and the "marketing character," this idea of a "loss of self" is the pivotal point, linking it to his argument as to the lack of true individuality in capitalist societies. In implicitly adopting the true/false self distinction, Fromm is cutting against the grain of most social theoretical thought today, which views such a distinction warily, if not with outright contempt. But, as with the other aspects already discussed, the opposition to this distinction is worth challenging. For, while we can acknowledge that our identity is an ongoing construction, a mixture of various internalizations, what is it in this that necessitates that we cannot speak of a more authentic form of construction? If we have the capacity for internal conversation, as we clearly do, then surely the clearer we can see the causes and motivations of the central aspects of this conversation the more clearly we can act with commensurate effort and agency. To speak of a "real" or "true" self in this context, then, is to refer to the *capacity* which mediates different internalizations and which enables us to have a greater sense of becoming the architect, actor, and subject of own life. This idea is basic to psychotherapy and to the older religio-philosophical ethical tradition.

The ideas of the self and the subject, then, each dependent on the other, are part of the defining features of what it is to be human. Fromm's humanism, in centering on the self and the removal of false consciousness (Freud and Marx, and the forces working behind our backs) is valid insofar as this is the case. Unsurprisingly for a psychoanalyst, especially one taken with Buddhism, Fromm sees the overcoming of alienation as consisting in the development of an increased awareness—the capacity for which, although culturally mediated, is nevertheless irreducible, and *requires* the positing of a self to make sense. The self as the experiential core is related to the subject as a means of development of the subject. In many respects—although not fully—the subject can be considered as the self, viewed from a different angle, or, perhaps better, as the *organized purpose* of the self. Having a clear, authentic view of the truths pertaining to one's self structure informs, and therefore offers, better possibilities for enabling the unification of the subject in what is a very often damaging external environment.

The idea of authentic selfhood is the crux of Fromm's thought. His radical humanism views the self as its radical goal, its telos, but also the means, in that it is through the radical authenticating of the self that we reach this end. This is a form of eudaimonia where the end and the activity coalesce. Crucially, psychoanalysis is set up to inform and assist this development, as a transtherapeutic instrument for the art of living. The overall aim can be seen as trying to restore the early Marx's focus on the individual and ethics to the forefront of socialist and social theoretical thought. While authentic selfhood is the goal, it is so with the recognition of the social embeddedness that frames this individual. Fromm was clear that the "self" of modern society is "essentially constituted by the role the individual is supposed to play," a "subjective disguise for the objective social function" (1969 [1941]: 117). But Fromm is important because of his parallel recognition that the irreducible entity that is the human individual/subject represents the appropriate realm of adjudication for concerns over health and illness; that the subject is therefore both the ultimate goal of attainment *and* bulwark against degradation. This recognition should not be confused with a rampant individualism, which posits an unbridgeable chasm between individual and society—it is clear that for Fromm the genuine needs of individuals are not the asocial or antisocial ones suggested by Freud or by utilitarian philosophy—but be taken as the evaluative decoupling of society and individual, so that, taken as nonidentical entities with potentially nonidentical needs, the individual considered from its own point of view becomes the teleological endpoint in the analysis of health and illness.

It should be noted here that this position is not necessarily a criticism of socialism or collectivism (and certainly was not intended to be such in the case of Fromm), but merely the methodological reminder that we should be ever vigilant against supposing that the goals and aims of society naturally mirror the goals and aims of the individual human being. This forms a crucial part of the future realization of humanism, and ties in with the goal of humanism as stemming from Judaic impulses. Fromm's is a humanism constructed through a synthesis of the religious questioning of how to live, how to be free, with contemporary evolutionary thinking and a psycho-existential interpretation of existence. The point, though, is the radical authenticating of the self through our interpersonal capacities for love and reason, which, in turn, are identical with the realization of the expression of the true self. The individual human subject, replete with self, is an entity possessed of certain properties, the said properties constituting the ground upon which value for human beings exists and upon which the very idea of ethics makes sense. This important issue will be returned to in chapter 6.

CHAPTER 6

The Renaissance of Humanism

At the end of *Beyond the Chains of Illusion*—a book that ranks among the most personal of his works—Fromm makes a call for the "renaissance of humanistic experience" (2006 [1962]: 128). In prose that combines Nietzschean and Heideggerian elements with the more constitutive humanistic religiosity that characterizes his own thought, he states that

> if the One World is not to destroy itself, it needs a new kind of man—a man who transcends the narrow limits of his nation and who experiences every human being as a neighbour, rather than as a barbarian; a man who feels at home in the world... Until now the One Man may have been a luxury, since the One World had not emerged. Now the One Man must emerge if the One World is to live. Historically speaking, this may be a step comparable with the great revolution which was constituted by the step from the worship of many gods to One God—or the One No-God. This step was characterised by the idea that man must cease to serve idols, be they nature or the work of his own hands. (2006 [1962]: 131)

For Fromm, our civilization is placed at the far end of the historical process in which we generally came to lose the religio-philosophical worldview, what he took be its central idea and experience—namely, man as an end—and the consequential reversion to an idolatrous worship of things. We had, he believed, regressed to a position that the turn to monotheism had, in principle at least, transcended, and thus to what can be seen as the *forgetting of humanism*. What this meant in practice was that we had fled, or *escaped*, from the promise of humanism as found most recently—and impressively—in Renaissance and Enlightenment thought. Fromm praised the Renaissance and, after it, the Enlightenment, as the culmination of the development of earlier, Judaeo-Christian and Greco-Roman humanisms, melding their spirit with a new democratic and scientific attitude, which furthered the case of prophetic messianism. Fromm's praise was not absolute, however, and he was certainly not naïve. Crucially stopping short of a "counter-Enlightenment" position, Fromm nevertheless saw the legacy of Enlightenment and Renaissance (and Reformation) thought as essentially divided, recognizing the ultimately inconsistent way "Western" civilization has dealt with the opportunity that was presented in these periods. From a concern with the idea of "the dignity of man," Fromm suggests that what reigns in contemporary capitalistic is a profound *indifference* to man, which is cloaked by an illusory individualism.

As a social critic influenced by the prophetic spirit, a large part of Fromm's work was centered on diagnosing what he saw as the spiritual malaise of modernity, and particularly the affluent alienation of postwar industrial capitalism. This analysis was centered broadly on American society but was, Fromm thought, indicative of trends that were becoming increasingly globalized. As manifestations of the forgetting of humanism, Fromm identified a deep-set reification, with man lost in a network of things in which means had become ends and ends had become means. In his discussion of the phenomena of "automaton conformity," the "marketing orientation," and the "having mode of existence," Fromm seeks to penetrate through the surface of contemporary life, following Freud's suggestion and engaging in the analysis of the "pathology of cultural communities." Growing out of this analysis is his concept of the "pathology of normalcy"—the idea that the normal functioning of a society (or part of a society) can be pathological—and the accompanying idea of a "socially patterned defect"—the idea that because the defect is shared en masse it is generally prevented from leading to neurosis. This application of psychological analytical categories to the social realm in the act of criticism represents the extension of his social psychology and raises him to "analyst of society" (2004 [1961]: 52). But while this may be so, Fromm's goals were ultimately *transtherapeutic*. Providing a solution to the malaise could not just be further adjustment, as further adjustment would merely be an additional adjustment to an inherently pathological state of affairs. Challenging the very *basis* of such a state of affairs was important. It was imperative, Fromm argued, lest we succumb completely to this process of dehumanization, that we *remember* what humanism was, retrieve it from its marginal status, and reintegrate it with the canons of our thought and practice such that we usher in a "renaissance of humanism" (2005: 29–30). The solution Fromm proposed essentially reduces to two connected aspects: a focus on the *art of living* and focus on the *humanization of all sectors of life*.

What was crucial for Fromm was that we return to the basic concern of the humanistic religious and philosophical tradition, that is, the questioning of what it is that makes us human and the idea of the individual human being as an end, not throwing out the developments of modern science (natural and social) but uniting them with these older concerns to create a humanistic "science of man," which would inform our relations with ourselves, others, and the world at large (2003 [1947]: 14–17; 1990 [1957]). This involves a concern with experiential humanism, but one which is generalizable in the form of a *normative humanism*, thereby undercutting excessively relativistic accounts while simultaneously avoiding a crass rationalism.

Both ideas—humanistic ethics as the applied science of the art of living based upon the theoretical "science of man" and the humanization of all sectors of life, which in effect call for the creation of a "New Man" and a "New Society" (2009 [1976])—have been criticized for their supposed naiveté, "utopianism," and conformism. These criticisms, in fact, say more about the critics than they do about Fromm or the ideas considered in themselves. The issue here is the location of a *true* radicalism, appreciation of which involves precisely the kind of conceptual and experiential change that Fromm speaks of as a precondition. What can certainly not be said is that these ideas were insufficiently serious. The creation of a "New Man" involves a resolute commitment to a personal quest and a deep level of honesty with oneself; the creation of a "New Society" involves a similar level of commitment and honesty, as well as deep faith and patience—what Fromm describes as the "paradox of hope." Ultimately, despite the bleakness of the situation and the low likelihood of change, as he perceived it, Fromm believed that a renaissance of humanism was still possible, that we had to hold on to faith in possibility lest we give over to a form of resigned paralysis.

The Forgetting of Humanism

Speaking in the early 1960s, after the two world wars and in the midst of a nuclear arms race, which was seemingly escalating toward conflict and ensuing holocaust, Fromm complained that humanism had become forgotten (2005). We had, he felt, come to lose the basic experience of humanism— that is to say, the experience of our own humanity as an end to be realized— and allowed an indifference to characterize our relations with ourselves and with others. The situation represented, for Fromm, the culmination of a tension that was set into motion with the demise of the medieval religiophilosophical worldview and in which an archaic regression reared its head. The splitting of science and ethics in the seventeenth century, the increasing dominance of inner worldly asceticism, and the development of capitalism with its ethics of egotism, are all seen as ushering in a process of dehuman-ization through which we gradually came to lose "the human substance of feeling" ("Concerning the Philosophy of Existence," lecture given by Fromm in Locarno, 1977—an audio copy is held at the Fromm Archives). This substance of feeling was, for Fromm, the basic experience of humanism, the experience, which accompanied older religious and philosophical thought in the questioning of existence, of our ability to connect with our existence and to recognize the norms and values which follow from it. The "solipsism," as Fromm describes it, which this loss engenders—an increasing cerebration at the expense of experience—repels reason,[1] and thought becomes increas-ingly characterized by technical framings in which means stand as ends and ends stand as means. Ethics recedes to an emotivism and thinking becomes a means for domination and power, as the concrete individual slips out of sight.

Risking accusations of "historical solecism" (Davies, 2008: 94) and "teleological thinking" (Foucault, 1984b, 2002a), Fromm reads human-ism back into human history as a definite and identifiable thread within ideational and material struggle. In his account, humanism as a mode of thought can be seen to develop out of prior humanistic developments in the major thought systems of the orient and the Occident in the last two thousand years, travelling, in European culture at least, in uneven loops of development and retardation through antiquity and the Middle Ages to the Renaissance and the Enlightenment and the thought of Marx, Freud, and Fromm himself. Such a view—which is self-consciously focused on the "West," but not without reference to the significance of similar develop-ments in the "East," particularly that of Buddhist and Taoist thoughts—is fairly unique today, and worth considering at length.[2]

In a lecture titled "Modern Man and the Future," given at the 1961 West German International Congress for Psychoanalysis and its Continued Development, Fromm briefly outlines five stages of Western history, each stage corresponding to developments in humanistic thought.[3] The first, inaugural stage, so to speak, occurs, according to Fromm, in the turn from idolatry found among the central thought systems of the "Axial Age" (Jaspers, 1951: 135)—the period between 800 BC and 200 BC, as identified by Jaspers, or between 1500 BC and the beginning of the Christian age, as Fromm suggests[4]—in India, China, and the Occident, in which the major world religions were founded and in which classical Greek philosophy rose to prominence. In the teachings of Akhnaten, the Mosaic religions, Taoism, Buddhism, and ancient Greek philosophers, Fromm locates a turning in which thought, hitherto directed outward, comes to focus upon the human individual as an entity capable of self-salvation (2005; 1966a). Where once totems and the gods of nature were to decide the fate of human history, it was now possible that real human beings, their powers and capacities, potentialities and limitations, could stand as the criterial referent for development. While Fromm is clear that this experience of human centering is partially overturned soon after being inaugurated in almost all cases, lost under the weight of what he calls the "fictitious additions" (1966a: 21) which accrue as the thought systems evolve, he is adamant that it is, nonetheless, the revolutionary introduction of an idea that has attained at least partial expression ever since.

The second stage in the development involves what Fromm describes as the discovery of the notion of *historical* redemption by the Old Testament prophets of Palestine. As was noted in chapter 2, Fromm reads Old Testament history from a position in which theology and religion are decoupled (or at least a position in which there is nothing necessary in their coupling) and where the evolution in the concepts of God and man can be reduced to the clear statement of the supreme value and the supreme goal for man as the finding of union with the world through the full development of his specifically human capacities of love and reason (1966a: 22). Fromm's Cohenian-inspired view of prophetic messianism and his reading of the Old Testament in line with its later interpretive traditions is evident here as the main source of this account. While some concerns over this view were raised in chapter 2, it should be stressed that Fromm is clear that he is only referring to a *tendency* that exists side by side with other more authoritarian tendencies—this is what his distinction between *authoritarian* and *humanistic* religion was primarily devised to explain and what is implicated in his historico-sociological, materialist account of the development. This stage, then, despite the evolution and retardation involved in the professed ideas, represents for Western civilization the explicit emergence of a view of history focused on human self-development.

The third stage Fromm outlines involves the transferal of this prophetic messianism from Palestine to Europe (and from Judaism to Christianity), leading in the process to an alteration of form: man's salvation no longer takes place within history but rather transcends it, the Kingdom of God understood not as a change in this world but as the establishment of a new, spiritual world that transcends it. Fromm argues that, in spite of this change, the revised dogma is still a continuation of prophetic messianism and, therefore, the incubator of the central humanist idea. Once more, the accuracy of Fromm's interpretation here can be questioned: some will clearly take issue with his respective characterizations of Judaism and Christianity (which do seem to betray an idealistic bias toward the former), but, as was explained in chapter 2, Fromm is dealing with the practice of each respective entity and searching for the dominant and most consistent representations thereof.

In the fourth stage, a "union of great historical significance" takes place, with the merging of message of the Gospels with that of the Catholic Church and, thus, the coupling of "the Jewish notion of reconciliation, in the form of prophetic messianism," with "the Greek idea of science, of theory" (2005: 19). Again, the process to which Fromm is alluding here—a process that stretched from fourth-century Rome to the end of the European Middle Ages—is not a simple process of ascension. In fact, in spite of the merger, Fromm contends that the idea that Europe was Christianized is largely a sham, arguing that a "new paganism" developed side by side with the professed humanistic elements (2009 [1976]: 118), the connections to stately power that characterizes the main part of Christian history and the poor fidelity to the core of the Christian message ensuring the effectual subsuming of the true messianic message to largely profane interests. But although a period of much struggle and tyranny and, ultimately, of an underlying but dominant paganism, Fromm maintains that the religio-humanistic element was never lost. In relation to this claim, Fromm cites the radical Christian thought of the late middle ages, which strongly criticized secular authority and the state from the standpoint of divine *and* natural law (2004 [1961]: 53). In particular, he stresses the role of the Christian sects and mystics who argued for a return to Christ's teachings: Thomism, the Cabbalists, Joachim of Fiore, and Meister Eckhart, among others. He also stresses the importance of the Reformation as giving repeated impetus to the historical liberation of man, particularly within the pre- and post-Reformation sects. Crucially, although Fromm reiterates that the failure of these movements in the thirteenth century meant that the short period of genuine Christianity ended and Europe returned to its paganism, the humanistic idea was not lost. In fact, this union of Greco-Roman and Judaeo-Christian concerns, which contained the basic idea, constituted something new that grew to fruition in Europe over course of the next one thousand years, giving birth to humanism as we recognize it and to the greatest flourishing of its central idea.

This development is evident in what Fromm describes as the fifth stage, the move to "modern" society and, in particular, the changes brought into existence during the Renaissance and the Enlightenment periods. In speaking of this stage, Fromm rephrases Burckhardt's famous formulation of the Renaissance as the "discovery" of the individual: "Perhaps instead of saying 'discovery,' one should more precisely say 're-discovery,' since it is the rebirth of much that Greek and Roman antiquity felt about man and nature" (2005: 19). In fact, Fromm praises the Renaissance as the flowering of ideas unheard of since the Middle Ages, where the idea of human dignity, the unity of the human race, and of universal political and religious unity found "unencumbered expression" (2009 [1976]: 118). Renaissance man, for Fromm, giving birth to a new scientific attitude, becomes more fully aware of his powers and begins to free himself from the shackles of nature, developing a new attitude toward life as a whole. In the subsequent centuries, this new attitude toward life leads to a radically new understanding of the world, and, in the seventeenth and eighteenth centuries, the new humanism reaches its apogee: "Western thought centered on man, on humanity, and on humaneness" (2005: 20). Here, first of all in Renaissance humanism, *humanitas* is understood in its natural "suchness" and as given the task of fully unfolding itself, a task embarked upon with great conviction among the Enlightenment humanists that followed (2005: 66). Among the central figures of these periods, Fromm cites the Catholic humanists such as Nicholas of Cusa, Ficino, Erasmus, Thomas More, and Siculo (1980 [1964]: 81) and, in the Enlightenment era, Rousseau, Herder, Lessing, and, particularly, Goethe. As Fromm interpreted them, the humanistic ideas of these thinkers were the extension of fundamentally religious groundings: although a time in which theistic concepts receded, "religious experience" (understood in Fromm's sense) is stronger than at any other time other than the thirteenth century. In addition to this, the prophetic messianic vision can be seen as maintained in the idea of Utopia and as underpinning the goals of the English and French Revolutions. But crucially, although underpinned by a religious spirit, the Renaissance and Enlightenment "enriched the Greek and Judeo-Christian traditions and developed them further, in humanistic rather than theological terms" (2006 [1962]: 129–130), thereby preparing the ground for the humanism of Marx and, eventually, Fromm himself.

In providing such a history, which by his own admission was suggestive and schematic (understandable given that the main thrust was offered in lecture form), Fromm is running against the vogue in social theoretical thinking, in conspicuous contravention of Foucault's warning against continuous history. While this is so, it must be stressed that Fromm is neither engaging in a form of historical solecism nor "teleological thinking"; nor, in fact, in a form of spurious "identity thinking." What Fromm is doing here is looking for roots, past connections and traditional crossovers, as well as accepting that fissures and disjunction have taken place. The fact that Foucaultians would criticize this reading-back, and would wish to stress that discourses arise afresh and in new connections, does not vitiate the fact that these ideas are often invoked specifically by explicit reference to past tradition and in self-conscious identification with (and development of) it—something that has certainly been the case in the development of humanism that Fromm outlined. In fact, the "apogee," as Fromm describes it, is so precisely *because* it occurs through the melding of medieval culture and Greco-Roman philosophy.

While Fromm's account may be said to be guilty of running close to an obtuse syncretism from time to time, it notably avoids the counter-Enlightenment equation of Enlightenment with terror. In fact, though the Renaissance and Enlightenment are praised by Fromm as great flowerings of humanism, he saw their legacy as ultimately divided. It is worth stressing here that Fromm said very little on the fact that the Renaissance and Enlightenment were also periods of European colonial expansion and slavery in which the banners of "progress" and "humanity" were used to legitimize terror and mass slaughter. While this is so, and while it is a failing in his account, it must be recognized that the crimes committed in these periods were committed in direct contravention of the central principles of humanist thought interpreted in consistent and robust fashion. It is an elementary part of Fromm's explanation of human history that there exists a tension between authoritarianism and humanism, and that the fact these humanist ideas coexisted with barbaric practices does not necessarily invalidate them, nor suggest that the thrust of his "apogee" characterization is misplaced. The point is that the ideas were expressed within the culture of the time to an extent never seen before. It did not amount to radical humanism, but it was nevertheless a great flowering of the humanist ideal, which Marx and, ultimately, Fromm himself was to build on. As if to underline this point, Fromm, in *Man for Himself*, describes an early–Middle Age battle between Augustine and Pelagius over the good or evil view of humanity. The victory of Augustine (who saw man's nature since Adam as corrupt) over Pelagius (who saw Adam's sin as purely personal and, therefore, the rest of the human race as untouched by it)—was to "determine—and darken—man's mind for centuries" (2003 [1947]: 158). Fromm identifies the replaying of this battle in the late–Middle Ages between Aquinas and thinkers of the Renaissance, who stressed human dignity and goodness, and Luther and Calvin, who revived the Augustinian position. Fromm's contention is that these two threads remain interwoven in the texture of modern thought, but that our lack of true conviction in the former leads to the effectual supersession of the latter.

With freedom comes responsibility and uncertainty; this is the fundamentally ambiguous nature of freedom. In the stripping away of traditional barriers (social and ideational), particularly the religious barriers that can be said to have been removed in the Reformation, Fromm identifies a powerful need to *escape* from freedom, a need based on what is essentially the *fear* of freedom.[5] Fromm charts what he sees as an "increase in isolation, doubt, and scepticism, and—resulting from all these—anxiety" (1969 [1941]: 48). This, he contends, is the same contradiction that is found in the philosophical writings of the humanists: "side by side with their emphasis on human dignity, individuality, and strength, they exhibited insecurity and despair in their philosophy" (1969 [1941]: 48). But while this dichotomy can be said to plague the legacy of the culture of the Renaissance and Enlightenment, Fromm cites the actual dissolution of this culture itself as one of the causal strands in the contemporary forgetting of humanism. These "escapes from freedom" develop outward into a new society with the relation of escape as its basis, a relation that is deepened through the relatively autonomous development of technology and ever greater dominance of capitalist relations. Importantly, Fromm views this as a *turn* from the inherent promise of the Renaissance and Enlightenment, not the inherent legacy bequeathed by these periods.

Whatever may be said of Fromm's thought here, he at least kept the good and bad firmly in view, managing to avoid a narrative of simple ascension while, at the same time, stressing the genuine stirrings and manifestations of the humanistic spirit in the various eras and movements in (generally "Western") history. His apparently simplistic humanist/authoritarian distinction is superior and more capable of accounting for the reality of this history than those who totalize the legacy in a unidirectional or one-dimensional focus on rationalization and instrumentalism. What is important in his account is the offering of the *other side*, a side that is largely underemphasized in the current intellectual climate. By maintaining a dynamic view of this process, Fromm is able to recognize the proclamation of the idea of the "dignity of man" pronounced by Renaissance and Enlightenment thinkers, and the use of this idea by progressive liberal thought of nineteenth century, alongside the idea of man's worthlessness found in authoritarian systems that were sustained by the instrumental rationality of formalist ethics. Democracy and authoritarianism, then, are the dual, contradictory legacy of this period. "Today," Fromm suggests, "we are adherents both of Augustine *and* Pelagius, of Luther [*and*] Pico della Mirandola, of Hobbes *and* Jefferson. We consciously believe in man's power and dignity, but—often unconsciously—we also believe in man's—and particularly our own—powerlessness and badness and explain it by pointing to 'human nature'" (2003 [1947]: 159).

What is particularly unique about Fromm's account is his observance of a related warping or hollowing out of these ideas, resulting in what he contends is essentially an *indifference* toward man that grows from the supersession of the idea of man's powerlessness and badness:

> Our moral problem is man's indifference to himself. It lies in the fact that we have lost the sense of the significance and uniqueness of the individual, that we have made ourselves into instruments for purposes outside ourselves, that we experience and treat ourselves as commodities, and that our powers have become alienated from ourselves. We have become things and our neighbours have become things. The result is that we feel powerless and despise ourselves for our impotence. Since we do not trust our own power, we have no faith in man, no faith in ourselves or in what our powers can create. (2003 [1947]: 185)

What is apparent to Fromm is that, in the loss of the humanistic experience, in its general replacement, we have come to lose real regard for ourselves:

> Each age has its own characteristic depravity; ours is perhaps not pleasure and indulgence, or sensuality, but rather a dissolute pantheistic contempt for the individual man. In the midst of all our exultation over the achievement of the age in the nineteenth century there sounds a note of purely conceived contempt of the individual man. In the midst of the self-importance of the contemporary generation there is revealed a sense of despair over being human. ("Concerning the Philosophy of Existence," 1977)

The identification of this society-wide and historically unique despair at being human, and the reification that goes with it, is the central feature of Fromm's analytical criticism of twentieth-century industrialized, late-capitalist society. It is the basis of his contention that we have *forgotten* humanism—a practical and ideological loss of the basic experience of humanism in modern society, which threatens to collapse potential avenues of retrieval.

Idolatry, Alienation, and the Pathology of Normalcy

But surely Fromm has it all wrong here—are we not, after all, the culture of individualism par excellence? Is our culture not one in which the uniqueness and significance of the individual is absolutely paramount, and unprecedented for being so? According to Fromm, this is far from being the case. The reality, as Fromm sees it, is that our (meaning "advanced," industrial, Western, Capitalistic) civilization is characterized by an *illusion* of individuality, which conceals an actual indifference, even *contempt*, toward the individual. In *Escape from Freedom*, Fromm remarks on the insignificance of the individual in the present era, arguing counter to the prevailing consensus that our apparently individualistic civilization is actually the result of an *escape* from individualism (which is itself an escape from freedom). What is taken as evidence of individualism, according to Fromm, is, in fact, largely compensatory activity engaged in so as to conceal an increasing sense of isolation and powerlessness. It is Fromm's contention that "the cultural and political crisis of our day is not due to the fact there is too much individualism but that what we believe to be individual has become an empty shell" (1969 [1941]: 269).

Central to Fromm's account of this situation is the secular employment of the religious concept of idolatry. What characterizes our civilization, Fromm contends, is an idolatrous relationship to the world in what is, in essence, a consumer society. Fromm speaks of the individual in such a society as *homo consumens*, "the man whose main goal is not primarily to own things, but to consume more and more, and thus to compensate for his inner vacuity, passivity, loneliness and anxiety" (1967 [1965]: 214). As Fromm understands it, *homo consumens* represents a milder variation of the psychopathological phenomenon found in many cases of depressed or anxious persons who flee into overeating, overbuying, or alcoholism, in order to escape from hidden anxiety and depression. Linked to this idea is Fromm's subsequent idea of the *having* mode of existence, in which there tends to be an obsession with things (and, in fact, a reified relationship to the world more generally[6]). Another facet of his transposed account of idolatry, the central feature of the relation to things in the having mode is the idea that "I have this, but also it has me," that "I am *controlled* by my irrational passion to have and am consequently unfree."

What these ideas describe are the effects of the preoccupation in advanced capitalist societies with crass materialism. In line with Fromm's characterology, these phenomena represent ways of *relating*—to everyone and everything, in terms of having and consuming. In addition to this—and as another facet of crass materialism—Fromm lays stress on the increasing extent to which *greed* governs our relations to the world. The point, as with the concepts of *homo consumens* and the having orientation, is that in greed we are driven, controlled by our passion to have and to consume, and that we flee into a greedy relationship with the world as a means of covering up increased anxiety, loneliness, insecurity, and lack of identity (1970 [1968]: 76). The corollary of idolatrous relating, our greed for "more food, drink, sex, possessions, power, and fame" (1997 [1973]: 281–282) works against true relating to the world and is "clearly a symptom of physical dysfunctioning, of inner emptiness and a lack of centre within oneself" (1997 [1973]: 282). In this connection, Fromm speaks of the failure of the "Great Promise of Unlimited Progress" and the radical hedonism and unlimited egoism that flow from it, fostered by consumerist culture, which in the end, leads to socially patterned and widespread rates of depression and anxiety (2009 [1976]: 1–8).

Connected to this picture—and illustrating the illusion of individuality further still—is Fromm's account of the prevalence of *narcissism*. As with greed, a relationship to the world in which narcissism predominates is one based on fear, but one in which *self-inflation* is chosen as the means of evading cognizance of this fear. In a narcissistic relationship to the world—a relationship that stands at the basis of all neurosis—the narcissistic person is preoccupied with him or herself and cannot truly perceive the reality within another (and, in fact, has little interest in doing so) (1980 [1964]: 68–69). As a consequence, objectivity and rationality suffer, with reason and love made more difficult to realize (1980 [1964]: 87). Fromm contends that narcissism is encouraged in our culture though an obsession with fame, celebrity, appearance, and the omnipotent but short-lived feeling we achieve through consumption. While it is commonly assumed that narcissistic persons are "very much in love with themselves, they are actually not fond of themselves, and their narcissism—like selfishness—is an overcompensation for the basic lack of self love" (1969 [1941]: 116).[7] What is important for the present discussion is the recognition that narcissism is essentially based on low self-esteem and involves the degradation of the kind of self-love that should accompany a real individualism; it is this that is the issue with so-called modern "individualism" as far as Fromm is concerned:

> The failure of modern culture lies not in its principle of individualism, not in the idea that moral virtue is the same as the pursuit of self-interest, but in the deterioration of the meaning of self-interest; not in the fact that people are *too much concerned with their self-interest*, but that they *are not concerned enough with the interest of their real self; not in the fact that they are too selfish, but that they do not love themselves.* (2003 [1947]: 104—emphasis in original)

Importantly, this deterioration of self-love leads to a denigration of sympathy. In advanced industrial society, where narcissism flourishes, separateness and antagonism exists between individuals—a separateness and antagonism encouraged by an economic system in which competitive advantage is sought over others as a means of its basic functioning—there is restricted room for concern and sympathy (1982 [1980]: 53). This issue is transferred onto the national and international plane in what Fromm terms *social*, or "group," narcissism (1980 [1964]: 78–80), that is to say, the transformation of personal into group narcissism, leading to the characteristic myopia that is found in most forms of nationalism (seen in phenomena ranging from the petty lauding of one's national traditions and "character" over others, to the use of this sense of superiority in justification of wars of aggression).

In addition to the concepts already discussed, Fromm proffers the idea of the increasing prevalence of the "marketing character" and *marketing orientation* to life in general. Related to the concepts discussed immediately above, the growth in the marketing orientation coincides with the growth in the "personality market" in employment and thus with more recent trends in the development of capitalism. In both instances, the value that counts is *exchange* value, and thus the qualities of the person that are valued are those that fulfill the condition of being *in demand*. What matters here is the respective weight of skill and personality as a condition for success, with personality being the factor that always plays the decisive role (2003 [1947]: 50–51). The premise of the orientation is, in fact, "emptiness, the lack of any specific quality which could not be subject to change, since any persistent trait of character might conflict some day with requirements of the market" (2003 [1947]: 57). What is required is a protean impermanence of attitude, a *centerless personality* devoid of passionate conviction and ever ready to meet the requirements of the role. In this commodification of personality, individuals become less-and-less concerned with their life and happiness and more and more with becoming saleable, everyone experiencing themselves (and everyone else) as a commodity.

Yet another of Fromm's concepts that draws out the illusion of individuality in our civilization is that which he has termed "automaton conformity" (1969 [1941]: 183). Describing a process very similar (and obviously related) to that of the marketing orientation, automaton conformity denotes the state in which "the individual ceases to be himself[,] adopts entirely the kind of personality offered to him by cultural patterns[,] and...therefore becomes exactly as all others are and as they expect him to be" (1969 [1941]: 184). Such a process involves the anonymous operation of authority through the mechanism of conformity, necessitated by the mode of production, which requires quick adaptation to the machine, disciplined mass behavior, common taste, and obedience without use of force—a situation made possible, Fromm contends, by the deep human desire to conform and not to be different, and linked to the powerlessness and aloneness of our existential condition. This, then, is the reality of the "individualism" in our culture:

Behind a front of satisfaction and optimism modern man is deeply unhappy; as a matter of fact, he is on the verge of desperation. He

desperately clings to the notion of individuality; he wants to be "different," and he has no greater recommendation of anything than that "it is
different"...All this indicates the hunger for "difference" and yet these
are almost the last vestiges of individuality that are left. (1969 [1941]:
254)

The phenomena discussed in the preceding part of this section could be
more simply described by the more familiar term: *alienation*—the estrangement of the human individual from its own self-affirming powers, and thus
from a true individualism. While this is so, there is a conceptual confusion
of sorts that arises in Fromm's work in relation to his inconsistent usage of
the term. This confusion stems from a lack of clarity over the term in relation to its connection to what can be called "existential" and "idolatric"
alienation—the first of which referring to what Fromm, in his reliance on
the biblical metaphor, describes as man's *original alienation*, and the second,
to what he denotes as the *alienation in the process of living*. Attention has
been drawn to this issue by Hammond (1965: 66–76); but while Hammond
was right to point to the problem insofar as there is an inconsistency in
relation to Fromm's language, the fact that Fromm's usage of the biblical
metaphor was precisely *metaphorical* as opposed to literal nullifies the force
Hammond seeks to apply with the criticism (that this is so is clearly borne
out by Fromm's atheism and attempt to ground his work in evolutionary
biology). Fromm's use of the idea of "existential" alienation (in the religious
sense) was figurative and can therefore be discounted from the final analysis, thus meaning that "alienation" and "idolatry" can exist as legitimately
interchangeable terms in his thought.

In addition to the instances of alienation already discussed, Fromm spoke
of alienation in a variety of other spheres of life, including those of work and
politics (2002 [1955]: 172–185). In the case of work, Fromm draws on the
Marxian analysis of alienated labor, citing alienation from the process of
decision making and from real control over and engagement in productive,
skillful activity. Fromm argues that this state of affairs breeds laziness and
a hostility to work, as well as a conscious (or unconscious) self-hatred at
allowing one's life to pass by (2002 [1955]: 177–178). In the case of politics,
Fromm argues that voting (the *symbol* of democracy today) is itself an alienated expression. If not the fact that this form of participation granted by the
political system is inherently alienated, with decision-making power ceded
to party machines and restricted to what is generally a four- or five-year
period of relative powerlessness, then the reality of automaton conformity,
coupled with the suggestive propaganda of the public relations machines
that control the interface between politicians and the public, means that

political ideas and leaders are thought of in the same manner as products are, and thus without the requisite objectivity and rationality required for true political engagement. In both instances, the problem is a detachment from real, meaningful participation in the activities concerned.

Fromm also spoke at length of alienation in relation to technology. Likening his thought here to that of Lewis Mumford and Jacques Ellul, Fromm was clear that although the technotronic society—"a completely mechanized society, devoted to material output and consumption, directed by computers" (1970 [1968]: 1)—was not here yet, he thought that our relationship with technology could make the leap to such a society possible. Ultimately, Fromm saw in our relationship with technology the evidence of an adherence to the following maxim: namely, that "something *ought* to be done because it is technically *possible* to do it" (1970 [1968]: 32). If it is possible to build nuclear weapons, we must build them, even if doing so may destroy us all; if it is possible to travel to the moon, even though doing so means that vast amounts of money and human ingenuity are spent on this task rather than dealing with problems on earth, we must do it. What this represented for Fromm was the negation of the central values of the humanist tradition and the triumph of reified ethics: "once the principle is accepted that something ought to be done because it is technically possible to do it, all other values are dethroned and technological development becomes the foundation of ethics" (1970 [1968]: 32–33).

What is most important in all of this, as far as Fromm is concerned, is that in this one-sided emphasis on technique and material consumption we lose touch with ourselves and with life. As he frames it in *Let Man Prevail* thus: "Where the roots of Western culture, both Greek and Hebrew, considered the aim of life the *perfection of man*, modern man is concerned with the *perfection of things*, and the knowledge of how to make them" (1960a: 17). This displacement—actual if not formal—of humanist evaluative criteria by thing-centered or technical-evaluative criteria, is the very crux of the tragedy of modernity for Fromm. It constitutes a central dehumanization that is efficacious in the realm of human relations. In the nineteenth century, one could say: "God is dead." In the twentieth, one must say that man is dead. Today, this adage rings true: "Man is dead, long live the thing!" (2005: 27). Lost in a network of things, a lopsidedness ensues in which an "intellectual-technical over-maturity" relates inversely to an "emotional backwardness" (1969 [1941]: xvi).

Linked to this emotional backwardness that stems from our worship of technique is what Fromm saw as the rise of *necrophilous-destructiveness*. Understood as a *secondary* potentiality (in the sense that it is primarily compensation for the lack of creative engagement with the world), necrophilous-destructiveness represents the substituting of an interest in living things with an attraction to mechanical, non-alive artifacts, which, if not checked, would lead to a destructive engagement with the world. What matters in this form of relating is not so much that someone may have an interest in machines or artifacts as such, but that their interest in machines or artifacts has replaced their interest in people, nature, and living structures, that it has become a *substitute* for interest in life (1997 [1973]: 455–457). Fromm is not saying here that an engineer, for instance, passionately interested in machines is necessarily necrophilous—he is explicit that such a person may be highly productive, with a great love of life that connects to his or her interest in machines (1997 [1973]: 456). What matters is the *characterological reality* underlying this interest, and thus whether it is geared toward love for life or toward indifference to life. Facilitated by what he sees as our emotional backwardness, Fromm identifies the prevalence of this form of relating to the world in what he contends is a decreasing sensitivity to destructiveness. Speaking during the nuclear crisis of the 1960s, he evokes the image of the neutron bomb, a weapon which "will destroy everything that lives and will leave everything that does not live—things, houses, streets—intact" (2005: 27). In addition to being the most ghastly and revealing example of this destructiveness, it is at the same time the most profound example of the alteration of the patterning of ethical consideration in our age: "Evil no longer exists in contrast to good; rather, there is a new inhumanity: indifference—that is to say, complete alienation, complete indifference vis-à-vis life" (2005: 27). As an illustration of his point, Fromm cites Herman Kahn's apparently calm question in *On Thermonuclear War* as to whether 50 million dead would still be "acceptable"—the apparent reasonableness of such a horrific calculation speaking for itself.

So while necrophilia, in its most extreme clinical forms, involves an interest in feces and corpses, what happens in its less extreme forms is a general turning away of interest from life. Our overemphasis on intellect at the expense of feeling leads ultimately to a bureaucratic spirit that governs general decision making, transferring the central ethical decisions to the realm of the administration of things. Fromm contends, in fact, that the split between thought and affect, which occurs in this process, leads to an increasingly pervasive "low-grade chronic schizophrenia" (1970 [1968]: 41). Our predominantly "cerebral-intellectual" approach, he argues, goes together with the absence of an affective response, leading to the withering of feelings, in that to the extent that feelings exist they are "not cultivated" and remain "relatively crude" (1997 [1973]: 468).

The situation that has been discussed in this section—an idolatrous alienation that has resulted in a desensitivization to life—has also been described by Fromm as a "pathology of normalcy." This idea, which has its genesis in something Freud first proposed in "Civilization and its Discontents"—namely, "research into the pathology of cultural communities" (Freud, 2001c: 144)—and which can be used to categorize any society in which what is pathological (in the psychological sense) has become normal, was formalized for the first time in *The Sane Society*. The premise of the idea is that a society can be "sick," which, taken on Fromm's terms, means that it is structured, and operates with values that are contrary to the healthy functioning of its individual members considered in themselves (as such, Fromm is not making an organicist argument, but one that relates predominantly to the psychological health of the individual). In Fromm's particular conception, this normalized pathology of twentieth-century advanced capitalist society consists in a reduced ability to experience affect, a relative loss of self, and the ever-increasing engagement in more passive (and "passivating," as Fromm describes it) activities.

In offering an account of the pathology of the cultural community of late-modern industrial capitalism (particularly in its American form—although with generic similarities that extend to all similarly advanced cultures), Fromm was acting in the role of "analyst of society." It is this—allied with the ethical and practical nature of his solutions (each of which will be discussed later)—which sets his account as particularly unique and separate from otherwise similar accounts. As Fromm himself noted in *The Sane Society*, his critique can be said to be grouped as part of wider critique of instrumental capitalist society, common to many thinkers stretching back to Burckhardt, Tolstoy, Proudhon, Baudelaire, Thoreau, Marx, Nietzsche, Kierkegaard, and Durkheim. It is clear also, therefore, that it adjoins more or less closely to the similar critiques offered by Weber, Heidegger, Horkheimer, Marcuse, Adorno, Mumford, Ellul, Christopher Lasch, and Zygmunt Bauman. Limitations of space prohibit detailed discussion of the connections between Fromm's critique and those of the authors mentioned above (although it must be stressed that Fromm's explicit evocation of idolatry as a conceptual analytical tool and the presence of a psychological depth to his analysis marks out his account as a unique fusion of inverted Judaic, socialized Freudian, and psychologized Marxian concerns). A few points that relate more generally to the accuracy of Fromm's account considered in itself will be dealt with presently.

First of all, it must be stressed that Fromm offers his account as a deliberately one-sided picture, framed so as to paint in stark colors what he saw as the underlying trend of global societies that might otherwise remain opaque. The extremity that might seem to pervade his account therefore leads to a sense of its seeming overwrought at times. But, as will be discussed in greater detail later, Fromm avoids the excessive view of reification found in Adorno, Marcuse (particularly in *Eros and Civilization* and *One-Dimensional Man*, but notably less so in *An Essay on Liberation* and *Counterrevoltion and Revolt*), and others. He was, in fact, explicit, on a number of occasions that he saw many signs of a culture that opposed the trends discussed above (something that will become clearer in the following discussion). The point of developing a one-sided account was so as to be able to outline what he felt were real and discernible trends that captured the direction of travel of changes in twentieth-century life, and to enable these trends to be challenged. While this may seem reasonable, Fromm's account has been accused of being somewhat outmoded, based on American society as it was in the mid-twentieth century. There initially seems to be more force in this criticism. The time and place at which Fromm's social criticism was offered—post–Second World War America—is generally considered to be a period of uncharacteristic affluence and relative homogeneity, with security in employment and a high degree of social conformity. The socioeconomic situation that developed over the ensuing decades and up until the present day is characterized by less security and the increased proletarianization of employment. As such, questions have to be asked of the relativity of Fromm's critique. Is his account of the marketing orientation, for instance, valid now, if indeed it ever was?

Michael Maccoby, who collaborated with Fromm on the Mexican social character study, argues that Fromm's concept of marketing character does not tally with the dominant social character today. In his introduction to the 1996 version of *Social Character in a Mexican Village*, Maccoby contends that Fromm's account of the character orientation is in fact an over-generalization of a particular character in American industrial society during a brief historical period (Maccoby, 1996: xxiii). In *Why Work? Leading the New Generation*, Maccoby describes what he sees as a more common, and more productive, variant of this new social character: namely, the "self-developer"—a character that is better adapted to the new world of work and its associated processes of restructuring, downsizing, and information technology proliferation, combining demands for teamwork and customer service with a lived uncertainty about employment. In comparison with what he contends is this more common character, Maccoby finds Fromm's marketing character to be the nonproductive and minority response to this new world of work, lacking a strong sense of self, trying to become what will sell in the marketplace rather developing new potentialities and skills. This idea has also been stressed by Richard Margolies, who suggests that marketing is "not an adequate description of a whole new class of educated managers and employees who are highly motivated regarding lifelong learning, gender inequality, and a balanced life" (Margolies, 1996:

374). But while Maccoby and Margolies are right to highlight the certain negative imbalance in Fromm's account, their criticisms run the risk of overcompensating with their emphasis on the positive side of adaptation to the new work arrangements that have taken place since the mid-point of the twentieth century. Maccoby's description of the "self-developer," for instance, comes close to falling into managerial euphemism and into the trap Fromm warns us of in *The Sane Society*, that is, of interpreting *the human problem of industrial relations* as *the industrial problem of human relations* (2002 [1955]: 176). Although the changes in the nature of employment to which Maccoby refers to are important for an accurate understanding of contemporary character, there is a real danger that behind words and phrases such as "downsizing" and "restructuring" is hidden the more brutal downgrading of employee rights and the imposition of compulsory redundancy, etc. In more a more "flexible" employment situation it is even more important that the "right package" is provided. This environment, because of its increased precariousness, coupled with relatively high levels of unemployment, will also be more competitive, thus intensifying farther the negative traits of the marketing orientation.

It might also be objected that Fromm's account of the life-indifferent, cybernetic society is excessive. Though he recognized that such a society was not realized, Fromm clearly felt that we were moving rapidly toward a fully industrialized, automated world where the 20-hour week would be standard (1967 [1965]: xii). Predictions in this area are notoriously difficult and identification of the causal elements in a particular social constellation always slippery; Fromm should not, therefore, be upbraided for apparently failing in this regard. Moreover, it is, it must be said, a little early to judge. The interaction of the causal elements, even when correctly identified, often take longer than expected to work toward the posited future state that their mutual relation suggests. While Fromm may have exaggerated the degree of cybernetic control, the relentless creep of computerized living suggests reason to be cautious before the cybernetic nightmare of the 1960s is completely written off as wholly unfounded. Similarly, while perhaps part of his critique of indifference might be said to be an overstatement motivated by the foreboding sense of nuclear holocaust, it could be plausibly countered that it is a somewhat open question as to the degree to which we differ from this age—the deployment of missile space stations and shields and the continued proliferation of nuclear weapons, while not conducted in a context as dramatic as the Soviet-American stand-offs of earlier decades, show that a definite connection to this way of thinking remains. What is more, the nature of modern warfare is such that, with the increased distanciation from killing afforded by new technological advances, as well as the accompanying rolling news coverage, sanitized media templates, talk of "precision weapons strikes," "shock and awe," etc., clearly encourages a cerebral-affective separation.

Importantly, Fromm did not restrict his analysis of this cataclysmic indifference to the nuclear issue. He saw the dangers of an ecological collapse as a critical contemporary issue—an issue, which today has largely replaced the apocalyptic dimensions of the nuclear fear. Fromm saw the ecological disaster we very likely face as resulting from the same failure to develop our emotional capacities, and to sufficiently appreciate and be motivated by the reality of the situation. As he put it in *Escape from Freedom* (in words meant for the coming crisis of fascism, but which are applicable to the issue at hand), there is a sense in which we seem to be "overcome by a profound feeling of powerlessness which makes [us] gaze toward approaching catastrophes as though [we] were paralyzed" (1969 [1941]: 254).

The Art of Living as a Normative Humanism

Having discussed what he refers to as the "deterioration of Western civilization" since 1914 (2006 [1962]: 126), it must be stressed that Fromm was not content with merely describing this deterioration: it was imperative that it be *reversed*. Concerned with how Western civilization could be prevented from destroying itself on account of its characteristic "discrepancy between intellectual-technical over-maturity and emotional backwardness" (1969 [1941]: xvi), Fromm called for a *renaissance of humanism*, which was first and foremost a "renaissance of humanistic experience" (2006 [1962]: 128). Central to this was the return to the basic concern of the humanist philosophical and religious tradition, the questioning of what makes us human, and the explicit ethical experience of human centering. More than anything, Fromm thought that life had ceased to be thought of as an art, that there was a general indifference as to the question of *how* to live, and an impoverished level of consideration of what it means to hold the human individual as an end. Fromm's thinking here is connected to the older religio-philosophical tradition in which ethics (in its humanistic application) was central. Inasmuch as this is the case, there is a connection to the humanist tradition of Judaism, to aspects of Buddhist thought, to Aristotelian and Stoic ethical philosophy, to Meister Eckhart and Spinoza, and to the humanistic philosophy of the "early" Marx. In each of these thought systems, the life of the individual was considered as fundamentally ethically centered, that is to say, as a realm in which life was experienced as involving the *question* of how to live and to realize well-being, and in which the human criterion was central. This is not ethics in its deontological sense, but something closer to the *eudaimonistic* conception, that is, ethics less as a formalistic conception of "duty," as opposed to ethics as a lived experience of concerned engagement with the harmony of the individual person (which, as will be shown, also means the harmony of the individual person as related to others).

In *You Shall Be as Gods*, Fromm attempts an encompassing if somewhat schematic description of what he takes to be the experience that underlies, and is common to, the various conceptualizations of humanistic ethical centering that influence his thought. He calls this common experiential substratum the "x experience" (1966a: 57) and lists its five characteristic aspects or goals: (1) the experience of life as a problem or question that requires an answer; (2) the presence of a definite hierarchy of values, the highest value being the optimum development of one's own powers of reason, love, compassion, and courage, with all worldly achievements being subordinated to these; (3) the belief that man alone is an end and never a means and that his whole attitude toward life is one in which each event is responded to from the standpoint of whether or not it helps to transform him in the direction of becoming more human; (4) the activity that can be described as the letting go of one's "ego," one's greed, and with it, one's fears (making one "empty" in order to fill oneself up with the world, etc.); and (5) the transcending— but not in the conventional sense in which the word is used—of the ego, leaving the prison of one's selfishness and separateness (1966a: 58–60).

It is clear from this outline that Fromm's thought here relates to what can be called an "experiential humanism," that is to say, a humanism based in lived experience and in engaged personal commitment. Existence under this mode of experiencing life will be characterized by the reduction of narcissism, greed, indifference, and the increase of what can be considered true individuality, that is to say, the experience of oneself as the author of one's own life. It will also be lived with what Tillich has described as an "ultimate concern" (Tillich, 1953: 14), something that "unifies man's mental life and gives it a dominating center" (Tillich, 1957: 107) such that any other concern will always be subordinated. Fromm used this phrase from time-to-time and it clearly expresses something of what he is trying to get across, although Fromm's usage of it is ultimately atheistic, whereas Tillich's is inescapably caught up in theistic problematics.

Central to the idea of the x experience is the bringing about of an increased freedom from controlling, damaging passions. Evidently, such freedom implies (and aims at) a degree of self-control, which in turn implies the development of reason, rationality, and objectivity. The "rationality" spoken of here, however, should not be confused with instrumental rationality; it is closer, in fact, to the Stoic ethical idea in which rationality seeks to conquer irrational, controlling passions. At the same time, it is also distinct from this idea in that passion is not seen as irredeemably irrational but in fact as potentially connected to rationality. In this sense, Fromm is closer to Spinoza, who was influenced by Stoic thought, but who refused the reason/emotion dualism found there. On Spinoza's account—an account which Fromm generally accepts—rationality and irrationality are considered *qualities* of emotion. As Fromm explains it, "reason flows from the blending of rational thought and feeling" (1970 [1968]: 40), such that not only thinking but also emotions can be rational. (Fromm held the Spinozean idea that rationality is that which furthers the growth and development of an organism, particularly, in this case, in relation to the harmonious balance of the human psychic structure.)[8] Fromm also shares with Spinoza a common conception of personal liberation from controlling, damaging passions: through understanding irrational passions we translate them into rational, active emotions ("active" here denoting the degree to which they are autonomous, spontaneous, noncontrolling). Such a process, of course, is the basis of psychoanalysis, with its fundamental working axiom that knowledge leads to transformation; that in the very act of knowing one transforms oneself. As with Spinoza's system, "knowledge" here is not understood as merely intellectual; it must also be affective. This point was crucial for Fromm, who stressed that the ultimate level of change escapes purely intellectual comprehension, that is, it is a pre-conceptual and fundamentally *experiential* phenomenon.

In addition to these systems, Fromm links his thought here to the experiential humanism of Buddhism (particularly Zen Buddhism) and mysticism (particularly the Christian mysticism of Meister Eckhart). In both systems of thought the overcoming of greed is central, with stress laid on the giving up of ego, being "empty" and "slaying" oneself—these descriptions understood in the positive sense of adopting an "openness to receive" (1960b: 41). Lack of space prohibits detailed discussion of the respective systems taken in themselves, but it must be stressed that Fromm's understanding of mysticism (Zen Buddhism being considered a mystical movement within Buddhism more generally) does not accord to the common pejorative understanding found in our culture, in which, as Fromm himself was aware, it is said "to suffer from a lack of rational clarity, to dwell in the realm of feeling and pious enchantment, and furthermore to imply flight from the social reality" (2005: 159). The fact that Fromm, with some historical justification, associated mysticism with radical autonomy and self-sufficiency, was discussed in chapter 2.

In all the influences Fromm draws upon, a central stress is laid on achieving greater awareness, becoming open and responsive and on the need "to experience one's self in the act of being, not in having, preserving, coveting, using" (1960b: 36). Common to all, then, is the goal of overcoming greed, narcissism, and egoism more generally (all irrational passions). In Fromm's own system, these ideas correspond to the concept of the *productive orientation* to life, which involves the spontaneous activity of one's own mental and emotional powers and the achievement of interpersonal relations based on the qualities of love and reason. As was discussed in chapter 3, biophilia (the love of life) and the being mode of existence are close extrapolations of this idea and are similarly centered on the move toward developing love and reason ("love" understood here as the achievement of interpersonal union on the basis of integrity and autonomy of self). This idea of achieving interpersonal union is crucial for Fromm. Influenced by religious and mystical thought and also by the Romantic concern with finding expressive unity, the x experience is concerned with finding harmony and solidarity *as well as* individuality. Living in accordance with the "x experience" provides us with the seemingly paradoxical task "of realizing [a true] individuality and at the same time transcending it and arriving at the experience of universality" (2003 [1947]: 136). On Fromm's account, Bauman's alternative of finding happiness through oneself or through others (Nietzsche vs. Levinas) is false. Concerned as he was with the reduction of narcissism, Fromm saw both as possible and, in fact, mutually implied (Fromm, as with Aristotle and Marx, saw man as a social animal for whom cooperation is fundamental, and that in order to remain sane man must be related to others). Making reference to the Judaic and Christian traditions once more, Fromm cited the injunction to "love thy neighbor as thyself" and, even more pointedly, to "love the stranger," as teachings essentially aimed at reducing narcissism. For Fromm, leaning on Hermann Cohen, "one discovers the human being in the stranger," for "if the stranger has become fully human to you, there is also no longer an enemy, because you have become truly human" (1980 [1964]: 89).

This idea has been sharply opposed by John Schaar, who questions Fromm's stress on the biblical idea of universal love. For Schaar, human love is "partial, selective, erratic…a valuable thing, not to be thrown about indiscriminately and given to all men regardless of merit" (Schaar, 1961: 132). Schaar goes on: "Love is not an affirmation of all mankind; it is the affirmation of a certain good and beautiful mankind which exists now in one person, the beloved…the essential feature of love is choice, decision, discrimination. It is false to think that the one who loves affirms mankind as such, respects all men equally, and takes everybody into his care and concern" (Schaar, 1961: 135–136). What is clear from the juxtaposition of Fromm and Schaar's views of love is that they are speaking about two different phenomena. Part of the problem in any discussion of "love" is the fact that the term stands for a variety of experiences which are not necessarily commensurable and not generally analytically separated. Although

Fromm does make a greater effort than most here, he must take his share of the blame for the confusion. What is important for Fromm is less "loving" everyone, in Schaar's sense, but increasing the sphere of concern and open relationship with others that is central to the biblical idea of "brotherly love." Fromm never says that realizing such a form of love is easy; it is a goal to be striven for, with much effort and dedication. The very fact that these ideas may seem remote and implausible to us is precisely the reason he called for the *art of living* to be resurrected and the "New Man" created.

The art of living as Fromm evokes it is understood in the ancient Greek sense as an activity requiring specific knowledge and skill; it is thus both theoretical and practical (the art is practical in that it is *lived* and *practiced*, something to be self-consciously worked at). Fromm's formulation here throws up a revealing difference between his understanding and that of Bauman. Whereas Bauman suggests that we cannot but practice the art of life, that "life can't *not be* a work of art if this a *human* life—the life of a being endowed with will and freedom of choice" (Bauman, 2008: 52–53), Fromm insists, like Foucault, that modern society has lost the concept of life as an art, and certainly that we generally do not practice it in the self-conscious and earnest way it could be said to be practiced in a life lived in accordance with the religio-philosophical humanist ideal. Part of the problem for Fromm is that to succeed at living well means that we need to know what living well means for *human* beings, and thus that we need to know something about human nature. As such, Fromm's account involves an explicit essentialism that is not found in either Bauman or Foucault. Moreover, because of this essentialism, the possibility of objectivity opens up. For Fromm, the axiom underlying art of living is objectively valid in that it is inherent in our nature and not the result of subjective value choice.

As such, the art of living implies what Fromm called the "science of man," which is given the task of constructing a "model of human nature." Fromm is adamant that such a task is not ruled out because we lack (and cannot ever get) complete knowledge of human nature; he points to the fact that other sciences commonly operate with concepts of entities based on, or controlled by, inferences from observed data and not directly observable themselves (2003 [1947]: 17). The task of the science of man is "to observe the reactions of man to various individual and social conditions and from observation of these reactions to make inferences about man's nature" (2003 [1947]: 16)—or as Fromm puts it in *The Sane Society*: "to infer the core common to whole human race from the innumerable manifestations of human nature" (2002 [1955]: 13). As was discussed in chapter 5, this is generally what happens in anthropological study, although the fact this is so is largely obscured by an excessive culturalist focus that disclaims the reality of universalism. That the idea might seem far-fetched is largely down to the fact that this excessive culturalism has come to dominate social theoretical and anthropo-logical thought. While there have been a number of studies countering some high-profile relativist claims, suggesting in the process at the existence of universal aspects of human life,[9] controversy remains and probably will con-tinue to do so, despite the fact that attempts to draw out human universals are not likely to go away and will surely only strengthen as the dominance of the anti-humanist paradigm, with its excessive culturalism, wanes.

The point of Fromm's talk about a "science of man"—which self-con-sciously references Aristotle, but is also connected to Enlightenment talk of the same name—is that it can assist in the creation of practical norms that can form the basis of a naturalistic ethics. The science of man, then, is seen as leading to a normative humanism from which an ethical naturalism forms. As with the idea of essentialism, normative humanism and ethical naturalism are much maligned concepts today, involving as they do the contention that there are objective norms and values stemming from the very nature of our existence. This position of opposition, based on a misunderstood conception of what is known as the "naturalistic fallacy" (the belief that values cannot be derived from facts—an argument traced either to David Hume or, more accurately, to G. E. Moore)—has become accepted as virtually unchallenge-able dogma. As Christian Smith has argued, however, drawing on the work of the virtue ethics revival in the later half of the twentieth century, this argu-ment neither makes sense (the very statement itself contravenes the principle), nor was it in fact what Hume said—as Smith shows, Hume, in the famous passage of *A Treatise of Human Nature* (Book III, Part I, Section I) does not state that is impossible to move from an is to an ought, but, rather, that moral arguments based on descriptive facts are all too frequently executed without sufficient thought or justification (Smith, 2010: 386–389).

Fromm quite openly bases his approach on the normative humanist idea that, as in any other problem, there are right and wrong, satisfactory and unsatisfactory solutions to the problem of human existence (2002 [1955]: 14). His contention is that there are in fact universal criteria for mental health, valid for the human race as such; that "moral norms are based on man's inherent qualities, and that their violation results in mental and emo-tional disintegration" (2003 [1947]: 4). The account of humanist ethics that he outlines contends that "good" is that which promotes life, spontaneity, individuality, and ultimately mental health, and that "bad" is that which leads to a lack of development of sense of self, to living in a narcissistic-indifferent way, and, ultimately, to dysfunction and pathology. As he puts in *Escape from Freedom*:

> We may not always know what serves this end, we may disagree about the function of this or that ideal in terms of human development, but this is

no reason for a relativism which says that we cannot know what furthers life or what blocks it. We are not always sure which food is healthy and which is not, yet we do not conclude that we have no way whatsoever of recognising poison. In the same way we can know, if we want to, what is poisonous for mental life. We know that poverty, intimidation, isolation, are directed *against* life; that everything that serves freedom and furthers the courage and strength to be oneself is *for* life. What is good or bad for man is not a metaphysical question, but an empirical one that can be answered on the basis of an analysis of man's nature and the effect which certain conditions have on him. (1969 [1941]: 265)

His humanistic ethics, then, is the "applied science of 'the art of living' based upon the theoretical science of man" (2003 [1947]: 12).

From this account it is clear that Fromm is opposed to subjectivist ethics. Fromm deals specifically with this issue in *Man for Himself*, rejecting the ethical hedonist position that uses pleasure as the criterion of value. It is not that Fromm denies the right of anyone to equate value with pleasure (or that they ever collide) but that he is clear that immediate gratification does not necessarily correlate to health and well-being, and thus to flourishing. What Fromm is opposing here is the "ethics of taste," in which there is no reason other than sentiment for choosing one particular course of action, or thing over another—a position that leads in the end to a radical subjectivism in which it is impossible to coherently hold, for instance, that freedom is preferable to slavery. Fromm's objectivist position, which is a corollary of his underlying essentialism, holds that there are objective criteria inherent in the facts themselves—that we have norms *because* we have values. What should be stressed in connection with this discussion is the fact that, unless we take a grounding position of some sort, value attributions will endlessly spiral back on themselves in tautological regresses. It is a fact of ethics (and of human existence itself) that we never pass a "pure" value judgment on anything. Fromm was not naïve on this score. He explicitly states that norms can only be deduced from theories on the premise that a certain activity is chosen and a certain aim is desired—in this case, the art of living, which has as its aim the *flourishing of the individual human being with a maximum vitality and intrinsic harmony*. It is clearly possible for someone who does not accept this particular value grounding, or who holds an anti-foundationalist position in general, to reject the premise. While this is so, it does not mean that this person is immune from the consequences of refusing to live their life in accordance with the dictates of the premise. As a depth psychologist, Fromm was convinced that though we can live life in a variety of ways, certain ways of living will cause certain reactions, quite independently of the intellectual position a person holds.

Fromm's idea of humanistic ethics as the applied science of man is explicitly framed in connection with the fact that all applied sciences deal with practical norms according to which things ought to be done. The fact that there are practical norms according to which things ought to be done is not to say that there is only one way of doing things in accordance with the norm, but that achieving the desired result is not a matter of arbitrary effort—"while there may be different ways of achieving excellent results in any art, norms are not arbitrary; their violation is penalized by poor results or even by complete failure to accomplish the desired end" (2003 [1947]: 12). The fact that we do not have complete knowledge here is precisely the reason to try to gain more. While there are few absolute certainties in such an enterprise, it seems preferable to the curiously uninquisitive attitude predominant in social theoretical circles where thinkers are apparently satisfied with holding back from making any significant discernment at all. Nevertheless, Fromm's ideas here will no doubt seem unacceptable to many: that in speaking of objective norms he is effectively ruling out individuality and freedom and is therefore overly restrictive (even ethnocentric); that his ethics, despite his pronunciations, is authoritarian; and that his stress on essential human qualities leads to the creation of a category of nonhuman and less-than-fully human, and the discriminatory attitudes that will stem from such distinctions. Something must be said about these criticisms.

Dealing with the first point, it must be stressed that Fromm explicitly states that man can affirm his human potentialities *only* by realizing his individuality, to become who one truly is—this is notably different to Bauman who says it is the task of the art of life to perpetually become *someone other* than one has been thus far (Bauman, 2008: 73). Fromm was clear in his acknowledgment of the diversity of human beings and human cultures and was not out to create a norm of bland uniformity; the objective point was to create a norm of flourishing as the kinds of beings that we are, a flourishing that is only possible in connection with the unfolding of human powers that are conducive to mental health. The simple but surely pertinent point here is that one is not truly "free" or living an "authentic" individuality if one is controlled by passions and cannot see clearly the causes of one's own actions. Similarly, one cannot be "free" if one has not developed the capacity for independent critical thought in a society that neither encourages nor fosters it. The idea that such an account is restrictive, or ethnocentric, is perhaps less easy to counter. But while there is something inescapably ethnocentric in a detailed human utterance of any sort, Fromm's ethics are aimed at purportedly universal aspects of humanity that can be realized in a variety of ways consistent with divergent historical and cultural situations. Although agreement has not yet been found on the specifics, it is fairly clear that, as Wilde has noted of Fromm, "his work on the productive character and the goal of the 'being mode' conveys a sense of liberated experience which is wholly consonant with the widest variety of cultural identities" (Wilde, 2000: 49).

In terms of the issue of "authoritarianism"—which has been raised by Petteri Pietikäinen in an article on Fromm titled "The Sage Knows You Better than You Know Yourself"—it is worth stressing at the outset that *force*, which is ultimately what the accusation of authoritarianism centrally implies, is the ultimate anathema to Fromm's whole manner of thinking and is explicitly ruled out on numerous occasions. Nevertheless, Pietikäinen, drawing on Isaiah Berlin (who made specific reference to Fromm in his *Four Essays on Liberty*), argues that there is "a disquieting element of authoritarianism in Fromm's commitment to human emancipation that is more in line with religious doctrines than with the kind of 'agonistic' value-pluralism that Berlin was concerned with" (Pietikäinen, 2004: 114). The problem Pietikäinen and Berlin evidently have with Fromm here is that in his proclamation that he knows what is harmful and healthy for human beings, he risks becoming, in Berlin's words, a "transcendent dominant controller" (Berlin, 1969: 134), manipulating the otherwise free will of individuals to his own desires. This, for Pietikäinen, as for Berlin, is to treat others as objects without any will of their own.

That this is a misleading picture of Fromm should hardly require stating. Fromm time and time again rails against the fact that human beings have become things in contemporary society and is adamant that we must defend the liberties that have been won over the last few centuries with the "utmost vigor" (1969 [1941]: 106). Fromm's point here is that the problem of freedom is not only a quantitative one but also a *qualitative* one; that is to say that, as well as constraints external to us, we need also to deal with constraints working *internally*, in our character structure and in the dynamic functioning of our psyche. The issue for Fromm, then, reduces to a need to transcend a concern with purely negative freedom, that is, "freedom *from*," to a concern with positive freedom, that is, "freedom *to*." When Berlin says that "if, although I enjoy the right to walk through open doors, I prefer to not to do so, but to sit still and vegetate, I am not thereby rendered less free" (Berlin, 1969: xlii), he is clearly right; but it is also clear that this says nothing about the qualitative aspect of freedom, nothing about the underlying psychological depth of human action that Fromm discusses. The difference between Fromm and Berlin (and Pietikäinen) is that Fromm sees freedom from political shackles as a necessary but insufficient condition; beyond this negative freedom we need "freedom to create and to construct, to wonder and to venture" and such freedom "requires that the individual be active and responsible, not a slave or a well-fed cog in the machine" (1980 [1964]: 52). The idea that force is implicated in Fromm's plea for the development of human capacities for positive freedom wholly ignores the voluntary nature of the plea and the humanist respect for the right of the individual. (That it may still be said to lead to a coercive moral authoritarianism is harder to counter—although Fromm's commitment to the inalienable rights of the human being and the deep empathy evidenced in his psychoanalytic approach which is expressed in his fondness of Terence's proclamation that "nothing human is alien to me" would, if strictly adhered to, surely work against this.) Talk of "techniques of self" (Foucault, 1984c) or "technologies of self" (Rose, 1999) does not side-track Fromm here either. Fromm understands cultural mediation, but posits a level of agentic, private experience that has some degree of autonomy from cultural forces.

As to the final criticism—that the focus on essential human qualities leads to the creation of a category of nonhuman and less-than-fully human—it must be stressed that while there is clearly a danger that singling out essential human qualities could lead to discrimination in certain situations, this idea, as with the previous concern over moral authoritarianism, sits poorly with the central thrust of Fromm's humanism, with its persistent call for human beings to be treated as *ends* rather than means. Although it is fair to note that Fromm did not deal explicitly with the issue of people with impairments, including severe mental impairments, speaking as he was to the majority of the society in which he lived in the role of prophet, it is clear that the basic humanist position demands respect, care, and assistance in the task of flourishing to the extent allowed by the inherent capabilities of person in question (the "capabilities approach" to justice, as outlined by Martha Nussbaum [2006], is an improvement in the sense of dealing specifically with the issue of people with impairments—although, as Wilde [2012] has pointed out, her reluctance to support a strong view of human nature reflects what appears a retreat from the spirited defense of essentialism contained in some of her earlier works). The point to be stressed here is that Fromm's idea of human nature is of a *capacity* as well as a principle. While it is an unfortunate fact that for some individuals the scope for certain otherwise characteristic human functions is inherently limited, this does not mean that the humanist idea of the search for perfectibility—which refers less to finding absolute "perfection" than the attempt to perfect existing potentials as much as is possible—must be ruled out. Moreover—and as I have tried to stress—it is also not a concern that could be consistently turned into discrimination, seeing as the basic maxim underlying this concern, and never altered by it, is the treatment of the individual in whatever condition fundamentally as an end.[10] Considering this, it is clear that discrimination could only occur in situations where the ideals of humanism were only nominally held.

As such, the argument that cautions us against defining the human, though important in dealing with purportedly humanist though in actual fact *non*-humanist thought systems, is not actually a damaging criticism of humanism itself. Moreover, the caution that stems from the concern to avoid discrimination actually tends to play into the hands of an inconsistent relativism that risks allowing and abetting violence; if we cannot say *why* freedom is preferable to torture, for instance, we are on shaky grounds for consistently upholding any other similar type of distinctions. The suggestion, made by many, that what is required is a perpetual inquiry into the human is certainly right (this is what Fromm suggests in his call for the science of man), but in this inquiry we need to have some reference points and to make some definite statements—for what does an inquiry amount to if not to making some consequential discernments that enable something definite to be said? Although we come to understand the human in different periods in different ways, to disavow any attempt to weigh these understandings against the thing we are trying to understand results in a hopeless form of radical skepticism in which it is impossible to speak of anything coherently at all.

Roads to Sanity (and the Paradox of Hope)

Despite the bleakness that pervades much of Fromm's critical account of the industrial-capitalist societies of his day, he held resolutely to the hope that a renaissance of humanism was possible. For the first time in history, he argued, there existed the potential to experience the "One World": with globalized communication, increased democratization, rising living standards, and the opportunity for increased education and transmission of ideas, we had the potential to put an end to national tribalisms and embrace the unity of humanity with common purpose and mutual respect. Fromm's goal here was *the gradual humanization of all sectors of society* such that external changes would facilitate and consolidate the personal transformations brought about through a renewed focus on the art of living. In *The Sane Society*, under the title "Roads to Sanity," Fromm discusses a range of practical measures that could be taken so as to enable such a renaissance of humanism in the world at large. These measures include suggestions to humanize work, consumption, politics—all of which framed around his normative humanist criteria. He returns to this practical discussion in *The Revolution of Hope* and once more in *To Have or To Be?*, each time repeating, summarizing, extending, or slightly reworking the preceding account.[11]

The humanization that Fromm speaks of essentially consists in "the change of the social, economic, and cultural life of our society in such a way that it stimulates and furthers the growth and aliveness of man rather than cripples it" (1970 [1968]: 96). This centers on increasing interest and participation through the deepening and expansion of the principles of democracy. In the case of the work situation, for instance, Fromm's aim was to make the situation itself as concrete as possible so as to ensure that it provided *meaning* for the employee. Importantly, merely transferring ownership into the hands of the state was insufficient; the point was to enact a form of what can be called "industrial democracy" (2009 [1976]: 147). Fromm's ideal was something like the Boimondau watch factory in France, a "Community of Work" based on communitarian socialist principles, which illustrated for Fromm the real possibilities of the transformation of our industrial organization; but he was adamant that, short of this ideal, it was still possible to increase meaning and concreteness, to which end he cited Elton Mayo's famous Hawthorne Works experiment, in which even a small degree of active participation within the existing Taylorist framework led to noticeable increases in motivation and satisfaction (2002 [1955]: 295–298). What was essential for Fromm was to strive for the *optimal* blending of centralization and decentralization such that active participation is facilitated to the highest level compatible with technical demands of the enterprise. Fromm spoke of comanagement and the participation of workers in day-to-day and long-term decision making. He was also vocal in his support for the role of Trades Unions, although he called for greater participation of the individual workers in the unions themselves (1969 [1941]: 126). Crucially, Fromm's idea of change in relation to work was of a gradual, evolutionary process, which would involve a *restriction* of property rights rather than an immediate revolution of them (although his overall aim was ultimately for revolution of these relations). The process would also be gradual in that Fromm noted that the first condition for active participation is that the worker is well informed, not only about his or her work but the performance of the whole enterprise. In line with this, Fromm advocated that formative and continuing education should be offered to all workers. Crucially, this education should not solely be geared to the requirements of the labor task, but to doing away with the "harmful separation between theoretical and practical knowledge" (2002 [1955]: 337).

Connected to these changes in work, Fromm called for changes in welfare. In a prescient suggestion, he called for the existing security system to be extended to a *universal subsistence guarantee* (2002 [1955]: 327), which would allow individuals the freedom to find a job most suited to them at any point in their career. Fromm suggested that this initiative would ensure that companies would be keener to make work more attractive to prospective workers. It would also be good for women previously financially tied to a husband or father (obviously Fromm was writing at time when women were more clearly dependent on a husband or father than is contemporarily the case). Fromm pointedly rejects what he sees as the myth of the inherent laziness of human beings, arguing that, aside from neurotically lazy people, there would be very few who would not want to earn more than the minimum and prefer to do nothing rather than work. As a means of mitigating fears, he suggested the scheme be limited to a period of two years so as to avoid any neurotic refusal of any social obligation (2002 [1955]: 328), and that this, added to the fact that it would provide only a relatively basic level of comfort, would mean that it would interest only those really interested in finding a more fulfilling career.

In relation to politics, Fromm explored ways and means to implement "active participatory democracy" (2009 [1976]: 148). Central to his thinking here was the creation of hundreds and thousands of face-to-face "clubs" consisting of 100 to 300 members, and much smaller "groups" of 25 or so. The idea behind these face-to-face groupings was that they would meet regularly, in a designated meeting space, with the purpose of exchanging information, engaging in discussion of the main issues of local and national concern, with any relevant practical work undertaken by all members. Fromm vacillated slightly on how the groups would be formed, suggesting initially that they should be formed on the basis of residence or work (2002 [1955]: 334) and, subsequently, that they should be formed by people with similar aims and interests so as to ensure there would be a variety of clubs to choose from (1970 [1968]: 156). Either way, Fromm stressed that the meetings should be carried out in a different spirit from traditional political groupings, with bureaucratic procedure kept to a minimum and ideological language generally avoided. The groupings should be autonomous and ideally achieve a mix of age and social status. Fromm envisaged the groups forming a true "House of Commons," sharing power with universally elected representatives on issues of fundamental principles of action (2002 [1955]: 335)—although moving toward this process would take time, as it is through the developmental potentials offered in the groups on the basis of discussion of impartial, good quality information that the best decisions can be made. Fromm's contention in advocating the formation of such groups was that "a good deal of the irrational and abstract character of decision making would disappear, and political problems would become in reality a concern for the citizen" (2002 [1955]: 335). In meeting regularly, and thereby coming to know each other, Fromm suggested that the participants would build up bonds of trust and develop their own sense of responsibility and self-consciousness. Ultimately, he thought that these groupings could form the basis for a mass movement of people, which would at the same time aim to move toward a personal transformation out of apathetic alienation and into active participation. Such a blueprint, he thought, could be extended to all collective enterprises, from businesses to the education or health sector (1970 [1968]: 112).

In the sphere of consumption, Fromm wanted to challenge the irrational manner in which we consume as well as the manipulation that encourages it. First and foremost, he called for the eradication of suggestive advertising and the manufacturing of needs by profit-seeking corporations. The first step in this would be to distinguish between "true" and "false" needs, that is to say, between needs that originate in our organism and that are an expression of the individual's growth according to the principles of normative humanism and needs that are forced upon the individual by industry and that lead to pathology and psychical ill-health (2009 [1976]: 144) (NB: Fromm speaks of "true" and "false" needs here from a position influenced by a humanist evaluative schema—he is not suggesting that one does not feel the "false" need, but analytically, it is a need *imposed* on the individual and/or which is ultimately detrimental to human flourishing. Although debate here is fairly intractable—see Soper [1981], Sayers [1988], and Benton [2009], for instance—Fromm's thinking in this connection is thematically linked to his criticism of The Great Promise: the idea being that the promise can never be met, premised as it is on never delivering general satisfaction but encouraging acquisitiveness, greed, narcissism etc., which are harmful to the individual. This is why not all needs/wants are "true," or good for mental health and autonomy. That this may still be regarded as a hypothesis to a certain degree at present, does not, of course, rule it out as a central aspect of theory.) In this connection, Fromm envisages a new humanist body of experts (comprised of psychologists, sociologists, anthropologists, theologians, as well as representatives of consumer groups) who would undertake a study of "humane" needs and the synthetic needs suggested by industry based on data developed in the science of man, and that the decisions realized here would be disseminated societally and discussed at face-to-face meetings. Importantly, this idea does not involve any obvious coercion, relying wholly on individuals deciding that they want to change their consumption patterns (2009 [1976]: 144). As part of his stress on the freedom and agency of the public, Fromm envisaged a militant consumer movement that would use the threat of "consumer strikes" as a weapon to challenge the power of the corporations.

Central to the changes Fromm envisions is the establishment of an effective system of dissemination of information. In relation to this, Fromm suggests the setting up of a nonpolitical national cultural agency with out-standing personalities from the fields of art, science, religion, business, and politics (Fromm titled this agency "The Voice of the American Conscience" in *The Revolution of Hope*, but "A Supreme Cultural Council" in *To Have or To Be?*). Fromm stressed that the members of the agency—who would be elected—would be people whose integrity and capability are unques-tioned, all sharing essentially humanistic aims. They would be charged with deliberating and issuing statements that would, hopefully, as a result of their rationality, win attention from at least a large section of the public (1970 [1968]: 151). Fromm also envisaged such councils being formed at the local level too, linking to subcommittees of the main agency for pointed debate of the issues, and thus engaging the wider public in the intricacies of the process.

The fact that Fromm, as a social theorist, risked offering such practical suggestions to the situation he was criticizing is as important as it is rare. In engaging in practical matters, the relatively free play of theory is cut short and one is opened up to attacks from a variety of angles. As it was, Fromm was criticized for "utopianism" (being superficially radical and hopelessly naïve) and for "gradualism" (being conformist and social democratic). For a committed socialist these are potentially pointed criticisms. Fromm has even been criticized on this matter by Lawrence Wilde, an otherwise keen cel-ebrator of his thought. Amid what is generally considered praise of Fromm, Wilde singles out his suggestions for the humanization of politics to be a "quaint mixture of Pericles and Plato," which is ultimately "impractical and somewhat naïve" (Wilde, 1998: 74–75). Normally judicious, it seems to me that Wilde may be a little too hasty here. Fromm's suggestions clearly have not been realized, but they were made in the full awareness of the difficulty of enacting real qualitative change in a society that is seemingly caught in the one-dimensional trap of affluent alienation.

Given this situation, what can be said of Fromm's suggestions is that they surely represent a crucial part of any genuinely progressive long-term strat-egy—and, despite the failure of any of them to be converted into reality, an eminently feasible part of such a strategy. This is not to say that they are *likely* to be realized, and that they are not a little wishful: is not almost everything in this regard a little wishful, given the apathy characteristic of affluent alien-ation? While it seems evident today that more concerted mass direct action will be required to raise consciousness sufficiently for these strategies to be effective, Fromm was writing at a time when consciousness was arguably raised to its highest point for the next 40 or 50 years, and certainly when radi-cal political policies were far closer to mainstream reality than they are today. In this situation, it seems that his suggestions should be viewed as nonviolent preconditions for any real and sustainable socialism, giving the space for a truly democratic socialist transition to occur (it is clear that Fromm's humanism was not a "militant humanism" [Schaff, 1963: 108; 1970: 170]—at least not in the general sense that the term "militant" can be said to have—and that he evidently refuted the idea that force was a permissible or even effective means of transcending such affluent alienation; that is not to say it is not a *committed* humanism, which is also what Schaff means by "militant"). Even today, when consciousness is historically deflated, Fromm's ideas here could still play a central part in any move toward realizing democratic socialism in practice. Either way—and this is crucial—Fromm did not think the process would be simple. He was clear, in fact, that the new social forms that will be the basis of the New Society "will not arise without many designs, models, studies, and experiments that *begin to bridge the gap between what is necessary and what is possible*. This will eventually amount to large-scale, long-run planning and to short-term proposals for first steps. The problem is the will and the humanist spirit of those who work on them"; however, he did believe that "when people can see a vision and simultaneously recognize what can be done step by step in a concrete way to achieve it, they will begin to feel encouragement and enthusiasm instead of fright" (2009 [1976]: 143). It is surely in this light that we should primarily judge Fromm's suggestions here.

The examples of Boimondau and Hawthorne Works show that it is possible to affect humanistic changes in the work situation. It is clear too that Fromm's ideas here are not merely accommodations to capitalism, but fairly realistic, immediate changes that will help prepare the ground for more significant changes further down the line. Fromm's suggestion of a *universal subsistence guarantee* has, as Wilde has pointed out, been adopted by a variety of thinkers, including economists, discussed under the name "basic income" (Wilde, 2000: 84). Fromm's call for consumer groups and advice agencies has proven prescient too, with a variety of consumer groups engaging in what is, admittedly, a fairly limited manner with industry and government advice agencies common to most welfare democracies. His call for weekly face-to-face club and group meetings was less prescient, though it has to be stressed that Fromm was writing at a time when similar groupings were spontaneously formed and genuinely considered to be the basis of a fundamentally transformed new society. The issue of a national cultural agency will perhaps seem the least prescient—and, to some, the most worrying—of his suggestions. It is clearly not hard to imagine such an agency, however, even though the move away from a committed, intellectually aspiring public sphere to an agonistic, populist one does make it seem more remote. Part of the problem with proposing such an arrangement is the resistance that accompanies our prevalent dislike of norms and of "being talked down to."[12]

Perhaps a greater, and certainly related, problem is the fact that the epistemological and methodological focus in current-day capitalist societies— a focus encouraged by tightly weaved political and financial interests—is largely aimed at technological improvement, or, as Fromm described it, the creation of "technological utopia" (2009 [1976]: 142). (This is not to suggest that there is no concern for improving the polity and society at large— clearly, in most welfare democracies, agencies exist with remits pertaining to certain aspects of societal and individual betterment; it is simply to stress that these efforts are largely swamped by the more dominant, instrumental concerns that dictate the flow of policy and political maneuvering that goes with it.) Were we to spend even the half the time pursuing *societal* utopia as we do technological utopia, Fromm's ideas would surely seem even less fantastic or quaint.

While this may be so, the charge of "utopianism" has been leveled at Fromm from another angle. For Pietikäinen, who acknowledges that Fromm's ideas for the creation of a New Society are not particularly fantastic (although, like Berlin, he worries over the possibility for coercion), what is fantastic and "utopian" about Fromm's account are his ideas for the restructuring of the human personality. Calling this a "psychological utopianism," Pietikäinen accuses Fromm of adopting a naïve Rousseauian position in which humans are seen as naturally altruistic at base, painting, in the process, a picture of an excessive harmony and suggesting that Fromm lacks any appreciation of the difficulties involved in issues pertaining to the incommensurability of constitutive goods (Pietikäinen, 2004: 106). Pietikäinen acknowledges that although Fromm was not arguing for a conflict-free society, "he never paused to think about the potential limitations of his Sane Society, nor about the reasons why anyone should disagree with him" (Pietikäinen, 2004: 113). Following Berlin, he asks, "What is to guarantee that the Sane Society will not educate its recalcitrant citizens to right living by coercion and make them obedient to the directives of an elite of Platonic guardians?" (Pietikäinen, 2004: 114). Schaar, 40 years prior to Pietikäinen, made a similar observation, saying of Fromm that he "lacks a clear and accurate conception of the political" (Schaar, 1961: 296).

While there is something to these criticisms—in that Fromm was not a political theorist per se and did not get as far as outlining a detailed political philosophy—it has to be stressed that Fromm was laying down *fundamental principles* on which such a philosophy could be developed, as well as making some important precursory suggestions as to how we might begin to go about realizing them. The point in Fromm's account relative to that of Pietikäinen, Berlin, and Schaar is that he was aiming for a much more substantive engagement with existential human reality beyond the negative agonistic liberalism that Pietikäinen, Berlin, and Schaar are content with. The idea that Fromm was oblivious to the incommensurability of goods is clearly wrong, as is evident from his recognition of precisely this point in *Man for Himself,* where he states that such incommensurability arises "necessarily in connection with existential dichotomies" (2003 [1947]: 179). What has happened is that Pietikäinen, Berlin, and Schaar, in their respective accounts of Fromm, attribute what seems to be the same thinness of their own views of personal human existence to Fromm and, from an analysis of the insufficiency of these views, conclude the insufficiency of Fromm's account. In their role as critics of Fromm they fail to respond in the appropriate way to his ideas: namely, to explore their political feasibility and to attempt to work out arrangements whereby they could be realized; the secondary, critical work ought to come *after* such an attempt. The point in Fromm's suggestions, it must be stressed, was to encourage debate and analysis of the state of contemporary consumer culture and how it might be improved. To call his idea of personal transformation "fantastic" without the requisite psychological and practical investigation suggests, on the basis of Fromm's own critique of our culture, the degree to which his idea of the "forgetting of humanism" could be said to be apposite. As Fromm puts it, "we have faith in the potentialities of others, of ourselves, and of mankind because, and only to the degree to which, we have experienced the growth of our own potentialities, the reality of growth in ourselves, the strength of our own power of reason and of love" (2003 [1947]: 156). Those who have had little experience of these phenomena may well have little reason to believe that they are real and possible.

Asides from seeming "utopian" and "gradualist," Fromm's suggestions and general approach to creating a New Society have drawn accusations of "conformism"—and none more prominently so than from Marcuse. In *Eros and Civilization*, Marcuse describes Fromm as a "sermonistic social worker," criticizing him for succumbing to the ideology that happiness could be achieved in contemporary society (Marcuse, 1966 [1955]: 6). Marcuse goes on, saying that Fromm "succumbs to the mystification of societal relations" and that his critique "moves only within the firmly sanctioned and well protected sphere of established institutions" (Marcuse, 1966 [1955]: 6). Echoing Adorno's earlier criticism of identity thinking, Marcuse says that Fromm's critique "remains ideological" and "has no conceptual basis outside the established system; most of its critical ideas and values are those provided by the system" (Marcuse, 1966 [1955]: 6). Ultimately, Marcuse takes issue with Fromm's idea of the development of personal potentialities and his stress on love as possible in the present social condition, contending that Fromm "revives all the time-honored values of idealistic ethics as if nobody had ever demonstrated their conformist and repressive features" (Marcuse, 1966 [1955]: 258).

Fromm was scathing in his response to Marcuse's criticism. As he pointed out, there is a great and unfortunate irony in his being accused of a lack of conceptual dialectics by a theorist who seems to forget that in any dialectical account of an alienated society, the said society must *already* contain within itself an element which contradicts it and thus can act to supersede it (1955: 348). It is worth quoting Fromm at length here:

> If it were not possible today to transcend the dominant personality pattern, it would never have been possible, and human progress could hardly have occurred...The development of personality can and does take place in the most adverse circumstances; in fact, it is stimulated by their very existence. But this holds true only for a minority who, for a number of reasons, can free themselves to some extent from the social mode of thought and experience, and react against it...As for the attempt to achieve some of the experience of the "new man" "prematurely," as it were, it is difficult but not impossible. And it must be tried precisely by those who are opposed to present-day society and are fighting for a world fit for man to live in. Political radicalism without genuine human radicalism will only lead to disaster. (1992: 127)

This is an issue that confronts the negative dialectical position of critical theory in general, Marcuse only imbibing it in part (in fact, by *An Essay on Liberation*, Marcuse seems to abandon the negative dialectical approach and adopt one with evident similarities to Fromm – an approach which in many ways is a consolidation of the humanistic aspects of his early approach as manifest in *Reason and Revolution*). Appropriately, Fromm turns round the barbed criticism that, as Adorno says of him in a letter to Horkheimer, he offers a mixture of "social democracy and anarchism" (March 1936, reported in Wiggershaus, 1994: 266), by drawing an equation with Marcuse (and, by implication, Adorno) to the effect that their neglect of the human factor mirrors the callousness toward moral qualities that led to the victory of Stalin (Fromm, 1955: 349). As Wilde notes, Fromm's position was closer to that of Rosa Luxemburg than it was to Lenin, Trotsky, or Stalin, and the social anarchist attempt to ensure an overtly ethical aspect, which was present in their social theory, was very appealing to Fromm as the basis for the realization of socialism with its human goals (Wilde, 2004a: 120–122). In Fromm's own words: "Since any improvement of the human situation will depend on the simultaneous change in the economic, political and in the human characterological spheres, no theory can be radical which takes a nihilistic attitude toward man" (1955: 349). In light of this view, Fromm describes Marcuse's position as "an example of human nihilism disguised as radicalism" (1955: 349), something that Marcuse virtually affirms when, in *One-Dimensional Man*, he says that "the critical theory of society possesses no concepts which could bridge the gap between the present and its future" (Marcuse, 1991 [1964]: 14).

As Fromm puts it in *The Revolution of Hope*, "if one is not concerned with the steps between the present and the future, one does not deal with politics, radical or otherwise" (1970 [1968]: 9). In outlining his practical suggestions Fromm was explicit on the need to avoid "dreaming" utopianism (2009 [1976]: 141) and to bridge the gap between present and future. His "gradualism," therefore, *is* a radical strategy, which begins the process of humanistic and socialistic transformation. The difference between Fromm and Marcuse here could be said to reduce to a difference between a *revolutionary* and *rebellious* stance, where revolution is conceived as a holistic approach that considers the relevance of the political, economic, social, and personal spheres (separately, and taken together) in a determined attempt to prize open opportunities for consequential social change, and where rebellion is conceived as a seemingly resigned and hopeless form of "happy consciousness" (although, as noted previously, Marcuse recants somewhat in *An Essay on Liberation* and *Counterrevolution and Revolt*, even singling out elements from the new social movements that might enable genuine revolution to occur). What Fromm was particularly scathing about was Marcuse's idea that anybody who studies the conditions for happiness and love inescapably betrays radical thought. Fromm believed that we must analyze the conditions of love and integrity in the present society and seek to strengthen them. Moreover, he believed that the attempt to practice these virtues amounts to "the most vital act of rebellion" (1955: 348–349). To acknowledge that there is a dearth of genuine love in contemporary society is not necessarily to rule out its possibility; for even if the possibilities for genuine love are reduced, it can always be actualized, developed, and built upon.

Fromm's stress on personal qualities in relation to social change is important and relatively unique. He recognized the degree to which liberation has become focused on the external world, without reference to the realities of inner change. His position was that we need to understand both inner and outer chains and that liberation must be based on "the liberation of man in the classic, humanist sense as well as in the modern, political and social sense" (2007 [1993]: 7–8). As Fromm points out, the evidence of history shows us that without this dual focus any given revolution tends to slide into authoritarianism. The only really revolutionary aim can be one of "total liberation" (2007 [1993]: 8)—the basic aim of Fromm's radical humanism—something which cannot consist in an ultimate focus on only one sphere of relevance at the expense of other spheres. Fromm's gradualist account of practical change and supposedly conformist account of personal change are in reality two aspects of the same strategy: to encourage the renaissance of humanism and, ultimately, the emergence of a New Man. It should be clear that this is not a shallow "exclusive pursuit of subjectivity" or a product of a "cult of subjectivity" as Jacoby claims (Jacoby, 1977: 105). Fromm is not calling for an examination and transformation of the self without changing the universe of the self: he is clear that we are social animals and that our physical constitution necessitates group living, which necessitates cooperation with others, which necessitates greater or lesser degrees of sanity, which in turn necessitates being related to others in some form of non-narcissistic union. He is also not suggesting "liberation now—without the sweat or grime of social change" (Jacoby, 1977: 47). Fromm stresses the necessity of practical measures, measures that are connected to the raising of subjectivity (yes, these measures are not as "militant" as those of others—Marcuse, Fanon, the Black Panthers, and the Situationists, etc.; Fromm avoids calls for violent revolution, but precisely because of what has been achieved, or what has not been achieved, by this in past century). All of this is preferable to Jacoby's critical theory claim that there is "no subjectivity" (1977: 80)—for if there is no subjectivity then it is hard to see how there can be any hope.

None of this is to say that Fromm was necessarily optimistic about the prospects of realizing these changes. In fact, Fromm's position in relation to social change was underlain with one particularly important idea that captures the spirit of this approach: namely, "the paradox of hope." As Fromm himself puts it,

Hope is paradoxical. It is neither passive waiting nor is it unrealistic forcing of circumstances that cannot occur. It is like the crouched tiger, which will jump only when the moment for jumping has come. Neither tired reformism nor pseudo-radical adventurism is an expression of hope. To hope means to be ready at every moment for that which is not yet born, and yet not become so desperate if there is not birth in our lifetime. There is no sense in hoping for that which already exists or for that which cannot be. Those whose hope is weak settle down for comfort or for violence; those whose hope is strong see and cherish all signs of new life and are ready every moment to help the birth of that which is ready to be born. (1970 [1968]: 9)

Fromm, in fact, stated that, despite the prerequisites for a renaissance of humanism being in place, he only saw a 2 percent chance of this change occurring (2009 [1976]: 160). He was fully aware that acceptance of this paradox is never easy, but that hope without expectation becomes a form of passive waiting, and that impatience rarely leads to long-lasting effective change. What is required, rather, is a form of "dynamic hope" (1966a: 153)—one must not "force the messiah" but expect him at each minute. A crucial part of this expectance is having faith: faith in the possibility of personal change that we are all generally capable of experiencing and which offers the essential complement to societal change. Faith for Fromm is like hope, it "is not prediction of the future; it is the vision of the present in a state of pregnancy...That is the paradox of faith: *it is certainty of the uncertain*" (1970 [1968]: 13). "Hope," Fromm continues, "is the mood that accompanies faith. Faith could not be sustained without the mood of hope. Hope can have no base except in faith" (1970 [1968]: 14).

The sentiments expressed here are surely a truer representation of the radical Marxian legacy than that offered by Adorno, Marcuse, and Jacoby—holding true to that legacy in the face of what is admittedly an apparently ever greater intensification of reification and apathy. So although it is clear that Fromm was neither an adherent of Hegelian necessity nor critical theory pessimism, he was in agreement with the religio-philosophical idea of socialism as the goal of history, that is to say, of history as the realm in which we realize the radical humanist promise of humanity. It must be clear that this is a utopian goal and that there is nothing untoward about this. To speak of utopianism, even less to speak of the "goal of history," in today's intellectual climate is to speak unfashionably, if not illicitly. Wary of notions of "teleology" and "progress," which tend to reflect back to theological absolutism or rigid organicist pan-logicism, on the one hand, or to myopic and self-congratulatory Whiggism on the other, this kind of talk is viewed as wishful at best, embarrassing at worst. But to speak of a "goal" here is not to give over to naïve progressivist thought; it is only to recognize the human capacity to realize at least part of our potential for reason, love, justice and, ultimately, solidarity; that when stripped of the unhelpful baggage of theological absolutism, talk of the "goal of history" can reduce to, as it does in Fromm, the recognition that the fact of human existence poses a problem, which must be resolved and whose resolution is best affected through the development of our love, reason, and justice and the concomitant creation of a peaceful and harmonious (or at least as far is possible) society. The fact this society is nowhere in sight does not obviate the heuristic function of the ideal that is posited—surely the point with an ideal is precisely that it is an ideal, either *rarely* found to exist or *not yet* found to exist. It does not follow from the fact that something has not yet been found to exist that it cannot exist, and certainly that it cannot exist as an ideal. Fromm very clearly held a non-naive developmental view of history, but he refused to give up (as others seemed to do) on the hope of significant improvements in this regard, whatever the chances.

Conclusion

It has been the central contention of this book that the radical humanism that emanates from Erich Fromm's writing is a unique and valuable contribution to social theory. This radical humanist social theory, which was insufficiently formulated as an explicit theory, but which saturates Fromm's writings nonetheless, is based on a policy of refined continuation in relation to the classical humanist tradition—a policy that enables him to engage in what is a fruitful mixture of essentialism and constructionism that is capable of reclaiming and reappropriating the analytical precepts of humanism at the same time as accommodating concerns over their naïve and ethnocentric application. Radical humanism, for Fromm, is a global philosophy grounded on the idea of the oneness of the human race; it emphasizes the capacity of the human individual to develop its own powers for love, reason, productiveness, and to realize the prophetic dream of messianic socialism; and it considers the goal of human life to be independence, in the sense that becoming aware of the origin of the structuring of one's character and passions enables greater levels of self-realization and freedom from internal and external sources of damaging determinations. As such, Fromm's radical humanism places a stress on the existence and importance of "man" (or the human being), the self, the subject, and the possibility of perfectibility and flourishing in the historical process. These concerns represent, in effect, the analytical precepts of classical humanist thought, and they exist in Fromm as the implicit and explicit presuppositions of this thinking.

As has been shown, the fact that Fromm's writings have such a focus sets them apart at the outset from the majority of writing that appears in the social sciences and humanities today, the essentialism they entail standing in direct contradiction to the antiessentialism that is fairly well lodged in most quarters. But rather than a weakness, this is their strength. Essentialism is a misunderstood term today, generally used pejoratively by those seeking to denounce ahistorical and pre-sociological views which are characterized by a naive lack of awareness of the importance of cultural construction, but also positively by those seeking to bring back its focus on natural entities and their characteristic capacities in conjunction with (and as the necessary complement of) cultural construction. Taken in the latter of these two senses, a basic essentialism is a necessary underlying component of any view of the world that recognizes the existence of relatively permanent entities, which are related to and distinguished from other entities by virtue of their particular constitution. In relation to radical humanism, then, essentialism pertains first of all to the issue of human universalism—the idea that human beings exist, are amenable to definition and are therefore capable of being meaningfully distinguished from other entities, and that thus there is a general human nature, common to the human race as a whole, which is nevertheless manifested in different cultures (and within the same culture) in different ways.

Such an idea is clearly paralleled along the long arc of the humanist tradition, in the religio-philosophical movements over the past two millennia, such as in the monotheistic and mystical religious traditions, in Greek and Roman philosophy, and in the dominant thinking in the Renaissance and Enlightenment periods. But the essentialism of Fromm's radical humanism is distinct in that it relates not only to the identification of the human being as a separate and definable entity, but to the understanding of this entity as resultant of the evolutionary history that defines the species Homo sapiens and, in particular, the culmination of evolutionary history that led to the creation of what Fromm terms the "existential dichotomy" that characterizes human existence. Although Fromm overstates his account of this dichotomy, positing it as the result of an evolutionary *discontinuity* (coming close in the process to an untenable dualism that makes it difficult to accurately conceptualize the change from pre-human to human form), the central features of his account *do* represent something of the nature of human existence, structured as it is by a series of fundamental "questions" that must be answered, the answers to these questions determining to a greater or lesser degree the satisfaction, happiness, and well-being of any given person. This essentialism relates at the same time to an acknowledgment of the theater of unconscious processes that work behind our backs—the phenomena of repression, transference, and the dynamism of character, for instance—as elementary facets of human existence considered in general terms. As such, Fromm's radical humanism is led to a concern with the development of the self, the construction of the subject and, thus, with the way social forces act on us as well as the way we internalize and react to these forces. This, it should hardly need stating, is clearly not the outlines of a "cult of subjectivity." In addition to its religio-philosophical groundings, Fromm's radical humanism is also explicitly and centrally aware of the historical and societal determination of ideas. A student of Marx as well as Freud, Fromm recognized the social and historical forces that shape our individual and collective life—his concept of social character, in particular, being an attempt to reconcile the play of forces within the individual, working on the elucidation of the dividing line that separates the personal and the structural. Fromm's radical humanism, therefore, was clearly not a naïve or "ideological" humanism, as Althusereans would have it.

Yet, Fromm's radical humanism is not cleaved from older humanist ideas in the way the accounts given by the anti-humanists are. Fromm spoke explicitly of a "renaissance of humanism" and can be seen as simultaneously reclaiming and reappropriating the ideas of past humanist thought. Indeed, Fromm's thought consists, at its most basic, of a syncretic attempt to complete and validate the ideas of the past. As such, something of the spirit of Fromm's thinking is expressed by Marx in the following excerpt from a letter sent to Arnold Ruge on the subject of the "reform of consciousness" in relation to socialism:

> It will then be clear that the world has long possessed the dream of a thing of which it only needs to possess the consciousness in order to really possess it. It will be clear that the problem is not some great gap between the thoughts of the past and those of the future but the completion of thoughts of the past. Finally, it will be clear that humanity is not beginning a new work, but consciously bringing its old work to completion. (Marx, 2000b: 45)

This sentiment, which has echoes of the Jewish practice of updating ancient texts so that they speak to modern times, also reflects Fromm's belief in the basic continuity of the essential human situation. Having said this, and as I have stressed, radical humanism is not merely a repetition of previous humanisms. In Fromm's radical humanism, what we primarily see is the translation and retranslation of Judaic, Marxian, and Freudian elements (all interpreted humanistically) such that each new system successively develops the previous system without supplanting the core of that system, this core working itself outward into the new system where it interacts with the new elements in that system to progressively develop the basis of humanism itself (it is in this sense that I have argued that Fromm's writings are *primarily* an expression of radical humanism). The Marxian and Freudian influences, although effectively functioning with what Fromm took to be the essential core of the Judaic tradition, add crucial theoretical and practical aspects that are not found fully formed in previous forms of humanistic thought (including Judaism) and which thus create the possibility for a greater realization of humanism.

Despite this, there will no doubt still be resistance to the idea of a renaissance of humanism. It will be objected that radical humanism, as with any form of humanism, is guilty of a fundamental selection bias, focusing always on certain selected human attributes that the selectors deem "good" and therefore "human," amplifying their presence at the expense of equally characteristic elements that they deem "bad" and therefore seek to minimize and classify as "inhuman." A cursory glance at Fromm's writings should disabuse anyone of the notion that such a bias can be attributed to him. A psychoanalyst with a depth-psychological approach who spoke of widespread destructiveness and neurosis and who saw strong strivings for greed encouraged and fostered in the pathology of normalcy of our time, Fromm's thinking is clearly not the product of a simplistic optimist. Neither is it triumphalist. Fromm's books are hardly paeans to flawlessly conquered internal and external reality. Nevertheless, he possessed hope and he possessed faith, and painted a deeply perceptive account of lived human experience in its genuine possibility. Such stress on possibility, undercut as it is in Fromm with a normative strain, is not a secret, subterranean form of authoritarianism. What Fromm views as the essence of human life is not reactionary and does not lead to the issuing of unduly restrictive proclamations on how human beings ought to live. As a humanist, Fromm's stress is primarily on human dignity, a stress that branches out into a universalism centered on the idea the potential to realize capacities for love, reason, creativity, and, ultimately, human flourishing based on underlying general psychological criteria that are nevertheless realized in varying ways in different social forms (and in varying ways within such social forms). Such a stress on human dignity and flourishing does not signal a vainglorious speciesism. Although Fromm's picture of the fundamental human existential dichotomy was certainly overwrought, even veering toward disrespect toward nonhuman animal capacity at times, his thought here was heuristically and didactically motivated and is undercut by the more substantive stress on loving and harmonious relations that informs his idea of the productive orientation and the being mode of existence (in fact, by his last work, *To Have or To Be?*, he is clear on his need for a relationship of balance and respect with nonhuman nature).

While all of this may be said in Fromm's favor, it is clear that he did not pursue his lines of enquiry to their end point. Whether this is possible or not, given the historical limitations to perception and local structurings of knowledge, it is certainly especially difficult for someone like Fromm who, in addition to being given to grand theoretical tendencies, worked as a practicing psychoanalyst not primarily concerned with theory and who saw his role largely in terms of prophetic mobilization. As a detailed theoretical body and developed empirical program, there are, therefore, inevitable insufficiencies in Fromm's writings. As such, his work does not represent a terminus. But while this is so, Fromm's writings are a solid beginning that calls us on toward further development. His genuinely humanist oeuvre is an immensely productive grounding source for thinking, which, despite being unfashionable, can still speak to us in late modernity. In many cases, his writings can be seen as well-framed, promising, and all-too-seldom encountered hypotheses pertaining to the nature of human existence in general and to human existence as it is found in advanced capitalist consumer society in particular. Ultimately, while the construction of his thought was imprecise at certain points and insufficient at others, it was sufficiently pointed (and sometimes markedly so) so as to facilitate refinements that enable the retention of its thrust and to allow it to be reappropriated for use in connection with a renaissance of humanism today. His essentialist and ethical normative stress, interacting as it does with elements of sociological constructionism, allows the return of an explicit ethical dimension to social theory without falling into reactionary moralizing. Such a stress broadens out into a concern with the art of living, which is informed by the idea of a science of man, both of which relate to his underlying normative stress. His focus on the individual is at once a crucial, dynamic component of the social process and the goal of this process, refocusing attention back onto to the self as potentially unifiable and the subject as a potentially pivotal force in social change. All of this serves to refocus social analysis onto the analytical correlates of humanism (that is to say, onto the human individual, with its hinterland of self- and subject-constitution), and thus to challenge the excessive culturalism and anti-personalism, which characterizes most "postmodern" thinking, whether it be structuralist, poststructuralist, or posthuman.

Clearly, Fromm's ideas need to be placed on a more adequate and explicitly drawn-out philosophical grounding and to offer a more thorough account of the structural determinations that are involved in the constitution of the individual and which play a central role in the social process. There are productive syntheses to make in this regard with certain thinkers today working under the "critical realist" banner.[1] Of particular importance here are thinkers such as Margaret Archer, Andrew Collier, Andrew Sayer, Christian Smith, Peter Dickens, and Ted Benton, who, in their various writings, have done much to prepare the field for what might be called the *dialectical supersession* of the anti-humanist paradigm. Although each thinker in this grouping has a particular focus, which is not reducible to the overly general description I am giving here, they are broadly united in using Bhaskar's critical realist "underlabouring" (Bhaskar, 1991; Bhaskar, 2011) to build a fairly coherent movement that has the potential to supplant the errors of "postmodernism" in the social sciences and humanities and, as Archer suggests, to "reclaim humanity"[2] therein (Archer, 2000: 2). While Fromm generally does not work at the level of conceptual sophistication found in these thinkers, he has covered some similar ground and is definitely related. Although not writing in the philosophy of science or philosophy of social science tradition, and making no reference to critical realism itself (and there is no biographical suggestion that he was familiar with it as a distinct theory), Fromm shared Bhaskar's opposition to positivism and his belief that the aim of science was to achieve the deepening our knowledge of nature (Bhaskar, 2008: 168–169). Added to this, like the majority of the thinkers mentioned, Fromm was a socialist whose virtue ethical position and underlying essentialism (which implies realism) have clear value implications for praxis in much the way that the critical realist position is said to have.[3] What is certainly the case is that the thinkers I have singled out are generally socialists with virtue ethical aspects to their thinking, and thus with definite affiliation to the humanist or ethical Marxist tradition.[4] In this sense, Fromm can be seen as definite a precursor to these thinkers and to the task of reclaiming humanity in dialogue with the anti-humanist thought that has sought to problematize it.

It is, then, as offering a timely mixture of acute clarification and a more rudimentary laying out of the terrain to be traversed that we should see Fromm's work today. In his development of an ethical normativism, in his discussion of what he saw as the existential needs characteristic of humankind, in his working out of a revised psychoanalytic system to rival that of Freud's (a system that he extended into a Marxian-influenced social psychology), and in his suggestions for humanistic reforms of public and private life, all of which form part of his attempt to displace excessive relativism from its strong foothold in intellectual life, Fromm has left an enviable and challenging legacy that ought to engage independent-minded thinkers seeking a path through the malaises of contemporary social theory. Nowhere should this legacy be felt more acutely today than in relation to Fromm's unfulfilled dream for the development of a truly humanistic 'science of man'. As anachronistic (and even pernicious) as such an idea will sound to many, it is surely in the interdisciplinary networking, compiling, and evaluating of ideas and research that we can best succeed in progressing beyond the excessive relativism that blocks and counters the liberatory thrust of humanistic thinking. Fromm's forgotten proposal of an *Institute for the Humanistic Science of Man* sought to rally thinking in this direction and to the task of bringing to bear concerted intellectual resources to understanding humanity in all its manifestations, with the goal of achieving real penetration into the essential nature of humankind. Reviving aspects of Enlightenment thinking, Fromm stresses in this proposal the need to establish the concept of human nature by a deepening and integration of historical and cultural knowledge of human existence, going "beyond a descriptive anthropology... to study the basic human forces behind the manifold varieties in which it is expressed" (1990 [1957]: 3). Central to this endeavor would be the study of values and, in particular, the demonstration that

> values are not simply matters of taste, but are rooted in the very existence of man. It has to be demonstrated which these such basic values are and how they are rooted in the very nature of man. Values in all cultures must be studied in order to find any underlying unity; and a study of the moral evolution of mankind must also be attempted. Furthermore, it is necessary to investigate what effect the violation of basic ethical norms has on the individual and on the culture. (1990 [1957]: 3)

Such an approach was grounded in a concern to supplant what he saw as the ineffective nature of the academic endeavor in the middle-to-end of the twentieth century, with its avowed concern to keep social science value-free and its reluctance to countenance the very idea of human universals. That there are practical consequences that follow from this is undeniable. As Amartya Sen (1999), Martha Nussbaum (2006), Doyal and Gough (1991), Assiter and Noonan (2007), among others, have argued, we are in need of developing a comprehensive systematic list of central aspects of human functioning and capabilities in relation to the universal goal of creating a fair, just, and happy One World, and in fighting the tyranny of "localisms" that work against this. This said, it is clear that the Foucaultian fear of disciplinary power will stalk such an enterprise, and demand a thoroughly reflexive and engaging approach. While this is so, it must be acknowledged that the power/knowledge couplet that underlies the Foucaultian fear throws up its own damning questions. Foucault—in many ways the most radical humanist of the anti-humanists—is confronted with the not so insubstantial fact that we have to ask what in the emancipation of the knowledge of the incarcerated and dominated this knowledge can become other than power itself? Since knowledge is always synonymous with power, fear of tyranny will undercut any attempt to discern, debate, and proclaim. Such an enterprise as the building of a contemporary science of man, if truly filled with a radical humanist spirit in all of the aspects that are evident in Fromm (including his apparently simple but, in the case of concerns over power/knowledge, highly instructive humanistic distinction between *rational* and *irrational* authority), is surely worth engaging in seriously, with the concerns of Foucault and others brought to bear against it to help ensure fidelity to the radical humanist spirit. The goal of reaching happiness, peace, and harmony—though never fully realizable—is, if pursued with humility, humor, and realistic expectations, essential to the discernable betterment of individual and social life that Foucault and others like him strive for.

Fromm's thought, then, in connection with related contemporary thinking, has the potential to assist in the rejuvenation of social theory by helping it to progress beyond certain impasses that threaten to overwhelm its once radical hopes. The strange slippage that has taken place between positivist and relativist (or idealist) epistemological and methodological positions has left social theory today largely bereft of real connection (either in thought or practice) to its historically associated goal of understanding, changing and improving the prevalent conditions of social life. Marx's famous insistence that the point is to *change* the world is generally only nominally adhered to, if it is adhered to at all, pushed out of consideration by a somewhat circular concern with working out what "the world," "knowledge," or "experience" can be said to be in the first place. While plumbing the depths of epistemological and ontological doubt in these areas is certainly a most valuable enterprise taken in and of itself, the paralysis it can induce demands a reappraisal of priorities and thus of the nature of social theory as a whole. Expressed in the most straightforward and revolutionary form by Marx, the idea of affecting change for the better ought to be inherently connected with social theory as an enterprise. What Fromm's radical humanism ultimately offers, in such a connection, is a refreshingly reconfigured form of humanism that can help humanism itself regain respect and be seen once more as a sensible, viable, and desirable explicit basis for social theoretical thought that is concerned with individual and social flourishing.

Notes

Introduction

1. Daniel Burston's *The Legacy of Erich Fromm*; Gerhard P. Knapp's *The Art of Living: Erich Fromm's Life and Works*; Mauricio Cortina and Michael Maccoby (eds.), *A Prophetic Analyst: Erich Fromm's Contribution to Psychoanalysis*; and Lawrence Friedman's *The Lives of Erich Fromm: Love's Prophet*, in North America; Svante Lundgren's *Fight against Idols*; Lawrence Wilde's *Erich Fromm and the Quest for Solidarity*; Adir Cohen's *Love and Hope. Fromm and Education*; Jürgen Hardeck's *Erich Fromm. Leben und Werk (Erich Fromm. Life and Work)*; Annette Thompson's *Erich Fromm: Explorer of the Human Condition*; and Domagoj Akrap's *Erich Fromm: ein jüdischer Denker (Erich Fromm: a Jewish Thinker)* in Europe and Israel. In addition to this, Rainer Funk, Fromm's literary executor and last assistant, has ensured the successive reissuing of some of Fromm's most central works alongside the publication of collections of previously unseen writings.
2. Birnbach says, in fact, that Fromm moved to a form of "ethical absolutism" (1962: 81)—a misconception that helps explain his failure to grasp the continuity in Fromm.
3. Wilde has also discussed Fromm in *Ethical Marxism and Its Radical Critics*, and a chapter in his collection *Marxism's Ethical Thinkers*.
4. Funk has also published *Erich Fromm: His Life and Ideas—An Illustrated Biography*.

1 The Life and Writings of a Radical Humanist

1. I use the term "Frankfurt School," and mention these thinkers (including Fromm) in relation to it, in full awareness of the problems that exist in terms of adequately characterizing the said thinkers as part of a "school" in the first place. I am, however, appealing to the sense of the existence of such a school and to the historical, biographical, and intellectual parallels that clearly do exist.
2. Rabinkov only published one article, "The Individual and Society in Judaism" (1929), which, besides being "poorly organized and often redundant" (Friedman, 2013: 17), is said to bear certain strong thematic similarities to

aspects of Fromm's mature thought, particularly the stress placed on the moral autonomy of the individual (Funk, 1988; Friedman, 2013: 17).

3. Interestingly, Fromm chose not to retrospectively translate and publish the pieces along with other early articles in *The Crisis of Psychoanalysis*.

4. The prospective piece was unearthed by Rainer Funk in 1991 among the section of Fromm's estate donated to the New York Public library. Its title was chosen by Funk to replace the original title—"A Contribution to the Method and Purpose of an Analytic Psychology"—which was felt to be too close to Fromm's 1932 "The Method and Function of Analytic Social Psychology."

5. Wiggershaus (1994: 266) points out that Adorno was fond of referring to Fromm as a "professional Jew." Fromm, in a letter to Raya Duyanevskaya (October 2, 1976), described Adorno as a "puffed up phrase-maker with no conviction and nothing to say."

6. This is, incidentally, is the same reason Fromm gives for Horkheimer's adoption of the title "critical theory" that came to be applied to the Institut's work in Fromm's absence: "These people, particularly Horkheimer, became so frightened after they had come to America of being considered radicals that they began to suppress all words which sounded radical" (letter to Dunayevskaya in Funk, 2000: 101).

7. Wiggershaus quotes Horkheimer in a letter to Pollock written toward the end of 1935, in which he says of Adorno that "despite a number of disturbing aspects, the source of which lies in his personality, it seems to me a matter of necessity for me to collaborate with him; he is the only person capable of collaborating on completing the logic, apart from the assistance I have from Marcuse" (1994: 159).

8. As Friedman notes, it is odd, especially considering this connection, that Fromm wrote so little about the situation of African Americans in the United states at the time (Friedman, 2013: 94).

9. Fromm claims that political developments—by which we can take him as referring to Nazism in Germany—caused him to interrupt a larger study on the nature of man and the social process. He felt that "the psychologist should offer what he has to contribute to the understanding of the present crisis without delay, even though he must sacrifice the desideratum of completeness" (1969 [1941]: x).

10. This is a rectification the anomaly whereby Buddhism and Confucianism are delineated as religions despite their lack of a theology.

11. Revealingly, Fromm in fact described himself as an "atheistic mystic" (Hausdorff, 1972: 3).

12. Hausdorff makes a similar observation, pointing out that in his "Der Sabbat" article, Fromm cited the prophetic concept that man and nature ultimately would be restored to harmony, and thus there is clearly far more continuity in his attitudes than may appear on the surface (1972: 65–66).

13. The comparatively early date of Fromm's criticisms here is worth noting, preceding as it does many later criticisms of a similar nature.

14. The following extract on Fromm's financial activism taken from an interview given by Lawrence Friedman to Lee M. Formwalt is illustrative of the way in which Fromm supported progressive politics in the United States: "He would sell anywhere from five million to thirty-seven million copies of each book. So one day I'm wondering where all this money goes, and I got hold of his tax returns, and he's giving it all away. He gives everything away to the civil rights movement, to the ACLU, to all these other groups which brought him considerable influence, and he was just writing out large checks all the time. So with this dimension I see somebody who has been an activist, a scholar, a donor, and I'm very comfortable with him, and it's a very wonderful life he lived" (Formwalt, 2007).

2 The Roots of Radical Humanism

1. Wilde divides Fromm's work into three "paths," or chronological stages: the social-psychological, the ethical humanist, and the political (Wilde, 2004a).
2. Rainer Funk has argued something very close to this in "The Jewish Roots of Erich Fromm's Humanistic Thinking," a lecture presented at the "Erich Fromm—Life and Work" Symposium, Locarno, Switzerland, May 12–14, as well as in personal communications. Domagoj Akrap (2011) also argues for this essential continuity.
3. Fromm here is giving over to the pejorative, theological sense in which something may be said to be metaphysical. This is surprising, given his familiarity with the thought of Aristotle and his later statement that "any metaphysical system is a conception of the world, a world perspective, a *weltanschauung*. Metaphysics is born out of the two questions already mentioned: 'Why, life?'; 'Life, what for?' Metaphysics tries to explain the place of man in the universe and thus tells us what the conduct of man should be in the process of living. In this sense metaphysical speculation is vital, not idle, speculation" (Fromm and Xirau, 1979 [1968]: 17). The word was used here merely to follow Fromm and to try uphold the immediate clarity of the distinction being made.
4. Both Funk (1982: 73) and Glen (1966: 116) have suggested that Fromm's Creation Story-Messianic Time narrative exhibits a strong affinity to the Hegelian dialectic of Absolute Spirit, and that this, understood in Feuerbachian or Marxian inversion, as opposed to Jewish theology, is perhaps the more accurate correlate of the view he presents of the history of man in his later writings on Judaism. Although it is impossible to settle this matter unequivocally, it seems pertinent to mention here the fact that Hermann Cohen, in his *Religion of Reason* (1995: 70), clearly states that the problem of creation is the problem of teleology, and that Maimonides, in *The Guide for the Perplexed* (1925: 13–16), suggests that the narrative of Adam's Fall is an allegory that employs homonyms which represent the relation that exists between man's physical faculties, that is, sensation, moral faculty, and intellect (and, as will be shown, both thinkers made a decisive influence on Fromm's interpretation of the Judaic tradition). What is certainly true is that, although Fromm's mature views may

be influenced by his later interests, it was nevertheless his "conviction" that his views had "at no point" broken from those of his fundamental rabbinical teachers of his youth, from which they initially grew (1966: 13). It seems, as will hopefully be shown, perhaps more accurate to view it as an expansion of these rabbinical ideas, or a translation of them, into nontheistic phraseology, and thus as an expansion of what is already there in Cohen.

5. Although a generic argument applicable in principle to all religions, Cohen argued for its applicability to Jewish consciousness in particular.

6. The idea here is that man's knowledge grows the more he succeeds in keeping false and inappropriate definitions away from God.

7. Certainly this is what Funk argues in *Erich Fromm: The Courage to Be Human*, a work composed in the final years of Fromm's life while Funk was employed as his assistant. In this work Funk outlines a series of connections between Fromm's and Hasidic ideas, pointing out some uncanny similarities (Funk, 1982: 203–204). Lack of space restricts the pursuit of these connections here; however, it must be stressed that Funk's statements in this regard should be accorded some respect, given his working relationship with Fromm. Funk is clear that Fromm gave extensive feedback on the book in the many conversations they had over this period, and, as such, he was surely privy to the fundamental nature of Fromm's conscious account of the roots of his thinking to a degree to which almost no one else has been.

8. Fromm notes that Maimonides actually reintroduces positive attributes, although not in the formal structure of his thought: by saying that God is not impotent Maimonides are at the same time implying that he is omnipotent, thereby indirectly voicing the very attributes which should not be voiced.

9. Wary of associations with Soviet communism, Fromm preferred to use "socialism" over "communism" in relation to his discussion of Marx.

10. While this is so, it must be noted that these thinkers bear the trace of messianic thought also. In addition to this, Fromm also points out that the only noncompulsory class Marx took as a student at university was on the prophets and that he told his wife, who was interested in attending lectures on religion given by a liberal minister, to "read the prophets instead of listening to banalities" (Marx, in Fromm, 2005: 166).

11. "Materialism" is used here in contradistinction to idealism, and not in the mechanical sense it can take in "vulgar" Marxism's.

12. Bloch himself expands on this in *Das Prinzip Hoffnung*, vol. II (1959). This recognition, being more common in continental European thought for a longer period of time, has increasingly permeated the English-speaking world. Of particular relevance here are Somerville (1968), Wood (1981), Meikle (1985 and 1995), Kain (1988), Peffer (1990), McCarthy (1992), Wilde (1998), and Meikle (2002).

13. While it is clear that Marx did not uncritically adopt the entirety of Aristotle's thought, Meikle nevertheless argues convincingly for a widespread and central appropriation of Aristotelian thought. Naturally leaving out things such as Aristotle's belief that slavery was just and natural, Meikle stresses Marx's undeniable appropriation of Aristotelian metaphysics in his discussion of the

commodity and the value form. Meikle also notes Aristotle's influence on Hegel, and the fact that Marx's critique of Hegel can in fact be seen as an attempt to use Aristotle to materialize Hegel's speculative elements (Meikle, 1985: 43). In addition to this, Meikle notes that Marx made the first German translation of *De Anima*—the work in which Aristotle had most to say about the specific essence of the human kind—and that it appears he had intended on publishing it (Meikle, 1985: 58).

14. Kate Soper (1986) gives a generally very fair and perceptive account of the contradictions that are manifest in Marx's thinking here.

15. Peter Gay, in his biography of Freud, gives some support to this idea, noting that Freud likened himself to Hannibal, Ahasuerus, Joseph, and Moses, among others and that he "took pleasure in being the unmasker of shams, the nemesis of self-deception and illusions" (Gay, 2006: 604). Gay also quotes a letter of Freud's to Silberstein in 1875 in which Freud, referring to Feuerbach, proclaims: "Among all philosophers, I worship this man the most" (Gay, 2006: 28). It would be hard to pass off such praise of a self-styled destroyer of illusions as Feuerbach as inconsequential.

16. Fromm uses the latter phrase in *The Revision of Psychoanalysis*. Considering his critique of both existentialism and phenomenology as philosophical doctrines, this is a little misleading. In the same work he also describes it as "sociobiological," which is perhaps more accurate—although proper discussion of his use of this bogey word is postponed until proper discussion can take place in the later chapters.

17. Burston (1991) does a good job of this, explaining also how Fromm was reluctant to acknowledge the similarities between his account and the accounts of Jung, Rank, and Adler.

3   Radical Humanist Psychoanalysis

1. There is an inescapable conceptual overlap between this and chapter 4. Because Fromm's revision of Freud's drive theory was prompted in large part through the attempt to apply his theory socially, the two aspects are mutually implicated. For the purpose of my argument, and for clarity more generally, I have separated the discussions somewhat forcefully—although not fully. This chapter is predominantly focused on radical humanist psychoanalysis considered in itself, that is to say, as a psychoanalytically based theory of human functioning. The following chapter is predominantly focused on the social application of this theory.

2. Fromm, in fact, refers to Freud's thinking as a form of "mechanistic physiologism" (1990a: 2).

3. Freud's contention in the *New Introductory Lectures on Psychoanalysis* is that masochism ontogenetically precedes sadism, and that sadism is the result of the externalization of the original masochistic impulse in the form of aggressiveness. He contends further that a "certain amount" of the original destructive impulse may remain in the interior, being bolstered by the return of the some

of the external aggression sent back by impediments to its realization in the exterior (Freud, 1964: 131).

4. Fromm (1997 [1973]: 599–600) cites Fenichel's account of the problematic nature of the death instinct in "A Critique of the Death Instinct." In this article, Fenichel stresses that the so-called death "instinct" cannot function as instinct in the previous sense, since the death instinct points towards the "total elimination of the social factor from the etiology of neuroses, and would amount to a complete biologization of neuroses" (Fenichel, 1954: 370–371).

5. The accuracy of this view—and the view of man as a "freak of nature" mentioned in the previous paragraph—will be discussed in more detail in chapter 5.

6. Fromm's opinion appears to have shifted over time. In *The Sane Society*, he speaks of the "passive" relationship to nature found in hunter-gatherer societies (2002 [1955]: 48). By *The Art of Being*, published posthumously by Rainer Funk but written in conjunction with *To Have or To Be?*, he points to the fact that "primitive" man (his scare quotes) is in "a constant process of learning," characterized by a "wide range of mental activities," and ultimately "sophisticated," so much so that "hunting was the school of learning that made the human species self-taught" (2007 [1993]: 90). Fromm concludes that "primitive" man had a "principle of greater activity" as compared to modern man and praises "primitive" art as "beautiful" and "a delight," stressing that hunter-gatherers were "very active in applying their own faculties of thinking, observing, imagining, painting, and sculpting" (2007 [1993]: 91–92).

7. This expression is a nod to Freud's expression in "The Ego and the Id," where he states that "we are 'lived' by unknown and uncontrollable forces" (Freud, 1984d: 13).

8. In *The Anatomy of Human Destruction*, Fromm adds a need for "stimulation and excitement," referring in doing so to neurobiological studies and the fact that the brain is spontaneously active (1997 [1973]: 324). Although, I will omit a detailed discussion of this need, it provides further evidence of Fromm's view of human life as fundamentally dynamically structured on the basis of existential (psycho-biological) reality.

9. In the studies already mentioned, Freud posits what are a series of speculative connections between the type of character a given person has and the organization of their instinctual sexual components. Through the identification of erotic zones (mouth, anus, and genitals) and the specification of stages of psychosexual development associated with them, Freud devised an etiology of generally permanent character traits as either "unchanged prolongations of the original instincts, or sublimations of those instincts, or reaction-formations against them" (Freud, 1959: 175). In this etiological schema, which is premised on the dual assumptions of libido (instinct energy or force) as the primary motivating structure of experience other than the nutritive drives, and of childhood experience as uniquely formative, the final outcome of psychosexual development is taken to be the normal, "genital" sexual life of the adult, that is, one in which "the pursuit of pleasure in accordance with reproductive function" is present, derived from "a firm organization directed towards a sexual aim

attached to some extraneous sexual object" (Freud, 2000: 63). Contrasted to this normal and healthy level of development is the "pre-genital" and neurotic level, understood as continued fixation (by any one of the means mentioned above) at the oral, anal, or phallic developmental stages.In each of these stages, the libido is said to become fixated on the given erogenous stimulus. Failure to adequately develop beyond the particular fixation is said to result in a relatively permanent character structure, which is trapped, as it were, in the particularities of the developmental stage. In a transposition of the traits synonymous with the activities associated with the various stages, either in toto or in inversion, Freud (aided by Abraham, Jones, and Fenichel) posits linkages between traits such as dependency, manipulativeness, a powerful urge to drink and smoke and what he calls an "oral character" and between traits such as orderliness, parsimoniousness, obstinacy, and what he calls an "anal character." In the case of the phallic stage (which, as the name suggests, is generally conceived in relation to the young boy), Freud conceives of libido as severing from its autoerotic base and turning outward toward the mother, prompting, at the same time, feelings of jealously toward the father (the well-known "Oedipus complex"). The feeling of jealousy toward the father, which the young boy feels, is seen as being accompanied by a concurrent sense of fear that becomes effective upon seeing the "castrated" female genitals, imagined by the boy as manifestation of the threat to his own. On making this recognition, a conflict is said to arise between the narcissistic interest in his own body and the libidinal cathexis of his parental objects, the former normally triumphing and the authority of the father or the parents becoming introjected into the ego (roughly, the rational and calm faculty of the mind), forming the nucleus of the superego, or ego ideal (roughly, conscience) necessary to reach the genital level. If the ego does not achieve more than a repression of the complex, the latter is said to persist in an unconscious state, manifesting eventually as neurosis (Freud, 1984a: 319; 1984d).

10. Fromm is not always consistent of the naming of this orientation. In choosing this name, I am following Rainer Funk's (1982) attempt to resolve the issue.

11. Lundgren suggests that Fromm was acquainted with this episode through Hugh Thomas's *The Spanish Civil War*, and that he in fact changes the word "necrophilistic" (used by Thomas) to "necrophilous" (Lundgren, 1998: 139).

12. This is an inconsistent presentation. In *Social Character in a Mexican Village*, Fromm lists *symbiotic relatedness, withdrawal-destruction*, and *narcissism*.

13. It is important here to note Fromm's distinction between neurotic and rational activity. In the latter case, the result is considered to correspond to the motivation of the activity; in the former, one is said to act out of compulsion, the activity therefore exhibiting a negative character, and generally with a result contrary to that which the person intended (1969 [1941]: 153).

14. Incidentally, this does not rule out a discussion of necrophilia more generally, despite how it might be viewed. Fromm was aware that "necrophilia" is customarily used to denote a sexual perversion, but held that, as is often the case, "a sexual perversion presents only the more overt and clear picture of an

orientation which is to be found without sexual admixture in many people" (1980 [1964]: 39).

15. In a parallel to Freud, Fromm points to "unification and integrated growth [as] characteristic of all life processes," from the level of the cell to thinking and feeling (1980 [1964]: 46).

16. Adorno had the earliest and perhaps deepest connection, undergoing a brief analysis with Karl Landauer and writing his initial *habilitation* on the relationship between psychoanalysis and the transcendental phenomenology of Hans Cornelius (Jay, 1972: 300).

17. In fact, there are a number of similarities between Fromm and Marcuse that Rickert (1986) brings out.

18. Incidentally, this was the only criticism on the matter to which Fromm responded to directly. Fromm replied to Marcuse's *Dissent* article with one of his own, "The Human Implications of Instinctivist 'Radicalism': A Reply to Herbert Marcuse," (1955), and issued a counter-rebuttal to Marcuse's rebuttal of Fromm's article, "A Counter-Rebuttal to Herbert Marcuse," *Dissent* (1956b).

19. Chodorow's criticisms of Marcuse are similar in nature to those that Fromm proffered. She goes beyond Fromm, however, in the level of detail she offers and, if anything, is more damning in her appraisal. Marcuse's account, in her view, exhibits an "extreme conception of instinctual malleability" (Chodorow, 1985: 290). As well as this, she notes that his stress on the polymorphous perverse pleasures is, in effect, an idealization of the narcissistic mode of relatedness and drive gratification which precludes intersubjective relations (Chodorow, 1985: 293).

20. Fromm had been working on this volume for some years, only diverting from completing it due to what he felt was the necessity to counter the arguments for an innate aggressiveness proffered by thinkers such as Lorenz. Rainer Funk has done his best to publish as much possible of what Fromm had written on clinical matters—see *The Revision of Psychoanalysis*, *The Art of Listening*, and *The Clinical Erich Fromm*, in particular.

21. But other than Willmott and Knights's article (1982) on Fromm and Habermas, there has been very little written in this connection. This is something that applies to Habermas himself, who, other than mildly praising the importance of Fromm's contribution to the early Institut in an interview with Marcuse, generally denigrates or ignores Fromm. The connection appears to have been more positive the other way around, Fromm recommending Habermas's *Knowledge and Human Interests* in *To Have or To Be?*.

4 Psychoanalytic Social Psychology

1. Fromm generally uses the phrase "analytic social psychology," broadened here to "*psycho*analytic social psychology" for sake of clarity.

2. Adler made an early attempt to relate Marx to Freud in a paper titled "On the Psychology of Marxism," delivered to the Vienna Psychoanalytic Society in 1909 (Jacoby, 1977: 21).

3. Lukács, in particular, seemed to grant the existence of a psychic dimension only to dismiss it (Jacoby, 1977: 77). For him, a psychological consciousness remains an immediate one, delineated in positivist terms.

4. Fromm, in fact, argued that Marx's dynamic psychology "came too early to find sufficient attention" (1970: 46) and that once his central concern—namely, man—has been fully recognized, its importance would be more clearly apparent (1970: 58). He noted its affinities to Spinoza (whom Marx read extensively) and cited an unabridged letter to Engels, which apparently exhibited a depth-psychological view of individuals, and which Fromm argued could be seen to anticipate Freud (1970: 56).

5. Reich, at this juncture, had argued against its applicability to social phenomenon. He had also, in his pamphlet "The Use of Psychoanalysis in Historical Research," criticized Fromm, arguing contrary to Fromm that psychoanalysis is competent only in explaining irrational social phenomena, that is, its function is "negative." In the same piece he erroneously attributes to Fromm the view that society has an id, ego, superego, etc. (Burston, 1991: 35–36).

6. As Fromm elaborates in his 1937 essay, "in Freud, the analysis of the impulse structure of individuals made a method of the hitherto unknown minute examination of all the individual life experiences and individual life practice. The use of the same principle for the analysis of the character structure typical of a social group requires a correspondingly exhaustive knowledge of the whole life practice of this group, and, in turn, [requires] analysis of the fundamental economic and social conditions within the life practice. The same role the individual life history plays in the analysis of an individual is played by the economic and social structure in the analysis of the character structure of a group. The understanding of the life practice of a group is, however, a far more complex and difficult undertaking than the understanding of the life history of an individual. It presumes the analysis of the economic and social structure of this group. A knowledge of 'the milieu,' that is, of certain manifest social and cultural phenomena, [but] without analysis of the dynamically decisive conditions is absolutely inadequate, just as is the knowledge of single isolated economic factors, such as plenty or scarcity of food, fruitfulness or barrenness of the soil, technical development etc. Understanding of the life practice means for us analysis of the dynamics of the social structure" (2010: 27–28).

7. In *Social Character in a Mexican Village*, Fromm claims that those individuals whose character is most fully equated with the social character receive also the social awards, which proper social behavior carries with it, in terms of material success and recognition of being "good" and "virtuous" (Fromm and Maccoby, 1996 [1970]: 18). They are also, if gifted, the most likely to become leaders of their respective groups.

8. Fromm, as with Reich and Horkheimer, stresses the role of the family, but, as was noted in chapter 2, he sees the need to go beyond the narrow sphere of the family to understand the wider societal influence.

9. Fromm stresses that the appeal of Lutheranism to the peasantry and the urban poor differed in line with their socioeconomic position: ruthlessly exploited

and deprived of traditional rights and privileges, what chimed with these lower classes was Luther's stress on the revolutionary spirit of the Gospels and his opposition to the Church (1969 [1941]: 79).

10. McLaughlin cites Richard Hamilton, who argues that it was proportionately those of the upper middle class, as opposed to the lower middle class, who were more likely to vote for the Nazi party (Hamilton, 1996).

11. In his introduction to the 1996 edition of the study, Maccoby claims that Fromm "wanted to silence critics who referred to him as an armchair sociologist by presenting solid empirical findings in support of his theory" (Maccoby, 1996: xxi).

12. Although Fromm is wrong to describe Weber's position as "idealistic," as he does at one point in *Escape from Freedom* (1969 [1941]: 294), the underlying point—that Weber brackets out psychological analysis, and that the brackets need to be removed—is valid.

5 Anti-Humanism: A Radical Humanist Defense

1. Interestingly, Althusser was approached by Fromm in relation to contributing a chapter to the *Socialist Humanism* volume. As it turned out, Fromm (who had contacted Althusser on the recommendation of Adam Schaff) found Althusser's piece "just terribly boring, and without any theoretical thought worth publishing" (letter to Schaff, February 8, 1964).

2. As was shown in chapter 2, this was not a reading with which Fromm concurred.

3. With Hume and Annette Baier, Rorty stresses that there is no such thing as the Platonic idea of a true self (Rorty, 1998).

4. See Habermas's obituary for Rorty (June 12, 2007), in which he said the following: "Nothing is sacred to Rorty the ironist. Asked at the end of his life about the 'holy,' the strict atheist answered with words reminiscent of the young Hegel: 'My sense of the holy is bound up with the hope that some day my remote descendants will live in a global civilization in which love is pretty much the only law'".

5. The former relates to the pro-social motives that have been shown to exist in humans and in other primate species; the latter relates to the phylogenetic retention by adults of traits previously seen only in juveniles.

6. See Benton (2009) versus Soper (1981) on the debate over exactly how far they have become modified.

7. Kate Soper has noted that most anti-humanisms "secrete humanist rhetoric" (Soper, 1986: 128). Nowhere is this easier to observe than in Rorty.

8. Adorno, in fact, states that there is no being without entities (Adorno, 1973: 135), but gives over very little time to discussing, in materialist fashion, the very entity that he posits as necessary for being. Similarly, although Adorno does offer a caveat in a piece of "Free Time" in a collection first published after his death—he says that "it is doubtful that the culture industry and the consciousness of its consumers make an absolutely symmetrical equation" (Adorno,

1989: 174)—the statement comes a little late, seems a little hesitant, and, to all intents and purposes, seems to call into question the stringency, if not very intelligibility of his earlier writings.

9. The following comes close to a confirmation: "Living in the rebuke that the thing is not identical with the concept is the concept's longing to become identical with the thing. This is how the sense of non-identity contains identity. The supposition of identity is indeed the ideological element of pure thought, all the way down to formal logic; but hidden in it is also the truth moment of ideology, the pledge that there should be no contradiction, no antagonism" (Adorno, 1973: 149).

10. Lyotard challenges the notion that everything is a text, proffering a corrective to deconstruction. He particularly challenges Derrida for presuming that there is only language (although this is not quite what Derrida says). In *Discourse Figures*, Lyotard seeks to move beyond the post-structural contentedness with pointing out the epistemic impasse of structuralism, by juxtaposing the Saussurean and structuralist account of linguistics with the phenomenology of vision as elaborated by Merleau-Ponty (Crome and Williams, 2006). His stress on the visible as the necessary yet heterogeneous complement to the textual is definitely an improvement on Derrida and Saussure in this regard.

11. This is the problem with process philosophy—the problem of bounded entities that develop, endure, and pass away. An account that does not feature them is hardly "materialist" (if we take materialist to mean what it originally meant), as Adorno claimed.

12. It might be objected that a "qualified relativism" might just as well be spoken of here; while strictly admissible, such an emphasis would undermine the stress of Fromm's radical humanism, seeking as it was to challenge the dominant relativist position.

13. Interestingly, Fromm himself made efforts to learn some of the fundamentals of neurophysiology in preparation for *The Anatomy of Human Destructiveness*, and, in *The Revision of Psychoanalysis*, contended that "the synthesis of psychoanalytic and neurophysiological data is to be expected one day" (1992: 6).

14. In connection with this, the elementary distinction between truth and falsity that human and animals make, which can be seen in behavioral studies (such as those studies which demonstrate the tracking of changes in the objects of perception), shows an implicit ontological understanding that pre-exists linguistic ability. Objective truth and falsity can become matters of cultural signification, but at a very simple level (and also less simple, I would contend) they are surely not.

6 The Renaissance of Humanism

1. As will be discussed, Fromm understands reason as transcending the equations of the merely logical. Logical thought is not rational if it is merely logical—paranoid thinking, for instance, is often "logical," yet it fails to really engage with reality.

2. In the account that follows, Fromm notably under-discusses the Muslim early medieval period and polytheistic and "primitive" cultures in general. While this is a failure of his account, he did, in the case of Muslim thought, hold Rumi, the Persian mystic poet, in the highest regard, writing the foreword to A. Reza Arasteh's *Rumi the Persian: Rebirth in Creativity and Love*, (1965). As for polytheistic and "primitive" cultures, it must be stressed that despite the fact that Fromm has far too little to say on this issue, the ultimate position he held seemed to be that such cultures were "sophisticated" and "very active in applying their own faculties of thinking, observing, imagining, painting, and sculpting" (2007 [1993]: 90–92). This issue was touched on in chapter 3, footnote 6.

3. Fromm's discussion here is expounded on in part at various other points in his writings; these instances will be drawn on as and when appropriate.

4. Fromm, perhaps prompted by Freud's *Moses and Monotheism*, suggests a potential lineage as far back as Akhnaten, the Egyptian Emperor from 1375–1358 BC (2005).

5. Incidentally, the original title of the British publication of *Escape from Freedom* was *The Fear of Freedom*.

6. Fromm rarely refers to the term "reification," largely, it seems, to avoid engaging in what he saw as unnecessarily technical language—at least this is what is suggested in "Medicine and the Ethical Problem of Modern Man," which appeared in *The Dogma of Christ and Other Essays on Religion, Psychology, and Culture*, where he uses the term in conjunction with the caveat: "to use a technical term" (1992 [1963]). While this is so, Fromm's thought is nevertheless clearly connected to the tradition in which this is a central concept.

7. Incidentally, this quote demonstrates that Christopher Lasch's criticism of Fromm in *The Culture of Narcissism*, which heavily leans on the prior criticisms of Marcuse and Adorno and suggests that Fromm fails to understand that narcissism for Freud does not involve self-love (Lasch, 1979: 31), is wildly inaccurate. In *Escape from Freedom*, after making precisely this point, Fromm goes on to criticize Freud for suggesting that this love is transferred onto others, arguing instead that the narcissistic person loves *"neither others nor himself"* (1969 [1941]: 116—emphasis added).

8. Incidentally, Damasio has given credence to this connection, noting that the apparatus of rationality, traditionally presumed to be neocortical, does not seem to work without the aid of biological regulation, traditionally assumed to be subcortical: "Nature seems to have built the apparatus of rationality not just on top of the apparatus of biological regulation, but also *from* it and *with* it" (Damasio, 1996: 128—emphasis in original). None of this is to deny that rationality extends beyond this bodily connection—the point is merely the more basic one that there *is* a connection.

9. Spiro's work here has been important—the main thrust of which is captured in *Culture and Human Nature: Theoretical Papers of Melford E. Spiro* (Chicago: The University of Chicago Press, 1987), as has the work of Ekkehart Malotki,

who counters the influential Sapir-Whorff hypothesis of relativity by amply documenting the richness of Hopi conceptions of time and their essential similarity to ours in *Hopi Time: A Linguistic Analysis of the Temporal Concepts in the Hopi Language* (New York: Mouton, 1983). Additionally, Paul Ekman and co-contributors have succeeded in documenting the universality of certain facial expressions—Ekman et al., "Pan-Cultural Elements in Facial Displays of Emotion," *Science* 164 (1969), and "Pan-Cultural Facial Expression of Emotion," *Motivation and Emotion* 10 (1986)—with Izard and Haynes developing this work in their "On the Form and Universality of the Concept Expression," *Motivation and Emotion* 12 (1988). In relation to color, Brent Berlin and Paul Kay in *Basic Color Terms: Their Universality and Evolution* (Berkeley: University of California Press, 1991), and (even) Marshal Sahlins in "Colors and Culture," *Semiotica* 16 (2) (1976), have contributed to the attempt to map out universalist experiences. Although, as was noted in chapter 5, there is clearly much more work to do here.

10. Although Fromm was not always fully explicit on this, it is clear that this attitude should be expressed to *all* life in as far as it is consistently possible to so express it—something called for by Schweitzer's concern with "reverence for life," (Schweizter, 1974) a concern which centrally motivated Fromm's own idea of "biophilia," that is, the *love of life*.

11. Lawrence Wilde has discussed these ideas thoroughly in *Erich Fromm: The Quest for Solidarity*. I cannot go into the same level of detail as Wilde here, and would direct the reader to Wilde's discussion of them in the aforementioned work. The present discussion, though certainly interested in the issues considered in themselves, is primarily concerned with them as part of the wider social theoretical focus of reappropriating traditional humanist analytical categories through Fromm.

12. Adam Curtis explains this latter point well in his film *All Watched Over by Machines of Loving Grace*, 2011.

Conclusion

1. Though generally known today as "critical realism," this is an adopted title for what can be seen as the "first-wave" development of Roy Bhaskar's system, consisting of his "transcendental" or "scientific realism," "critical naturalism," and theory of "explanatory critique" (Hartwig, 2011: vii). It does not necessarily (nor generally) include what can be seen as Bhaskar's "second-wave" development of "dialectical critical realism," with its quasi-mystical negative philosophy.

2. I have listed Ted Benton last in the list above, primarily due to his apparently ambiguous connection to this issue of reclaiming humanity. Although Benton, like the others, is a democratic socialist (and therefore clearly has humanistic leanings), the main thrust of his work has been to challenge the overemphasis placed on human exceptionalism and thus to criticize "humanism" understood in terms of its anthropocentric excesses. This, it should be noted, is not

at all inconsistent with a radical humanist, essentialist understanding (despite Fromm's equivocation on the matter of the human/animal relationship). In fact, Benton's work in this regard can be seen as correcting Fromm's overdrawn account of evolutionary discontinuity and thus helping us reclaim the animality in humanity (which, of course, is a part of reclaiming humanity in itself).

3. In saying this, I am aware of Gregor McLennan's argument—which draws, in fact, on Benton—that the claims of critical realism have been consistently overstated, to deleterious effect (McLennan, 2009: 47). McLennan suggests that we need to see that critical realism is *not* best regarded as either an elaborate philosophical ontology or as offering prescriptive methodological criteria for sound research practice and good theorizing. He is also explicitly critical of the claim that realism is intrinsically critical or necessarily radical in a political-ideological sense, saying that "realism offers nothing more—but also nothing less—than a powerful heuristic conception of the *goals* of systematic enquiry, and that it represents the ethos of explanatory *naturalism* within the human sciences" (McLennan, 2009: 47–48).

4. This is so in spite of Bhaskar's doubts over the work of the humanist Marxist tradition. Influenced by Althusser, who he holds in high regard, Bhaskar lumps together Fromm with Lefebvre, E. P. Thompson, Sartre, Merleau-Ponty, Kolakowski, Schaff, and K. Kosic, in virtue of the fact that they all share a renewed emphasis on man and on human praxis as the center of authentic Marxist thought (Bhaskar, 1991: 177). While for Bhaskar this signals a partial return from Marx to Feuerbach, and thus a degradation in socialist thinking, I hope it has been shown that, in Fromm's case at least, this is an unfair assessment, and that it is the structuralist (and poststructuralist) problematic—particularly because of its relative dominance—that requires a greater materialization in terms of the adequate theorization of biological and psychological aspects of the social process—something that Fromm can contribute toward.

Bibliography

Adorno, Theodor. (1967). "Sociology and Psychoanalysis (Part I)." *New Left Review* 46 (November/December).

Adorno, Theodor. (1968). "Sociology and Psychoanalysis (Part II)." *New Left Review* 47 (January/February).

Adorno, Theodor. (1973). *Negative Dialectics*. London: Routledge.

Adorno, Theodor. (1989). *Critical Models: Interventions and Catchwords*. Translated by Henry W. Pickford. New York: Columbia University Press.

Adorno, Theodor. (2003). *The Jargon of Authenticity*. London: Routledge.

Adorno, Theodor. (2005). *Minima Moralia Reflections on a Damaged Life*. London: Verso.

Adorno, Theodor, et al. (1982). *The Authoritarian Personality*. New York: W. W. Norton & Company..

Adorno, Theodor. and Max Horkheimer. (1997). *Dialectic of Enlightenment*. London: Verso.

Akrap, Domagoj. (2011). *Erich Fromm: Ein Jüdischer Denker*. Vienna: LIT-Verlag.

Althusser, Louis. (1969). *For Marx*. London: Allen Lane.

Althusser, Louis. and Étienne Balibar. (1970). *Reading Capital*. London: New Left Books.

Althusser, Louis. (1976). *Essays in Self-Criticism*. London: New Left Books.

Althusser, Louis. (1977). *Lenin and Philosophy and Other Essays*. London: New Left Books.

Anderson, Kevin. (2000). "Erich Fromm and the Frankfurt School Critique of Criminal Justice." In Kevin Anderson (ed.), *Erich Fromm and Critical Criminology: Beyond the Punitive Society*. Chicago: University of Illinois Press.

Archer, Margaret S. (2000). *Being Human: The Problem of Agency*. Cambridge: Cambridge University Press.

Archer, Margaret S. (2007). *Making Our Way through the World: Human Reflexivity and Social Mobility*. Cambridge: Cambridge University Press.

Arasteh, A. Reza. (1965) *Rumi the Persian: Rebirth in Creativity and Love*. Lahore: Shmuhammad Ashraf.

Aristotle, (1995). *Politics*. Translated by Ernest Baker. Oxford: Oxford University Press.

Assiter, Alison, and Jeff Noonan. (2007) "Human Needs: A Realist Perspective." *Journal of Critical Realism* 6 (2).

Bauman, Zygmunt. (2008). *The Art of Life*. Cambridge: Polity Press.

Bell, Daniel. (1959). "The 'Rediscovery' of Alienation: Some Notes along the Quest for the Historical Marx." *Journal of Philosophy* 56 (24).

Bentall, Richard P. (2003). *Madness Explained: Psychosis and Human Nature*. London: Penguin.

Benton, Ted. (1991). "Biology and Social Science: Why the Return of the Repressed Should Be Given a (Cautious) Welcome." *Sociology* 25 (1).

Benton, Ted. (1999). "Evolutionary Psychology and Social Science: A New Paradigm or Just the Same Old Reductionism." In Lee Friesse (ed.), *Advances in Human Ecology*, vol. 8. Stanford: JAI Press.

Benton, Ted. (2001). "Why are Sociologists Naturephobes?." In José Lopéz and Garry Potter (eds.), *After Postmodernism*. London: Athlone Press.

Benton, Ted. (2009). *Natural Relations: Ecology, Animal Rights and Social Justice*. London: Verso.

Berlin, Brent, and Paul Kay. (1991). *Basic Color Terms: Their Universality and Evolution*. Berkeley: University of California Press.

Berlin, Isaiah. (1969). *Four Essays on Liberty*. Oxford: Oxford University Press.

Bernfeld, Siegfried. (1972). "Psychoanalysis and Socialism." In Wilhelm Reich's *Dialectical Materialism and Psychoanalysis*. London: Socialist Reproduction.

Bhaskar, Roy. (1991). *Philosophy and the Idea of Freedom*. Cambridge: Blackwell.

Bhaskar, Roy. (2008). *A Realist Theory of Science*. London: Verso.

Bhaskar, Roy. (2011). *Reclaiming Reality: A Critical Introduction to Contemporary Philosophy*. London: Routledge.

Birnbach, Martin. (1962). *Neo-Freudian Social Philosophy*. London: Oxford University Press.

Bloch, Ernst. (1952) *Avicenna und die Aristotelische Linke*. Berlin: Rütten und Loening.

Bloch, Ernst. (1959). *Das Prinzip Hoffnung*, vol. II. Frankfurt: Suhrkamp.

Bonss, Wolfgang. (1984). "Introduction." *The Working Class in Weimar Germany: A Psychological and Sociological Study*. Cambridge, MA: Harvard University Press.

Bourdieu, Pierre. (1984). *Distinction: A Social Critique of the Judgement of Taste*. London: Routledge and Keegan Paul.

Buber, Martin. (1960). *The Origin and Meaning of Hasidism*. New York: Horizon Press.

Bronner, Stephen Eric. (1994). *Of Critical Theory and Its Theorists*. Oxford: Blackwell.

Burston, Daniel. (1991). *The Legacy of Erich Fromm*. London: Harvard University Press.

Burston, Daniel. (2014). "Humanism." In T. Teo (ed.), *Encyclopedia of Critical Psychology*. New York: Springer.

Cortina, Mauricio. (1996). "Beyond Freud's Instinctivism and Fromm's Existential Humanism." In Mauricio Cortina and Michael Maccoby (eds.), *A Prophetic Analyst: Erich Fromm's Contribution to Psychoanalysis*. London: Jason Aronson.

Cortina, Mauricio, and Giovanni Liotti. (2010). "Attachment is about Safety and Protection, Intersubjectivity is about Sharing and Social Understanding." *Psychoanalytic Psychology* 24 (4).

Cortina, Mauricio, and Giovanni Liotti. (Forthcoming). "An Evolutionary Outlook on Motivation: Implications for the Clinical Dialogue." *Psychoanalytic Inquiry.*

Chodorow, Nancy. (1985). "Beyond Drive Theory: Object Relations and the Limits of Radical Individualism." *Theory and Society* 14 (3).

Chodorow, Nancy. (1999). *The Power of Feelings: Personal Meaning in Psychoanalysis, Gender, and Culture.* London: Yale University Press.

Craib, Ian. (1989). *Psychoanalysis and Social Theory: The Limits of Sociology.* London: Harvester Wheatsheaf.

Crome, Keith, and James Williams. (2006). *The Lyotard Reader and Guide.* New York: Columbia University Press.

Cohen, Herman. (1995). *Religion of Reason.* Atlanta: Scholars Press.

Damasio, Antonio. (1996). *Descartes' Error: Emotion, Reason and the Human Brain.* London: Macmillan.

Damasio, Antonio. (2000). *The Feeling of What Happens: Body, Emotion and the Making of Consciousness.* London: Vintage.

Damasio, Antonio. (2003). *Looking for Spinoza: Joy, Sorrow, and the Feeling Brain.* Orlando: Harcourt.

Davies, Tony. (2008). *Humanism.* London: Routledge.

Depew, David J. (2002). "De Anima and Marx's Theory of Man." Reprinted in Scott Meikle (ed.), *Marx.* International Library of Critical Essays in the History of Philosophy. Aldershot: Ashgate.

Derrida, Jacques. (1976). *Of Grammatology.* Baltimore, MD: John Hopkins University Press.

Derrida, Jacques. (1981). *Positions.* Translated and annotated by Alan Bass. London: Athlone Press.

Doyal, Len, and Ian Gough. (1991). *A Theory of Human Need.* London: Macmillan.

Durkin, Kieran. (Forthcoming/2015). "Erich Fromm: Studies in Social Character." In Alex Law and Eric Royal Lybeck (eds.), *Sociological Amnesia: Cross-current in Disciplinary History.* Farnham: Ashgate.

Eagleton, Terry. (2003). *After Theory.* London: Allen Lane.

Ekman, Paul, Richard E. Sorenson, and Wallace V. Friesen. (1969). "Pan-Cultural Elements in Facial Displays of Emotion." *Science* 164.

Ekman, Paul, and Wallace V. Friesen. (1986). "Pan-Cultural Facial Expression of Emotion." *Motivation and Emotion* 10 (2).

Elliott, Anthony. (2002). *Psychoanalytic Theory: An Introduction.* London: Blackwell.

Erikson, Erik. (1958). *Young Man Luther: A Study in Psychoanalysis and History.* London: Faber and Faber, 1958.

Fenichel, Otto. (1944). "Psychoanalytical Remarks on Fromm's Book 'Escape from Freedom.'" *Psychoanalytic Review* 31 (January).

Fenichel, Otto. (1954). "A Critique of the Death Instinct." In Hannah Fennichel (ed.), *The Collected Papers of Otto Fenichel.* London: Routledge.

Feuerbach, Ludwig. (1957). *The Essence of Christianity.* New York: Harper and Row.

Fishbane, Michael A. (1997). "Introduction" to Nahum N. Glatzer's *The Memoirs of Nahum N. Glatzer.* Cincinnati, OH: Hebrew Union College Press.

Formwalt, Lee. W. (2007). "Balancing Scholarship and Activism: An Interview with Lawrence J. Friedman." *Organization of American Historians Newsletter* 35 (1) (February).

Foucault, Michel. (1978). *The Will to Knowledge: The History of Sexuality,* vol. 1. Translated by Robert Hurley. London: Penguin.

Foucault, Michel. (1982). "Afterword" to Hubert L. Dreyfus and Paul Rabinow's *Michel Foucault: Beyond Structuralism and Hermeneutics.* London: Harverster Wheatsheaf.

Foucault, Michel. (1984a). "What is Enlightenment?" In Paul Rabinow (ed.), *The Foucault Reader: An Introduction to Foucault's Thought.* London: Penguin.

Foucault, Michel. (1984b). "Nietzsche, Genealogy, History." In Paul Rabinow (ed.), *The Foucault Reader: An Introduction to Foucault's Thought.* London: Penguin.

Foucault, Michel. (1984c). "On the Genealogy of Ethics: An Overview of Work in Progress." In Paul Rabinow (ed.), *The Foucault Reader: An Introduction to Foucault's Thought.* London: Penguin.

Foucault, Michel. (1986a). *The Use of Pleasure: The History of Sexuality,* vol. 2. Translated by Robert Hurley. Harmondsworth: Viking.

Foucault, Michel. (1986). *The Care of the Self: The History of Sexuality,* vol. 3. Translated by Robert Hurley. London: Allen Lane.

Foucault, Michel. (1989). *Madness and Civilisation.* London: Routledge.

Foucault, Michel. (2002a). *The Archaeology of Knowledge.* London: Routledge.

Foucault, Michel. (2002b). *The Order of Things: An Archaeology of the Human Sciences.* London: Routledge.

Foxbrunner, Roman A. (1992). *Habad: The Hasidism of R. Shneur Zalman of Lyady.* London: University of Alabama Press.

Freud, Sigmund. (1953). *On Aphasia: A Critical Study.* London: Imago.

Freud, Sigmund. (1959). "Character and Anal Eroticism." James Strachey (ed.), *The Standard Edition of The Complete Psychological Works of Sigmund Freud,* vol. IX. London: Hogarth Press.

Freud, Sigmund. (1964). *New Introductory Lectures on Psycho-analysis.* New York: W. W. Norton.

Freud, Sigmund. (1967). *Moses and Monotheism.* New York: Vintage Books.

Freud, Sigmund. (1984a). "Beyond the Pleasure Principle." In Angela Richards (ed.), *On Metapsychology: The Theory of Psychoanalysis.* The Penguin Freud Library, vol. 11. London: Penguin.

Freud, Sigmund. (1984b). "Two Principles of Mental Functioning." In Angela Richards (ed.), *On Metapsychology: The Theory of Psychoanalysis.* The Penguin Freud Library, vol. 11. London: Penguin.

Freud, Sigmund. (1984c). "Instincts and their Vicissitudes." In Angela Richards (ed.), *On Metapsychology: The Theory of Psychoanalysis.* The Penguin Freud Library, vol. 11. London: Penguin.

Freud, Sigmund (1984d). "The Ego and the Id." In Angela Richards (ed.), *On Metapsychology: The Theory of Psychoanalysis*. The Penguin Freud Library, vol. 11. London: Penguin.

Freud, Sigmund. (1991a). "Thoughts for the Times on War and Death." In Albert Dickinson (ed.), *Civilization, Society and Religion*. The Penguin Freud Library, vol. 12. London: Penguin.

Freud, Sigmund. (1991b). "Group Psychology and the Analysis of the Ego." In Albert Dickinson (ed.), *Civilization, Society and Religion*. The Penguin Freud Library, vol. 12. London: Penguin.

Freud, Sigmund. (2000). *Three Essays on the Theory of Sexuality*. New York: Basic Books.

Freud, Sigmund. (2001a). *Totem and Taboo: Some Points of Agreement between the Mental Lives of Savages and Neurotics*. London: Routledge.

Freud, Sigmund. (2001b). "The Future of an Illusion." In James Strachey (ed.), *The Standard Edition of the Complete Psychological Works*, vol. XXI. London: Vintage.

Freud, Sigmund (2001c) "Civilization and Its Discontents." In James Strachey (ed.), *The Standard Edition of the Complete Psychological Works*, vol. XXI. London: Vintage.

Frie, Roger. (2003). "Erich Fromm and Contemporary Psychoanalysis: From Modernism to Postmodernism." *Psychoanalytic Review* 90 (6).

Friedman, Lawrence. (2013). *The Lives of Erich Fromm: Love's Prophet*. New York: Colombia University Press.

Fromm, Erich. (1939a). "Selfishness and Self-Love." *Psychiatry: Journal for the Study of Interpersonal Processes* 2.

Fromm, Erich. (1927). "Der Sabbat." *Imago* 13.

Fromm, Erich. (1930). "*Die Entwicklung des Christusdogmas, Eine Psychoanalytische Studie zur Sozialpsychologischen*." Translated in Fromm, 1992 [1963].

Fromm, Erich. (1932a). "*Über Methode und Aufgabe einer Analytischen Sozialpsychologie: Bemerkungen über Psychoananlyse und historischen Materialismus*." Translated in Fromm, 1970.

Fromm, Erich. (1932b). "*Die psychoanalytische Charakterologie und ihre Bedeutung für die Sozialpsychologie*." Translated in Fromm, 1970.

Fromm, Erich. (1934). "*Die sozialpsychologie Bedeutung der Mutterrechtstheorie*." Translated in Fromm, 1970.

Fromm, Erich. (1935). "Die gesellschaftlicthe Bedingtheit der psychoanalytischen Therapie." *Zeitschrift für Sozialforschung* 3.

Fromm, Erich. (1937). "Zum Gefühl der Ohnmacht." *Zeitschrift für Sozialforschung* 6.

Fromm, Erich. (1939b). "The Social Philosophy of 'Will Therapy'." *Psychiatry: Journal for the Study of Interpersonal Processes* 2.

Fromm, Erich. (1948). "For a Cooperation between Jews and Arabs." *New York Times*, April 18.

Fromm, Erich. (1949). "Psychoanalytic Characterology and Its Application to the Understanding of Culture." In S. Stansfeld Sargent and Marian W. Smith (eds.), *Culture and Personality*. New York: Viking.

Fromm, Erich. (1950). *Psychoanalysis and Religion*. London: Yale University Press.

Fromm, Erich. (1955). "The Human Implications of Instinctivist 'Radicalism': A Reply to Herbert Marcuse." *Dissent* 2 (4).

Fromm, Erich. (1956a). *The Art of Loving: An Inquiry into the Nature of Love*. New York: Harper and Row.

Fromm, Erich (1956b) "A Counter-Rebuttal to Herbert Marcuse," *Dissent* 3 (1).

Fromm, Erich. (1959). *Sigmund Freud's Mission: An Analysis of His Personality and Influence*. New York: Harper and Row.

Fromm, Erich. (1960a). *Let Man Prevail: A Socialist Manifesto and Program*. New York: Call Association.

Fromm, Erich. (1960b). *Psychoanalysis and Zen Buddhism*. London: Unwin.

Fromm, Erich. (1961). *May Man Prevail? An Inquiry into the Facts and Fictions of Foreign Policy*. New York: Anchor.

Fromm, Erich. (1963). *War Within Man: A Psychological Inquiry into the Roots of Destructiveness*. Philadelphia, PA: American Philadelphia Service Committee.

Fromm, Erich. (1966a). *You Shall Be as Gods: A Radical Interpretation of the Old Testament and Its Traditions*. New York: Holt, Rinehart, and Winston.

Fromm, Erich. (1966b). *Dialogue with Erich Fromm*. Interview by Richard Evans. New York: Harper and Row.

Fromm, Erich. (1967 [1965]). "The Application of Humanist Psychoanalysis to Marx's Theory." In *Socialist Humanism: An International Symposium*. London: Allen Lane.

Fromm, Erich. (1969 [1941]). *Escape from Freedom*. New York: Holt Paperbacks.

Fromm, Erich. (1970). *The Crisis of Psychoanalysis: Essays on Freud, Marx and Social Psychology*. New York: Holt, Rinehart and Winston.

Fromm, Erich. (1970 [1951]). *The Forgotten Language: An Introduction to the Understanding of Dreams, Fairy Tales and Myths*. New York: Holt, Rinehart and Winston.

Fromm, Erich. (1970 [1968]). *The Revolution of Hope: Toward a Humanized Technology*. New York: Harper and Row.

Fromm, Erich. (1980 [1964]). *The Heart of Man: Its Genius for Good and Evil*. New York: Harper Colophon Books.

Fromm, Erich. (1982 [1980]). *Greatness and Limitations of Freud's Thought*. London: Abacus.

Fromm, Erich. (1984) *The Working Class in Weimar Germany: A Psychological and Sociological Study*. Cambridge, MA: Harvard University Press.

Fromm, Erich. (1986 [1983]). Interviewed by Hans Jürgen Schultz, *For the Love of Life*. New York: Free Press.

Fromm, Erich. (1989 [1929]). "Psychoanalysis and Sociology." In Stephen Eric Bronner and Douglas Kellner (eds.), *Critical Theory and Society: A Reader*. London: Routledge.

Fromm, Erich. (1989 [1931]). "Politics and Psychoanalysis." In Stephen Eric Bronner and Douglas Kellner (eds.), *Critical Theory and Society: A Reader*. New York: Routledge.

Fromm, Erich. (1990 [1957]). "The Humanistic Science of Man." In *Yearbook of the International Fromm Society: Wissenschaft vom Menschen-Science of Man. Jahrbuch der Internationalen Erich-Fromm-Gesellschaft*, vol. 1. Münster: LIT—Verlag.

Fromm, Erich. (1992 [1963]). *The Dogma of Christ and Other Essays on Religion, Psychology, and Culture*. New York: Henry Holt.

Fromm, Erich. (1992). *The Revision of Psychoanalysis*. Rainer Funk (ed.). Oxford: Westview Press.

Fromm, Erich. (1994). *The Art of Listening*. London: Constable.

Fromm, Erich. (1997 [1973]). *The Anatomy of Human Destructiveness*. London: Pimlico.

Fromm, Erich. (1997). *Love, Sexuality, and Matriarchy: About Gender*. New York: Fromm International.

Fromm, Erich. (2000 [1930]). "The State as Educator: On the Psychology of Criminal Justice." In Kevin Anderson (ed.), *Erich Fromm and Critical Criminology: Beyond the Punitive Society*. Chicago: University of Illinois Press.

Fromm, Erich. (2000 [1931]). "On the Psychology of the Criminal and the Punitive Society." In Kevin Anderson (ed.), *Erich Fromm and Critical Criminology: Beyond the Punitive Society*. Chicago: University of Illinois Press.

Fromm, Erich. (2002 [1955]). *The Sane Society*. London: Routledge.

Fromm, Erich. (2003 [1947]). *Man for Himself: An Inquiry into the Psychology of Ethics*. London: Routledge.

Fromm, Erich. (2004 [1961]). *Marx's Concept of Man*. London: Continuum.

Fromm, Erich. (2005). *On Being Human*. Rainer Funk (ed.). New York: Continuum.

Fromm, Erich. (2006 [1962]). *Beyond the Chains of Illusion: My Encounter with Marx and Freud*. London: Continuum.

Fromm, Erich. (2007 [1993]). *The Art of Being*. London: Constable.

Fromm, Erich. (2009 [1976]). *To Have or To Be?* London: Continuum.

Fromm, Erich. (2009). *The Clinical Erich Fromm: Personal Accounts and Papers on Therapeutic Technique*. Rainer Funk (ed.), New York: Rodopi.

Fromm, Erich. (2010). "Man's Impulse Structure and Its Relation to Culture." In Rainer Funk (ed.), *Beyond Freud: From Individual to Social Psychology*. New York: American Mental Health Foundation.

Fromm, Erich. (2011 [1960]). "Man's Needs." Interview with Huston Smith. The Literary Estate of Erich Fromm.

Fromm, Erich, and Michael Maccoby. (1996 [1970]). *Social Character in a Mexican Village: A Sociopsychoanalytic Study*. London: Transaction.

Fromm, Erich, and Ramon Xirau. (1979 [1968]). *The Nature of Man*. London: Collier Macmillan.

Frosh, Stephen. (1987). *The Politics of Psychoanalysis: An Introduction to Freudian and Post-Freudian Theory*. Basingstoke: Macmillan.

Funk, Rainer. (1982). *Erich Fromm: The Courage to Be Human*. New York: Continuum.

Funk, Rainer. (1988). "The Jewish Roots of Erich Fromm's Humanistic Thinking." Lecture presented at the "Erich Fromm—Life and Work" Symposium, Locarno, Switzerland, May 12–14.

Funk, Rainer. (1990). "Humanism in the Life and Work of Erich Fromm. A Commemorative Address on the Occasion of his 90th Birthday." Lecture delivered at the Annual Congress of the International Erich Fromm Society, University of Heidelberg.

Funk, Rainer. (2000). *Erich Fromm: His Life and Ideas—An Illustrated Biography.* New York: Continuum.

Funk, Rainer. (2005) "Productive Orientation and Mental Health." Lecture presented at the International Conference on the Occasion of the twentieth anniversary of the International Erich Fromm Society.

Gay, Peter. (2006). *Freud: A Life for Our Time.* London: Max Press.

Giddens, Anthony. (1979). *Central Problems in Social Theory, Action, Structure and Contradiction in Social Analysis.* London: Macmillan.

Geertz, Clifford. (1984). "From the Native's Point of View: On the Nature of Anthropological Understanding." In Richard A. Shweder and Robert Alan LeVine (eds.), *Culture Theory: Essays on Mind, Self, and Emotion.* New York: Cambridge University Press.

Gellner, Ernest. (1982). *Postmodernism, Reason and Religion.* London: Routledge.

Geras, Norman. (1983). *Marx and Human Nature: Refutation of a Legend.* London: NLB.

Geras, Norman. (1995). *Solidarity in the Conversation of Humankind: The Ungroundable Liberalism of Richard Rorty.* London: Verso.

Glen, J. Stanley. (1966) *Erich Fromm: A Protestant Critique,* Philadelphia: The Westminster Press.

Gojman, Sonia. (1992). "A Socio-psychoanalytic Intervention Process in a Mexican Mining Village." In *Wissenschaft vom Menschen-Science of Man. Jahrbuch der Internationalen Erich-Fromm-Gesellschaft,* vol. 3. Münster: LIT-Verlag.

Gojman, Sonia, and Salvador Millán. (2001). "Attachment Patterns and Social Character in a Nahuatl Village: Socialization Processes through Social Character Interviews and Cideotaped Attachment Current Methodology." *Fromm Forum* 5.

Gojman, Sonia, and Salvador Millán. (2004). "Identity in the Asphalt Jungle." *International Forum of Psychoanalysis* 13 (4).

Greenberg, Jay R., and Stephen A. Mitchell. (1983). *Object Relations in Psychoanalytical Theory.* London: Harvard University Press.

Habermas, Jürgen. (1987). *Knowledge and Human Interests.* Cambridge: Polity Press.

Habermas, Jürgen. (2007, June 12). "Philosopher, Poet and Friend." Obituary for Richard Rorty. http://www.signandsight.com/features/1386.html (Accessed June 4, 2014).

Hamilton, Richard. (1996). *The Social Misconstruction of Reality: Validity and Verification in the Scholarly Community.* New Haven, CT: Yale University Press.

Hammond, B. Guyon. (1965). *Man in Estrangement: A Comparison of the Thought of Paul Tillich and Erich Fromm,* Nashville: Vanderbilt University Press.

Hardeck, Jürgen. (2005). *Erich Fromm: Leben und Werk.* Darmstadt: Primus Verlag und Wissenschaftliche Buchgesellschaft.

Hartwig, Mervyn. (2011). "Introduction" to Roy Bhaskar's *Reclaiming Reality: A Critical Introduction to Contemporary Philosophy.* London: Routledge.

Hausdorff, Don. (1972). *Erich Fromm.* New York: Twayne.

Heidegger, Martin. (1998). "Letter on 'Humanism.'" In William McNeill (ed.), *Pathmarks (Texts in German Philosophy)*. Cambridge: Cambridge University Press.

Held, David. (1980). *Introduction to Critical Theory: Horkheimer to Habermas*. London: Hutchinson.

Hegel, G. W. F. (1977). *Phenomenology of Spirit*. Oxford: Clarendon Press.

Horkheimer, Max. (ed). (1936). *Studien ü ber Autorität und Familie*. Paris: Felix Alcan.

Horney, Karen. (1937). *The Neurotic Personality of Our Time*. London: Routledge and Kegan Paul.

Izard, Carroll E., and O. Maurice Haynes. (1988). "On the Form and Universality of the Concept Expression: A Challenge to Ekman and Friesen's Claim of Discovery." *Motivation and Emotion* 12 (1).

Jacoby, Russell. (1977). *Social Amnesia: A Critique of Conformist Psychology from Adler to Laing*. Sussex: Harvester Press.

Jacoby, Russell. (1983). *The Repression of Psychoanalysis: Otto Fenichel and the Political Freudians*. New York: Basic Books.

Jaspers, Karl. (1951). *Way to Wisdom: An Introduction to Philosophy*. London: Victor Gollancz.

Jay, Martin. (1972). "The Frankfurt School's Critique of Marxist Humanism." *Social Research* 39 (2).

Jay, Martin. (1996). *The Dialectical Imagination: A History of the Frankfurt School and the Institute of Social Research, 1923–1950*. London: Heinemann.

Kain, Philip. (1988). *Marx and Ethics*. Oxford: Clarendon Press.

Kellner, Douglas. (1998). *Critical Theory, Marxism and Modernity*. Oxford: Polity Press.

Kessler, Michael and Rainer Funk (eds.). (1992). *Erich Fromm und die Frankfurter Schule*. Tübingen. A. Francke Verlag.

Knapp, Gerhard P. (1993). *The Art of Living: Erich Fromm's Life and Works*. New York: Peter Lang.

Korsch, Karl. (1974). "Fundamentals of Socialization." In Douglas Kellner (ed.), *Karl Korsch: Revolutionary Theory*. Austin: University of Texas Press.

Lacan, Jacques. (2001). *Écrits: A Selection*. London: Routledge.

Lasch, Christopher. (1979). *The Culture of Narcissism: American Life in An Age of Diminishing Expectations*. New York: W. W. Norton.

Lévi-Strauss, Claude. (1966). *The Savage Mind*. London: Weidenfeld and Nicolson.

Lévi-Strauss, Claude. (1969). *The Raw and the Cooked: Introduction to a Science of Mythology*. London: Pimlico.

Lévi-Strauss, Claude. (1977). "Jean-Jacques Rousseau, Founder of the Sciences of Man." *Structural Anthropology*. London: Allen Lane.

Lichtman, Richard. (1982). *The Production of Desire: The Integration of Psychoanalysis into Marxist Theory*. New York: Free Press.

Lukács, Georg. (1971). *History and Class Consciousness: Studies in Marxist Dialectics*. London: Merlin Press.

Lundgren, Svante. (1998). *Fight against Idols*. Frankfurt am Main: Peter Lang.

Lyotard, Jean-François. (1984). *The Postmodern Condition*. Manchester: Manchester University Press.

Lyotard, Jean-François. (1988). *The Differend: Phrases in Dispute*. Minneapolis: University of Minnesota Press.

Lyotard, Jean-François. (1993). *Libidinal Economy*. London: Athlone Press.

Lyotard, Jean-François, and Jean Loup Théduad. (1979). *Just Gaming*. Theory and History of Literature, vol. 20. Minneapolis, MN: University of Minneapolis Press.

Maccoby, Michael (1976) *The Gamesman. The New Corporate Leaders*, New York: Simon and Schuster.

Maccoby, Michael. (1996). "Introduction to the Transaction Edition." *Social Character in a Mexican Village*. London: Transaction.

Maimonides, Moses. (1925). *The Guide for the Perplexed*. London: Routledge.

Malotki, Ekkehart. (1983). *Hopi Time: A Linguistic Analysis of the Temporal Concepts in the Hopi Language*. New York: Mouton.

Marcuse, Herbert. (1941) *Reason and Revolution: Hegel and the Rise of Social Theory*. London: Oxford University Press.

Marcuse, Herbert. (1955). "The Social Implications of Freudian 'Revisionism.'" *Dissent* 2, (3).

Marcuse, Herbert. (1966 [1955]). *Eros and Civilization: A Philosophical Inquiry into Freud*. Boston, MA: Beacon Press.

Marcuse, Herbert. (1969). *An Essay on Liberation*. Boston: Beacon Press.

Marcuse, Herbert. (1972). *Counterrevolution and Revolt*. London: Allen Lane.

Marcuse, Herbert. (1991 [1964]). *One-Dimensional Man: Studies in the Ideology of Advanced Industrial Society*. London: Routledge.

Margolies, Richard. (1996). "Self Development and Psychotherapy in a Period of Rapid Social Change." In Mauricio Cortina and Michael Maccoby (eds.), *A Prophetic Analyst: Erich Fromm's Contribution to Psychoanalysis*. London: Jason Aronson.

Marx, Karl. (1970). "A Contribution to the Critique of Hegel's Philosophy of Right: Introduction." *Critique of Hegel's Philosophy of Right*. Joseph O'Malley (ed.). London: Cambridge University Press.

Marx, Karl. (1977). *Economic and Philosophic Manuscripts of 1844*. London: Lawrence and Wishart.

Marx, Karl. (1990). *Capital: A Critique of Political Economy*, vol. 1. London: Penguin Classics.

Marx, Karl. (1991). *Capital: A Critique of Political Economy*, vol. 3. Harmondsworth: Penguin, in association with New Left Review.

Marx, Karl. (2000a). "The German Ideology." In David McLellan (ed.), *Karl Marx: Selected Writings*. Oxford: Oxford University Press.

Marx, Karl. (2000b). "Letter to Ruge." In David McLellan (ed.), *Karl Marx: Selected Writings*. Oxford: Oxford University Press.

Marx, Karl, and Friedrich Engels. (1956). *The Holy Family or Critique of Critical Critique*. Moscow: Foreign Languages Publishing House.

McCarthy, George. (ed.). *Marx and Aristotle: Nineteenth-Century German Social Theory and Classical Antiquity*. Savage, MD: Rowman and Littlefield.

McLaughlin, Neil. (1996). "Nazism, Nationalism, and the Sociology of Emotions: Escape from Freedom Revisited." *Sociological Theory* 14 (3).

McLaughlin, Neil. (1998). "How to Become a Forgotten Intellectual: Intellectual Movements and the Rise and Fall of Erich Fromm." *Sociological Forum* 13 (2).

McLaughlin, Neil. (1999). "Origin Myths in the Social Sciences: Fromm, the Frankfurt School and the Emergence of Critical Theory." *Canadian Journal of Sociology* 24 (1).

McLaughlin, Neil. (2000). "Revision from the Margins: Fromm's Contribution to Psychoanalysis." *International Forum of Psychoanalysis* 9.

McLaughlin, Neil. (2001). "Critical Theory Meets America: Riesman, Fromm, and *The Lonely Crowd*." *American Sociologist* 32 (1) (Spring).

McLaughlin, Neil. (2007). "Escape from Evidence? Popper and Psychoanalytic Social Theory." *Dialogue* 46.

McLennan, Gregor. (2009). "'FOR Science in the Social Sciences': The End of the Road for Critical Realism." In Sandra Moog and Rob Stones (eds.), *Nature, Social Relations and Human Needs: Essays in Honour of Ted Benton*. Basingstoke: Palgrave Macmillan.

Meikle, Scott. (1985). *Essentialism in the Thought of Karl Marx*. London: Duckworth.

Meikle, Scott. (1995). *Aristotle's Economic Thought*. Oxford: Clarendon Press.

Meikle, Scott (ed.). (2002). *Marx*. International Library of Critical Essays in the History of Philosophy. Aldershot: Ashgate.

Mitchell, Stephen A. (1993). *Hope and Dread in Psychoanalysis*. New York: Basic Books.

Nussbaum, Martha C. (2006). *Frontiers of Justice: Disability, Nationality, Species Membership*. Cambridge: Harvard University Press.

Obeyesekere, Gananath. (1990). *The Work of Culture: Symbolic Transformation in Psychoanalysis and Anthropology*. Chicago: University of Chicago Press.

O'Brien, Ken. (1997). "Death and Revolution: A Reappraisal of Identity Theory." In John O'Neill (ed.), *On Critical Theory*. London: Heinemann.

Pietikäinen, Petteri. (2004). "'The Sage Knows You Better than You Know Yourself': Psychological Utopianism in Erich Fromm's work." *History of Political Thought* 25 (1).

Peffer, R. G. (1990). *Marxism, Morality, and Social Justice*. Princeton: Princeton University Press.

Rickert, John. (1986). "The Fromm-Marcuse Debate Revisited." *Theory and Society* 15.

Reich, Wilhelm. (1972). *Dialectical Materialism and Psychoanalysis*. London: Socialist Reproduction.

Rose, Gillian. (1978). *The Melancholy Science*. London: Macmillan.

Rose, Nikolas. (1999). *Governing the Soul: The Shaping of the Private Self*. London: Free Association Books.

Rorty, Richard. (1980). *Philosophy and the Mirror of Nature*. Oxford: Blackwell.

Rorty, Richard. (1989). *Contingency, Irony, and Solidarity*. Cambridge: Cambridge University Press.

Rorty, Richard. (1998). *Truth and Progress*. Cambridge: Cambridge University Press.

Sahlins, Marshall. (1976). "Colors and Culture." *Semiotica* 16 (2).

Sayer, Andrew. (1992). *Method in Social Science: A Realist Approach*. London: Routledge.

Sayers, Sean. (1998). *Marxism and Human Nature*. London: Routledge.

Schaar, John. (1961). *Escape from Authority: The Perspectives of Erich Fromm*. New York: Basic Books.

Schaff, Adam. (1963). *A Philosophy of Man*. New York: Monthly Press Review.

Schaff, Adam. (1970). *Marxism and the Human Individual*. New York: McGraw-Hill.

Scholem, Gershom. (1971). *The Messianic Idea in Judaism: And Other Essays on Jewish Spirituality*. London: Allen and Unwin.

Schweitzer, Albert. (1974). *Reverence for Life*. London: S. P. C. K.

Sen, Amartya. (1999). *Commodities and Capabilities*. Dehli: Oxford University Press.

Smith, Christian. (2003). *Moral Believing Animals: Human Personhood and Culture*. New York: Oxford University Press.

Smith, Christian. (2010). *What is a Person? Rethinking Humanity, Social Life, and the Moral Good from the Person Up*. Chicago: University of Chicago Press.

Somerville, John. (1968). "The Value Problem and Marxist Social Theory." *Journal of Value Inquiry* 2 (Spring).

Soper, Kate. (1981). *On Human Needs: Open and Closed Theories in a Marxist Perspective*. Sussex: Harvester Press.

Soper, Kate. (1986). *Humanism and Anti-Humanism*. London: Hutchinson.

Spiro, Melford. (1984). "Some Reflections on Cultural Determinism and Relativism with Special Reference to Emotion and Reason." In Richard A. Shweder and Robert Alan LeVine (eds.), *Culture theory: Essays on Mind, Self, and Emotion*. New York: Cambridge University Press.

Spiro, Melford. (1987). *Culture and Human Nature: Theoretical Papers of Melford E. Spiro*. Benjamin Kilborne and L. L. Langness (eds.). Chicago: University of Chicago Press.

Spiro, Melford. (1993). "Is the Western Conception of the Self 'Peculiar' within the Context of the World Cultures?" *Ethos* 21 (2).

Stevens, Richard. (1983). *Freud and Psychoanalysis: An Exposition and Appraisal*. Milton Keynes: Open University Press.

Taylor, Charles. (2005). *Hegel*. New York: Cambridge University Press.

Tillich, Paul. (1953). *Systematic Theology*, vol. 1. London: Nisbet.

Tillich, Paul. (1957). *Dynamics of Faith*. New York: Harper and Row.

Thompson, E. P. (1991). *The Making of the English Working Class*. London: Penguin.

Thompson, E. P. (1978). *The Poverty of Theory and Other Essays*. London: Merlin Press.

Thompson, Annette. (2009). *Erich Fromm: Explorer of the Human Condition*. Basingstoke: Palgrave Macmillan.

Thornhill, Chris. (2005). "Karl Jaspers and Theodor W. Adorno: The Metaphysics of the Human." *History of European Ideas* 31 (1).

Weber, Max. (2003). *The Protestant Ethic and the Spirit of Capitalism*. Translated by Talcott Parsons. Mineola, NY: Dover Publications.

Weiss, Joseph. (1985) *Studies in Eastern European Jewish Mysticism*. Oxford: Oxford University Press.

Wells, Harry. (1963). *The Failure of Psychoanalysis—From Freud to Fromm*. New York: International Publishers.

Wiggershaus, Rolf. (1994). *The Frankfurt School: Its History, Theories and Political Significance*. Cambridge: Polity Press.

Wilde, Lawrence. (1998). *Ethical Marxism and Its Radical Critics*. London: Macmillan.

Wilde, Lawrence. (2000). "In Search of Solidarity: The Ethical Politics of Erich Fromm." *Contemporary Politics* 6 (1).

Wilde, Lawrence (ed.). (2001). *Marxism's Ethical Thinkers*. New York: Palgrave.

Wilde, Lawrence. (2004a). *Erich Fromm and the Quest for Solidarity*. New York: Palgrave.

Wilde, Lawrence. (2004b). "A Radical Humanist Approach to the Concept of Solidarity." *Political Studies* 52 (1).

Wilde, Lawrence. (2012). "Marx, Morality and the Global Justice Debate." in Matthew Johnson (ed.), *The Legacy of Marxism: Contemporary Challenges, Conflicts and Developments*, London: Continuum.

Willmott, Hugh, and David Knights. (1982). "The Problem of Freedom: Fromm's Contribution to a Critical Theory of Work Organisation." *Praxis International* 2.

Winnicott, Donald. (1965). *The Maturational Process and the Facilitating Environment: Studies in the Theory of Emotional Development*. London: Hogarth Press.

Wood, Allen W. (1981). *Karl Marx*. London: Routledge and Kegan Paul.

Archival Material

The following is a listing of the archival material (letter excerpts and audio material) cited, all held at the Erich Fromm Archives, Tübingen, Germany:

Letter to Adam Schaff, February 8, 1964.

Letter to Adam Schaff, March 18, 1965.

Letter to Lewis Mumford, April 29, 1975.

Lecture titled "Concerning the Philosophy of Existence," 1977.

Letter to Raya Duyanevskaya, October 2, 1976.

Index

Printed and bound in the United States of America